Germany in the Later Middle Ages

Germany
in the
Later Middle Ages

by

F. R. H. Du Boulay

THE ATHLONE PRESS
London

First published 1983 by The Athlone Press Ltd
58 Russell Square, London WC1B 4HL, England

© F. R. H. Du Boulay 1983

Published in the USA and Canada by
St Martin's Press Inc
New York

British Library Cataloguing in Publication Data

Du Boulay, F. R. H.
  Germany in the Later Middle Ages.
  1. Germany — History — 1273–1517
  I. Title
  943'.02   DD166
  ISBN 0-485-11220-5
  ISBN 0-485-12042-9 Pbk

Typeset by Top Type Phototypesetting Co. Ltd, London W1.
Printed in Great Britain by Nene Litho, Earls Barton,
                    Northants.
Bound by Woolnough Bookbinding, Wellingborough,
                    Northants.

Contents

Contents

Illustrations

Dedicated to
The Religious, Royal and Ancient Foundation of
Christ's Hospital
where my interest in German history and
letters was first awakened

Acknowledgements

In the most general way the subject-matter of this book had occupied my mind since as an English schoolboy during the *Hitlerzeit* I had wondered why those I felt to be cousins were so different as well as so similar. Specifically, the attempt to write it was set in motion by the manifest regrets of my English university undergraduates that there was little to read in their own language and mental idiom on this period of German history. Modern German history has long been a historical magnet but, as Marc Bloch was always trying to explain, the present can only be understood through a past which is sometimes very distant. An Englishman might add that there is an English way of doing this as well as French and German ones.

This is an English effort, of a difficulty perhaps hopeless. However that may be, the first I would acknowledge are the young who encouraged me. I make bold to thank my son Tom, but he stands for others who also have laboured in the vineyard of the BA in history.

My professional colleagues (and friends) at College spent a long time reading various drafts, making constructive criticisms and, of course, talking to me. I thank them too for their practised judgement and their characteristic generosity, and should allude in particular to Dr N.M. Sutherland, Dr Penelope Corfield and Dr Caroline Barron.

I owe very great thanks to Dr Henry J. Cohn of the University of Warwick for his expert and positive help, bibliographical and factual, and to Professor Michael Wilks for some powerful and valuable criticisms.

At various stages I was privileged to have useful conversations and/or correspondence with the late Professor Dr Peter Classen, Professor Dr Günther Franz, Mr John Gillingham, Dr A.E. Hollaender, Dr Peter King, Dr Rosl Philpot, Professor Steven Rowan, Fräulein Dr Sibylle Schüler and Dr Tom Scott. Help on certain textual points was kindly given by Dr Sylvia Ranawake, Dr Bruce Watson, Professor Frank Goodyear and Frau Annaliese Hofmann. I am grateful for material sent from Germany and Switzerland by Dr Stuart Jenks (Berlin) and Mrs Sarah Metzger-Court (Zürich).

Friendly help was given by the staffs of the Bildsammlung des

Instituts für Agrargeschichte, Universität Hohenheim (Stuttgart), of the manuscript department of the Germanisches Nationalmuseum at Nuremberg, and of the German Historical Institute in London.

Permission to reproduce pictures was also most kindly granted by the following institutions: the Uffizi Gallery, the Curator of the Hohenheimer Bildsammlung, Agrarhistorische Bildsammlung, Universitätsarchiv Hohenheim; the Württembergisches Landesmuseum Stuttgart; and the Landeskonservatorim, Germanisches Nationalmuseum, Nürnberg.

Two of my former postgraduate pupils have my affectionate gratitude for intelligent conversation and practical help, in England and Germany: Dr Ann Brown and Dr Michael Burleigh.

Miss Sheelagh Taylor typed much of the text, and with unfailing cheerfulness.

Mistakes and errors of judgement are obviously mine, and so too were the benefits of being allowed two summer terms of study leave by my departmental colleagues, of a British Academy grant towards visiting libraries and cultural centres in Germany, and of receiving the constant support of my wife.

Finally, grateful acknowledgment is made to the Publications Fund of the University of London, and to the Isobel Thornley Bequest, for subventions in aid of this publication.

Abbreviations

Angermeier	Heinz Angermeier, *Königtum und Landfriede im deutschen Spätmittelalter* (Munich, 1966).
Ausgang	*Die Stadt am Ausgang des Mittelalters,* ed. Wilhelm Rausch (Linz/Donau, 1974).
CDS	*Die Chroniken der deutschen Städte vom 14. bis ins 16. Jahrhundert* (Historische Kommission bei der Bayerischen Akademie der Wissenschaften, 1862–).
Der Deutsche Territorialstaat	*Der Deutsche Territorialstaat im 14. Jahrhundert,* 2 vols., ed. Hans Patze (Vorträge und Forschungen hg. vom Konstanzer Arbeitskreis für mittelalterliche Geschichte, XIII, XIV, 1970, 1971).
HZ	*Historische Zeitschrift* (Munich).
JNS	*Jahrbücher für Nationalökonomie und Statistik* (Jena und Stuttgart).
MGH	*Monumenta Germaniae Historica.*
MIÖG	*Mitteilungen des Instituts für österreichische Geschichtsforschung* (Innsbruck).
Quellen	Günther Franz (ed.), *Quellen zur Geschichte des deutschen Bauernstandes,* vol. 1 (Berlin, 1967).
Stadtherr	*Stadt und Stadtherr im 14. Jahrhundert,* ed. Wilhelm Rausch (Linz/Donau, 1972).
TRHS	*Transactions of the Royal Historical Society.*
VSWG	*Vierteljahrschrift für Sozial- und Wirtschaftsgeschichte* (Wiesbaden).
ZGO	*Zeitschrift für die Geschichte des Oberrheins* (Heidelberg).

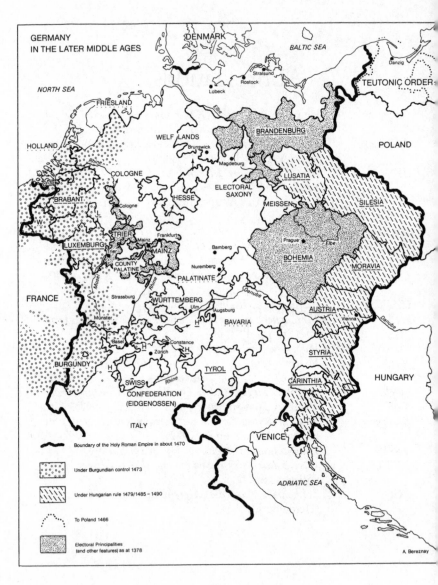

Habsburg lands <u>underlined</u> or indicated by H

Luxemburg lands <u>underlined</u> or indicated by L

Wittelsbach lands <u>underlined</u> or indicated by W

1

Language
and Mental Communication

For an Englishman or a Frenchman there is not much difficulty in identifying his country if he wishes to write about its medieval past. In spite of disputed areas like the Anglo-Scottish border or Lorraine, and in spite of regional dialects, there were vast lengths of coastline round these western kingdoms where the sea determined the realm without argument, so that is possible to speak about medieval England and France in a geographically coherent sense as well as a political one. With Germany it is otherwise, and 'central Europe' is a concept to bewilder the student for a number of good reasons: uncertain frontiers, political fragmentation, and the flood and ebb of colonization. Partly (but only partly) as a consequence of this uncertainty of boundary there are few 'history books' about medieval Germany in the western sense, that is to say, general treatments from several viewpoints in the same volume which bring together information and ideas about the monarchy, the principalities and the societies of the portions which formed so blurred and complex a whole. Nor have German scholars been very bold in attempting introductory works of synthesis which take account of different regional and technical specialisms.

It is probably best to begin with language in the search for German identity. Jacob Grimm said that through language a society enters history,[1] and speech was at least one characteristic which Germans had in common during the later medieval period. Furthermore, they realized that they possessed this common bond of literary German over and above the variations of regional dialect and colloquial talk. To be sure, the sense of linguistic brotherhood claimed by educated Germans was sometimes over-optimistic. Those grouped under the

1

German 'nation' at the Council of Constance (1414–18) included men who spoke Czech, Polish, Hungarian and Scandinavian tongues as well, and this faint pre-echo of a later *Reich* was heard again with clarity, though softly, in 1497 at the University of Bologna, where many central Europeans congregated to study law, and where the proctors of the German nation declared that 'all who have the native German tongue, even if their domicile is elsewhere...shall be understood as the college of the German nation', while almost in the same breath they claimed Bohemians, Moravians, Lithuanians and Danes as their own.[2] We are reminded of a stirring song which with the aid of a Haydn melody declared:

From the river Maas to Niemen,
From the Adige to the Belt,
Germany is to us the country
Best of all throughout the world.

When Professor Hoffmann, a native of the duchy of Brunswick, wrote *Deutschland über alles* in 1841 he was adapting for his own purposes the words of Walther von der Vogelweide, probably an Austrian, and a court poet of the thirteenth century:

From the Elbe to the Rhine
And further to Hungarian ground,
That is where you'll find the best
Who on this earth are to be found.[3]

But neither the one man nor the other was writing of more than an emotional reality. Hoffmann's patriotism extended to four waterways which had little political meaning as boundaries of Germany at the time of writing, and Walther was gallantly praising German women. The sentiments need not sound discreditable, even in the ears of a foreigner, but they do not help an understanding of the historical limits of German speech.

In this respect it seems that a German language may be traced to the eleventh century if we realize that it was confined to courtly, cultured circles. The *Annolied* of c.1090 is an epic poem from the Cologne region, under Archbishop Anno, which emphasized the favourite idea of Germany's former conquest by Rome and referred to the German land to which a common German language (*diutischin sprechin*) belonged. It has been called 'the birth-certificate of German'[4] because the concept of *Deutschland* and a *deutsche Sprache* never afterwards disappeared. Hence it is possible to allow from a time much earlier than that covered in this book a common *literary* language in which men and women of the courtly class could understand and enjoy poetry. If it was not yet a very rich language it was at least common currency over what may be called Germany. As chivalric speech it was influenced by French, and French has made a lasting present to German of several chivalric words which happen also to be much the same in English, like 'tournament', 'lance' and 'adventure'.

Written German was, then as now, something very different from the dialect and colloquialism needed to communicate with provincial and unlettered people, and even written German, accepted over wide areas, was divided into broad families of Low and High German, which were used along the northern littoral and over the remainder of Germany respectively. High German itself was by no means uniform; in 1440 the Grand Master of the Teutonic Order described the three 'tongues' into which the Upper German members were divided as those of the Rhineland, of Meissen-Thuringia-Saxony, and of Swabia-Franconia-Bavaria.[5]

But the process of standardization was at work, and a German speaker of any sort knew well enough that he differed from linguistic foreigners. Barbarossa could order in 1158, according to Otto of Freising, that a German soldier in Italy might have an Italian as a comrade only if the latter could speak German.[6] Ultimately, the Meissen-Saxony variety of High German became the language of the chancelleries at the expense of Latin. The chancellery of the Emperor Charles IV (1347-78) was one of the most important. Charles was a cultivated man, brought up in French-speaking courts, who yet lived much of his life in Bohemia and founded the Charles University of Prague in 1348. His court and this first of the 'German' universities lay, of course, in a country where Czech and German mingled, so his place in the development of the German language is rather paradoxical. It is even arguable that he did not regard Low German as German at all.[7] However that may be, his chancellor, von Neumarkt, a noted prose stylist from Silesia, recruited most of his 138 known officials from Germany, and specifically from the region between Trier and the River Main, and it was from this heartland, near the Luxemburgers' dynastic territory, that official German took its shape.

From then onwards towns as well as courts were adopting this language. The town chancery of Eger, on the western Bohemian-German border, was one of the leading ones.[8] Another centre of written communication was Meissen, near Dresden, in Saxony. This was in the territory of the great house of Wettin, after 1423 rulers of the electoral duchy of Saxony, whose chancellery took up and spread the imperial German language emanating from Prague. Meissen in the fourteenth century was still a transit area between west and east[9] and consequently a meeting-place for men from western, southern and middle Germany, and it came to form an intellectual centre between Nuremberg and Lübeck. Here too developed the skills of written government under the chancellor Konrad von Kirchberg, who had studied at Bologna and later became bishop of Meissen. Chancery records were kept, district officials continually informed in writing, and in 1349 a great feodary was made from this centre. When in the fifteenth century Saxony suffered partition, the electoral portion was ruled from Wittenberg. It is therefore not surprising that administrative German grew up within the triangle Trier-Prague-Wittenberg, and encroached victoriously into the written language of the whole country. 'I have no special language of my own', wrote Luther from Wittenberg; 'I use the common German language, so that both High and Low Germans may understand me equally well. In speech I follow the Saxon chancellery which is imitated by all the princes and kings of Germany.'[10] This statement takes us beyond our period, but it suffices to show that Luther was not the father of the German language, as is sometimes said, but one who vastly popularized and enriched a tongue already widely used. With a little simplification it can be said that the linguistic map of Germany by 1500 corresponded with that of Germany in 1939.

Speech is never static, but it can become geographically diffused enough to be referred to as 'standardized' while continuing to change slowly in standard form in the written as well as the spoken word. This process was at work in German vernacular writing, which greatly increased in quantity during the fourteenth and fifteenth centuries. As in England there was a long tradition of chronicle writing in all parts of Germany, moving in the late middle ages into the vernacular, notably in towns. [11] Town chronicles grew out of a historiography which was clerical and frequently in the hands of the friars. As town communities developed under their governments of mayor *(Bürgermeister)* and council *(Rat)* in the thirteenth century, the writing-office *(Schreibstube)* was formed with custody of the town archives.[12] These began to keep books of council records, and what had been begun by clerics was continued in some larger towns by laymen who had either been trained to write in the town school or hired from outside. By way of comparison, the keeping of annals by English townsmen from the late fourteenth century onwards is a familiar development, but outside London it was insignificant and even London writers were few compared with the enormous and variegated activity of German town writers. Almost every German town worthy of the name had scribes by the late fifteenth century, and many had had them since the thirteenth. In south-western Germany, comprising just Swabia, western Franconia and the Swiss Confederation, there were 140 towns with medieval scribes.[13] Their work was not curtailed by the military defeats suffered at the hands of the princes. On the contrary, the Great Town War of 1388 seems to have increased the need for urban administrative writers. As time went on, such men ceased to be drawn from the ranks of schoolmasters and humble notaries and came increasingly from more exalted families, often with diplomatic experience, with members prominent in the affairs of several cities. They belonged to the many-sided town secretariat and were likely to be conversant with politics, administration and legal matters. They were trained as scribes rather than writers of narrative, and the chronology and scale of their existence is an eloquent comment on two things: on the need for German towns, unlike English ones, to fend for themselves in a hostile world, threatened rather than protected by princes, and depending for affluence and for life itself upon well-armed and administered self-government; and on the fluent and copious use of the written German language to communicate with German friends and enemies. Certainly the London writers were interested in the doings of king, pope and lords as well as their own co-citizens. But among German town writers there is an astonishing variety of motive at work. Early compilers, as at Nuremberg, seem intent chiefly on recording the memorable doings of a particular patrician family, and wrote for the benefit of that family's successors and friends, who might compose a large audience. Others wrote campaign reports on the occasion of expeditions against hostile knightly castles (not an English requirement). Others again wrote to glorify a military victory, a royal ceremonial visit or a more general but equally intense civic patriotism. Some, like Sigmund Meisterlin, ex-monk of Augsburg, even wrote (of Nuremberg) just for money. Town histories sometimes built up gradually in time, as when scribes

5

became fond of adding private comments to their official work, treating of what they might earnestly describe as the 'eternal things' *(ewige Dinge)*, meaning events rather than the processes of law or copies of letters and privileges. At times chroniclers may appear learned or flowery, like Gerold Edlibach of Zürich; but that did not necessarily mean they were familiar with the secrets of the Latin declensions or the phrases of classical poets.[14] By the fifteenth century both patrician families and lesser gildsmen were interested in such annals. Literacy was encouraged by trade, warfare and town administration and it is easy to see why such official town books were at first compiled in an unsystematic way and contained pell-mell entries about citizenship, pledges, feuds, debts and demarcations as well as personal observations. The earliest known of such books seems to be the Council Book of Rostock (1258–1323). There are others from Hanseatic towns in the later thirteenth century, while down to the south the Nuremberg Act Book begins in 1285. In the course of the fourteenth century town books tended to become specialized according to subject-matter: for example, records of feuds *(Fehdebücher)* in Nuremberg and Brunswick, and here and there particular books noting punishments meted out by the town courts. But by the fifteenth century there were also numbers of vernacular town chronicles in a broad sense. Those of Augsburg, Nuremberg and Lübeck are good examples.

Burkhard Zink, merchant of Augsburg, wrote his private observations on local events between 1450 and 1468. He had been born in 1396 at Memmingen and received a clerical education, but by 1415 he was in Augsburg in the service of a trading-house for which he undertook journeys to Rhodes and to Italy, especially Venice. Soon he started his own business and acquired property and citizenship in Augsburg. His chronicle was a product of his later life and was written for his own interest rather than as an official commission or within an existing tradition. He had access to earlier reminiscences, however, for he began from the year 1368, but as he went on he incorporated more of his own experience from the time he had settled in Augsburg. As will be seen, Zink was only one of quite numerous men, townsmen and even knights, who at the end of the middle ages were seized by a desire to write down their memoirs.[15] He thought of himself as a historian — *'geschicht'* — though his work is a formless annal which notes travels, marriages and deaths in his own family, the fall of towers, the price of wine and so on. Hearsay is recorded: sentences often begin 'it is said' (*man sagt*), and the mind behind the pen was a fanciful one. Yet it was reflective too in its microcosmic musings and shows warm feeling for the town he had made his home, and is laced with angry comments on its enemies. At its broadest, Zink's political world was Christendom or 'the holy empire', but in practice his vision was bounded by the River Main to the north and follows the trade-routes over southern Germany, Bohemia, Hungary and northern Italy which he and his business friends had been accustomed to traverse.

He communicates to his readers a world of towns, princes and lords, not of the poor or the peasants, who appear only marginally as victims of politics, worthy of fleeting sympathy. The princes feature as the worst enemies, especially Duke Ludwig of Landshut (Bavaria), for such men were wickedly hostile to cities and ever ready to bar off precious trade-routes. It is interesting that Zink did not dwell on rivalry between cities themselves but thought of them in general as representing, even being, the empire in a political world where disruption was essentially the doing of lords. Writing of Mainz, which was conquered by its own archbishop, Adolf of Nassau, in 1461–2, he observed: 'Dear men of Augsburg, man the gates with pious people, for you have many wicked neighbours who would gladly see you dead'. Both historical evolution and political geography were beyond him; he never realized that Augsburg had changed from being an episcopal city to an imperial one only late in the thirteenth century. For him it embodied the empire as did other imperial towns, and the empire was hardly the person and court of a great king, still less a gigantic realm, but a mass of rights. Perhaps he was accidentally right in his naive expression of a sophisticated historical truth. At least he voiced the precise and widespread civic wish to be subject directly to the emperor and hence free of local seignorial claims, and in writing he was communicating these ideas to others, contemporary and future. His world was urban and German. Of foreign parts he knew little; Tuscany was astounding for its heat and strange crops. The city provincialism of which he was a mouthpiece brings us nearer to understanding the meaning of 'Germany' at that time.

Nuremberg also possessed family annals which were brought together by a citizen, in this case a brewer called Heinrich Deichsler who began to consolidate and continue them after 1469 (when he was about forty) until the end of the century. The geographical horizons were similar in stopping at Germany north of the Main, and the political outlook was equally simple in regarding princes as foes, the nearer the worse, and the empire as an idea with an urban embodiment. Sigismund's coronation in Rome was treated as a Nuremberg event. After all, the city had been entrusted with the imperial regalia: *insignia que imperium dicuntur*. The world beyond was felt to be acutely threatening, but its boundaries were blurred — the Turkish sultan was 'king of all possible Asiatic towns' — and Rome, symbol of salvation, could hardly be conceived in more concrete terms than the seven designated churches of Nuremberg where Roman indulgences might be earned. If the writing reflected the thought, then the death of Frederick III in Linz and the suicide of a lunatic in Nuremberg formed part of a single stream of consciousness, visually two-dimensional and formless in its notion of time, since Nuremberg's privileges were eternal, and every cold winter was 'the coldest for fifty or a hundred years'. For Deichsler the Turks and disease were alike the consequences of sin, and in betraying this view we may possibly have again a simpleton who lights on a mysterious truth. But there was no sense of cause and effect, only of occurrence.

The third example is the Council Chronicle of Lübeck, which was added after 1438 to the chronicle of a Franciscan reading-master who had composed his own story from older materials going back to 1101. In this case the non-clerical portion (1438–82) was written by the town scribe as part of the official annal, carried to 1469 by Johann Hertze, to 1480 by Johann Wunstorp, and finally to 1482 by Dietrich Brandes. It is a mixture of judicial proceedings, political reports and rumours. Imperial events and the wars against the Turks were known through papal legates who brought indulgences and through the emperor's agents. A long account of Charles the Bold's Swiss war of 1475–7 was copied verbatim from a Basel document, but it is only in relation to Burgundy that any trace of German national sentiment enters. As might be expected, the area of knowledge shown in the Lübeck chronicle was mainly confined to northern Europe, stretching from England and Flanders in the west, Scandinavia in the further north, across northern Germany to Livonia, with excursions into middle Germany and occasionally outward to Hungary, Switzerland and Italy. For the writer there was no 'Germany' as such but a series of interacting authorities: emperor, pope, princes and other cities, which encountered each other in conference or feud. Lübeck was clearly a juridical entity under its council, which had responsibility for the safety of trade and the freedom of the streets, and if roads were barred or convoys robbed the injury done was seen as an offence to God, honour and justice. Again, the architects of villainy were authorities who hindered commerce, whether Count Gerd of Oldenburg for his robberies, the council of Lüneburg which levied a new and 'treasonable' toll in 1472, the Teutonic Order as a manifold oppressor, or most of all King Christoph of Denmark. All these enemies of Lübeck were summed up in the adjective 'arrogant'.

These town writings make it clear that there was a network of vernacular intelligence over Germany which was urban, and specifically patrician, in its sentiments. The empire was understood and referred to in terms of the town, and the town stood to benefit from the imperial privileges it had long since been accorded by emperors who were theoretically competent yet without continuous geographical location. According to this pre-national universalism the empire, the kingdom and Christendom were identical yet served as a cloak for the actual power of the individual city. The enemies were princes and lords who were trying to modernize and round out their states and territories, and in doing so they were felt vaguely but strongly to be the servants of anti-Christ no less than Turk or Hussite.

Local and patrician though they were, the town sources allow views other than those of the rich merchants to be heard, for the later fourteenth and earlier fifteenth century was an era of rebellion by townsmen excluded from the cities' ruling circles.[16] The causes and course of these revolts do not fall within the subject-matter of this chapter, but the immediate point is the use of town chronicles as listening-points for other German voices, namely those of lesser merchants, artisans, mercenary captains, clerks, lawyers and taverners who felt their interests to be in some way blocked by the ruling establishments. True, men not engaged in long-distance trade were usually less able to write, but in some towns successful opposition brought new men on to the councils, and the discussions that got them there can be pieced together well enough to show German negotiating with German, townsman with townsman, class with class, in tones of voice contrasting with each other as radically as those heard in modern confrontations between established authorities and their critics. In Lübeck, for instance, the patrician council assumed that it must be acting in the interest of all and that lesser men were like a crowd of

9

schoolboys who simply did not understand what was at stake. Authority spoke in measured, civil tones: 'we don't mind what stupid people say but are distressed to be accused wrongly'; 'you will recall that....' 'as you well know...', and 'this will upset all decent people'. To such grave men, accustomed to handle diplomacy and levy taxes, the activity of high politics was not for every Johann and Heinrich. Councillors knew how things worked. They had access to town books and documents, and it probably did not even cross their minds that they enjoyed power. The oppositions, however, gave vent to a medley of complaints which can be extracted from recorded letters, and although they were numerous and varied they can mostly be summarized in angry cries of 'what has happened to our good money?' and 'it has been wasted by business-sharks and incompetents' who promote each other and go crawling to the town's foreign enemies. When it came to the point, the rebels were as scornful as any patrician of the anarchical mass of people below them whose arrogance and inflexibility were reflected obliquely in the documents but are never quoted verbatim. So we are left aware of quarrelsome discussions between patricians and those who were fighting to break into the patricians' literate world, and of vast areas in German town society which were inarticulate.

If this is true of towns, it also applies, in a rather different way, to countrysides. But here too the historian need not be disappointed by a wholly blank silence, for there are many surviving evidences of written rural communication. From the earlier twelfth century the practice began of discovering or agreeing about local customs such as boundaries in common fields, services due from peasants, and the rights of peasants themselves. These meetings were called *Weisungen* and the written document which embodied such agreements was a *Weistum*. In England it would be called a 'custumal'.[17] The number of these documents rose steeply in the fourteenth century to a peak in the sixteenth, and they originate from all over Germany except the colonial lands east of the Elbe. They are commonest from the Rhineland, Alsace, the Tyrol, Switzerland and Lower Austria, and rarest from southern Bavaria, Thuringia, Saxony, Bohemia and Moravia. In the course of time the *Weisung* changed from being mainly an oral interview between humbler villagers and the lord's steward, who would have the proceedings summed up in a Latin text, to being a two-sided question-and-answer consultation that involved the better-off and sometimes even permanent representatives of the local community, and which was written down in the vernacular. This is, of course, a generalized statement of the change to which all sorts of exceptions could doubtless be found, but the growing dominance of villager leaders or jurors *(Schöffen)* seems clear from the tests. A twelfth-century *Weistum* from the Cologne area remarked that justice had suffered because the selected villagers had been miserable-looking speciments and should in future be taken from amongst 'the better-off, more powerful and more prudent men'.[18] But by the fourteenth century the higher status and greater articulateness of villagers was being matched by lords who sometimes sent trained notaries to the meetings, and by the earlier fifteenth century villagers were beginning to object to this method of proceeding, preferring a vernacular rendering under their own control of what they deemed to be 'good old customs'. At a meeting in 1427 in western Germany 'jurors observed that a notary was present and refused to make any more statements, saying it was not customary to have such a man before them, and they got up and went away.'[19] The story demonstrates a strengthening rural resistance to late medieval lordly dominance, but in this context it illustrates the movement of written communication into the countryside.

Town chronicles and country custumals are only two contrasting kinds of developing written communication in medieval Germany. By the fourteenth century literacy was becoming widely extended in many territories, both in quantity and in specialization.[20] At the top of the scale, the number of imperial charters had increased enormously under Frederick II, but lack of effective centralization in Germany meant that the continuing increase in official writing was centred in principalities and towns no less than in the royal chancery, wherever that happened to be. In the Palatinate, for example, the fourteenth century saw a striking rise in the number of letters from the count to the king, especially those concerned with property pledged for money by the count, whose sheer lack of cash led him to use written instruments and bits of land as much as currency. There are also a good many written settlements of frontiers, as various leagues required and got precise delineations of areas in which troops, contributions, booty, protection and trade were to be administered. Such arrangements were constantly being changed, and scribes were learning to be briefer in recording the necessary descriptions. In its

11

own way the competition for scarce economic resources and the spread of literacy helped the 'administered' territory's emergence out of the older feudal lordship, operated solemnly by witnessed charter and more routinely by word of mouth. Most surviving letters of instruction or grant were, of course, one-way matters, passing from higher to lower officials, and it is far clearer that taxes were demanded than how effectively they were paid. Central archives pre-date local ones. In the archbishopric of Mainz many registers were kept from the mid-fourteenth century onwards, but only the minority were about spiritual matters. Most were about the administration of the archbishop's territorial state, about pledges, castles, treaties, payment of soldiers and about those all-important river tolls to which the financial liquidity of the Rhineland princes owed so much. Far away to the east the Teutonic Order was the most homogeneous German principality in its basic legal and administrative procedures, though a prolific correspondence between central and local officials developed only after c.1350. In the fourteenth century many accounts and memoranda were still kept on waxen tablets, of which a handful have survived. But the Order was developing a postal system worked by mounted couriers, runners and 'letter-boys' *(Briefjungen)*, and when written letters were thus sent they were endorsed with timings and route-plans.

Development in written administration meant not only specialization in the varieties of document but more use of the vernacular. This can be seen beginning in the fourteenth and even thirteenth century, when lay officials *(Amtmänner)* sometimes reported back to their masters on the action they had taken in German but with a formal Latin ending to the letter. More complex discussion between lesser officials called for personal meetings, but town schools were playing a part in the spread of German official literacy, teaching their pupils to write quickly and in small characters. There were links between popular speech and this informal business-writing of the lay world. Princes and lords were sending more letters than before, but letters less formal in their nature and starting with the first person, singular or plural. This began in the early fourteenth century in the archbishoprics of Mainz and Trier where Latin was used, but it was taken up in the vernacular first by lay princes. German formularies were being compiled in fourteenth-century Lübeck. A side-effect of the ten-years' war between Luxemburg and Wittelsbach in mid-century was the register of land-holding *(Landbuch)* compiled by order of the Emperor Charles IV in 1373-5 for Brandenburg. The procedure expanded later into records of possessions and dues in the Mark based on questionnaires put by travelling officials, so that mere villages were woven into the administrative unity of the territory. Likewise in 1414 the Teutonic Order began its Great Rent Book *(Grosses Zinsbuch)*, arranged by districts and noting under each the villages, whether inhabited or depopulated. Books of grants or enfeoffments were specialized out of general official registers in the fourteenth century in order to centralize the prince's information. Many earlier ones come from ecclesiastical territories, though the Meissen registers were prepared by clerks trained in Bologna. The first German-language feodary or *Lehnbuch* derives from Brunswick in 1383-5.[21] Administration takes a leap forward when copies of documents are kept. Triplication is a stock joke today against bureaucracy, but even to a clerk of Archbishop Baldwin of Trier (1307-54) it brought, in his own words, 'an almost hopeless amount of work'. The practice was learned from the more advanced French chancery through the Luxemburg dynasty to which both Archbishop Baldwin and the Emperor Charles belonged. To an English historian this is nothing new, for already in the thirteenth century Archbishop John Pecham of Canterbury was lodging copies of titles in Canterbury and taking other copies round with him on his journeys through his province. But in the great territorial archdiocese of Trier in the heart of the Rhineland the copying of documents in the fourteenth century was an administrative advance. The portion that the archbishop took round with him was inscribed 'that you know you have this and that as a grant'. The significance of this will be better realized when in a later chapter Baldwin's state-building is discussed, and it is seen how this outstanding man was buying up and affirming his rights to castles and other kinds of property which had fragmented into the hands of lesser but dangerous nobles. Similar methods of recording and enregistration were being used by the Teutonic Order after 1360.

The keeping of financial accounts also came later in Germany than in England, and there are few from the fourteenth century even in the greater principalities. Some of the earliest also occur in Trier. The provosts of Mainz, beneficed by the Avignon pope, showed some skill in this field too, and proved to be hard task-masters in keeping their clerks up at night. Likewise the bishops of Passau had the costs of journeys noted down as well as the expenditure of household and officials. The Teutonic Order kept rather sophisticated accounts, and some others in the fourteenth century come from the Tyrol. All betray the usual 'immaturity' of medieval accountancy in northern Europe, in that they failed to distinguish plainly between receipts, costs and inventories, and rendered economic statements of incomings and outgoings in Latin sentences and Roman numerals instead of arithmetical columns. Yet, as Professor Basil Yamey has remarked, men make do with the accounts they need, and even in modern times an individual entrepreneur may well hold in his head what is required for quite complex operations.[22] As might be expected, the earliest German financial documents derive from mercantile concerns. From the thirteenth century more merchants began to sit at home and send their goods to be sold by agents, often working on commission. Naturally this could not be done without record, even less so when credit was used. The first surviving merchants' books date from the 1340s in Lübeck and Rostock, though they lack the sophistication of the Italian method with its division into day-book and ledger.

Whether we are thinking of accounts, acts, proceedings, or registers of copies, however, it would be a mistake to suppose that princely and urban writing developed quite separately. Notaries and scribes were employed by both noble and civic authorities. Many were clerical and trained in ecclesiastical or princely chancelleries or in Bologna, but an increasing number were laymen who learned their craft in town schools like that of Lübeck, which was physically attached to the town's administrative buildings, and there was some interchange of personnel between the writing-offices of Germany.

The expense of parchment and the laboriousness of using it were obvious hindrances to speedy, copious and informal writing. It is interesting that the use of paper became common at least as early in Germany as in England, perhaps earlier, despite England's more advanced administration. This may owe something to the fact that England was a great sheep-raising country, but at all events it underlines again the technical as opposed to the political skill of Germans. Paper, a Chinese invention, came to Italy earlier than to northern Europe, and it was in Italy that Germans began to buy it. Some registers belonging to the Luxemburg dynasty were already made of paper in the fourteenth century. But the big advance in the imperial chancellery came with the Emperor Rupert (1400–10), and from this time smaller offices, both of princes and towns, went over increasingly to paper. It made communication speedier and cheaper and is another instance of the way in which technical advance is brought about in times of disturbance and hostility, when lists, agreements and messages of all kinds are more urgently required. Italy was near at hand, and the connections enjoyed there by German merchants made import an easy matter. It also made the spread of technical knowledge easy. The first German paper-mill was probably got going by an ingenious piece of industrial espionage, but at any rate there was a converted metal workshop owned by the great Nuremberg family of Stromer which was put to paper manufacture in about 1390. King Sigismund heard of it and was anxious to exploit the discovery, and soon afterwards paper was being made in many German centres.

There are historical connections, not always realized, between the development of paper manufacture and the much more publicized invention of printing. These links are as much personal as technical. And it is a curious fact that, while the secret of paper-making was stolen from Italy by Germans, the printing which was to revolutionize mental communication was a German invention.

What is known of the origins of movable-type printing is too familiar to rehearse here.[23] The personal contacts by which these discoveries were mediated, however, are worth noting in an introductory chapter on communication, even though the urban setting will be explained more fully and with some repetition later on.

The acknowledged inventor of printing belonged to the patrician family of Gensfleisch in Mainz and took his personal name, (Johann) Gutenberg, as medieval people so easily did, from the property in Mainz where he lived. He was a skilled worker in precious metals, so his family circumstances were not unlike those of the Stromer of Nuremberg, the paper-makers whose firm also worked as bladesmiths, as apothecaries, and in commerce. Nuremberg was a more stable city than Mainz, from which Gutenberg was exiled in 1428 to live many years as a resident alien in Strassburg. But in 1448 he was back in Mainz, in association with the money-lending lawyer Johann Fust, who got taken into partnership in 'the work of the books'. Another Mainz family, the Zum Jungen, were Gutenberg's friends and helpers who at one time had his printing presses standing in their house. The Zum Jungen were also friends of the Stromer of Nuremberg.

In 1455 Gutenberg was made bankrupt and his stock taken over by Fust. It is interesting that the notary who received Fust's affidavit against Gutenberg at Mainz in 1455 was one Dr Ulrich Helmasperger, clerk of the diocese of Bamberg, because it was to a Bamberg man that Gutenberg disposed of some of his bankrupt stock. This was Albrecht Pfister,[24] the first printer to illustrate his books with pictures. Clearly, there was a wide German network of families or people working in Nuremberg, Mainz, Strassburg, Bamberg and doubtless other places as well, as rivals but also as friends, interested in producing, amongst other things, the consumer goods of communication.

Pictures are another medium of this activity which must not be wholly ignored here. To paint illustrations of manuscript books is a commonplace of the medieval scene. More particularly, Charles IV attracted foreign artists to Prague.[25] His son and successor, Wenzel IV, made use of Bohemian book illustrators, who worked on Bibles, books of entertainment, and astronomical, geographical and military texts. By the fifteenth century there were numerous princely bibliophiles, and many townsmen also, who wanted illustrated books and archives, holy pictures on single leaves, playing cards and the like.

This popularization of the hand-illustrated book is important for our understanding of late medieval German minds. A single, outstanding example will be helpful, though it is not unique. This is the so-called *Medieval Housebook (Das mittelalterliche Hausbuch)*, preserved in the ownership of the princes of Waldburg-Wolfegg, in Swabia.[26] It is a parchment manuscript book of miscellaneous contents which one would expect to find of interest to well-off burghers or noblemen, and deserving of greater fame for its vivid skill. The book has been cut about since its first making in about 1480, but there are now some four dozen illustrated pages, including pen-and-ink drawings, engravings, and painted coats of arms, tournament scenes and mineworks. The first owner was probably a well-to-do townsmen of a Rhenish city, technically minded, interested in warfare (he took part in the siege of Neuss), and accustomed to a conventional family life in which the father looked up to the emperor, taught his grown-up sons how to behave, viewed with cynicism the marriage of partners of very disparate ages for the sake of money, and enjoyed the entertainments of hunting, fishing, mild gambling and the antics of jugglers. A series of detailed drawings illustrates the characters of people born under the sign of each one of the planets, and in so doing

16

portrays many daily activities: cultivation of fields, butchering, studying, practising archery, flirting, executing criminals, playing musical instruments, wrestling, bathing and the savage looting of villages in the course of war or feud. There is a courtly element in the Garden of Love, and in tournaments where both the blunt and the sharp lance was used. Many drawings convey the technology of peace and war: coining, metallurgy, the military encampment and the siege-train, early pieces of ordnance, levers, bolts and brakes. This genre was not uncommon. Konrad Eyser of Eichstätt composed his *Belli fortis*, a picture-book on the military arts, in 1405, and prefaced it with views of the planets. The creator of this *Housebook* is sometimes called the 'Master of the Amsterdam Cabinet' because engravings by the same hand are in the print-room of the Rijksmuseum there. But whether or not he was Netherlandish, his mature work seems more at home in the middle Rhine area. Above all, the humorous subtlety and naturalism of his drawing of men and animals put him firmly in the world of Dürer.

Just as technicians in metal took the world from manuscript to printed text, so it passed also from crayon and brush to the mechanically reproduced picture. The illustrated books begun by Albrecht Pfister start with the *Ackermann aus Böhmen* of 1460 in wood-cut, and from then the flood grew. At Augsburg, Günther Zainer and Johann Bämler continued what Pfister had begun. In the later fifteenth century a favourite theme was the 'mirror of human life', which in one form or another illustrated the joys and sorrows of various human callings, secular and spiritual, juxtaposed in contrast with each other. In such a mirror we see the interior life of German people as deeply moralistic, aware of hierarchy and degree, accustomed to violence, rejoicing mainly in the cruder pleasures, and resigned to the mysterious turns of fate in which the influence of heavenly bodies somehow operated within the Christian scheme of man's free will to pursue vice or virtue.

It is a truism to observe that this was the world into which Luther was born, but we are historically deprived if we can see it only from the sixteenth century backwards. Late medieval Germany was, at one and the same time, individualistic and anonymous in its modes of communication. Illustrators were often independent and itinerant and used their print-blocks in different places. Some were creative but many were skilled copyists. They had the tantalizing habit of

17

identifying their works, if at all, by initials or monograms. Production required capital-organization and money troubles were frequent. Hence, by reason of plagiarism, sale, bankruptcy or inheritance, it is extremely difficult to be sure who executed the pictures and where. At the same time the huge number of surviving pictures possess generic qualities which indicate clearly what people liked. Over and over again the portrayal of life, work and death suggests that many educated and half-educated Germans lived in a world half satirical, half fantastic, in which humour played a stronger part than wit, and folly was castigated with a solemnity that placed a higher value on right order than on simple pleasure. Hedonism was for peasants, who are depicted guzzling and vomiting without restraint. The burgher gave more thought to aping noble style, but interrupted his efforts constantly by sombre reflections on the discipline of work and the folly of desire.

2

Kings and their Politics

(a) *The general nature of the German kingship during the later middle ages*

This book is an introductory study of a little-known epoch in the history of the German-speaking lands. Whether these can at that time be called a country is an interesting point of speculation. In 1350 *Deutschland* was not common usage, but the plural, *deutsche lande*, might often be found.[1] In the later fifteenth century 'German nation' overtook 'German lands' and appears in the time of Frederick III in conjunction with 'empire': for example, 'the holy empire and our German nation'. But whatever the political, national or ethnic characteristics of late medieval Germany, it certainly had a king.

At least two objections may be raised against writing a chapter like this on the German monarchy. The first is that the king was also the emperor of the so-called 'holy' or 'Holy Roman' empire, and that these two royal overlordships, by no means all German, were historically so bound together that it is misleading to write at all of one without the other. The second objection is that a political narrative of the German kingship may give the impression that royal policy possessed the same sort of overriding importance within the realm as it did in more centralized monarchies, even in the middle ages, whereas in reality Germany differed from kingdoms like England or France in that the monarch's politics, often weak, remote or muted, formed a continuing counterpoint to those of the great princes.

These are powerful objections. But despite an accepted danger of doing violence to a complex whole, the risks are going to be taken. The purpose is to write about German society at a particular phase of its development, and German historians themselves give good reasons for separating the history of Germany, regional though it was, from a

19

history of the empire.[2] The price will be a short excursion into the remoter past which, it is hoped, will have the effect of justification as well as explanation for those unfamiliar with the scene. As to a narrative treatment of the monarchy, it will serve as a footpath in country which has not yet many tracks for ordinary walkers.

The great stem-duchies of the ninth and tenth centuries were ruled by dukes who were of equal status but who elected one of their number king. Henry I (the Fowler), duke of Saxony, was elected king in 919, and his son Otto I succeeded him. This Saxon dynasty was unsurpassed in wealth and continued till it died out in 1024.[3] It acquired the central duchy of Franconia as royal territory and came to control other duchies with the support of great prelates who were enriched.

After 962 the kings, who had been crowned in Aachen, were also crowned as emperors by the pope in Rome, as had first been done for Charlemagne in 800. This practice continued across the changes in German royal dynasties.

In 1024 the Franconian count Conrad, by descent both a Frank and a Saxon, was chosen king and became the first member of the Franconian or Salian dynasty, which lasted till 1125. Then, with the intermission of Lothar of Saxony (1125–37), came the six generations of (Hohen)staufen kings, dukes of Swabia, who reigned from 1138 till the death of Conrad IV in 1254.

One must ask of whom or what these Germans were king. The earlier Saxons had been called kings of the East Franks, or Franks and Germans, or Germans. Henry II (1002–24), anxious to further his Italian claims, started calling himself king of the Romans even before his imperial coronation by the pope in 1014, and this became the chancery style and usual title of the king after Lothar. Towards the end of the thirteenth century, however, a German scholar observed that since Barbarossa's time (Frederick I, 1152–90) the political weight of the empire had been displaced so much to the south that people had started to talk about *regnum Alamanniae* rather than *regnum Germaniae* or *Theutoniae* or *Romanorum*. He was, of course, referring to the south German duchy of Swabia. For some contemporaries *Alemannia* was an old name for this duchy. The practice of referring to the kingdom of Alemannia was observed by others in the late thirteenth century, including Pope Gregory X and papal curialists in respect of Rudolf of Habsburg, and also by Germans like the archbishop of Mainz who were anxious to emphasize the boundary between Germany and

20

Bohemia. Even as emperor, Lewis of Bavaria (1314–47) was occasionally called *imperator Alemanniae*.[4]

The empire through its medieval history had various shades of meaning. To some men of the tenth century like the Saxon Widukind, acclamation of the king appeared actually to create the empire directly under God,[5] but if further definition was required they referred themselves to the empire of the Franks, bequeathed by Henry I in 936 to his son Otto. Otto I in fact used the title *Imperator Augustus* without making any prior connection with Rome. But when he and his successors entered Italy and became involved with Rome, the theme of the succession to the Roman empire was soon elaborated. Territories outside Germany were included in the empire: northern Italy, Burgundy and a suzerainty over Bohemia.

Popes from the time of Innocent III (1198–1216) thought of the emperor as a sort of ordinand, to be approved by them, as was explained in the famous decretal *Per Venerabilem* of 1202 which reversed previous church teaching and called the elected king 'the king who is to be promoted emperor' *(rex in imperatorem promovendus)*. Innocent IV, at the First Council of Lyons in 1245, even declared the emperor deposed.

Royalist resistance to the claims of clerical and papal superiority have a long and complex history. The thinking behind *Per Venerabilem* was never generally accepted. More to the present discussion, imperial politics themselves were becoming increasingly unpopular in the late thirteenth century. This is true of Germany itself as well as of the world outside, where Angevins and Lombards were sometimes heard wondering what purpose the empire served any longer.

Concurrently, the distinction between the king and the emperor was becoming blurred rather than clarifed. One writer, Mathias von Neuenburg, wrote: 'King Albert [I]...was powerful in the kingdom of Alemannia...[but] took no account of other parts'.[6] Rudolf of Habsburg (1273–91), who wanted to defend the imperial idea, wrote that certain castles belonged to the king 'by reason of the empire *or kingdom of Alemannia*'. In 1355 Pope Innocent V used the phrase 'the princes of Alemannia who have the vote in the election of the king of the Romans'. Indeed, it is strongly arguable that under Lewis of Bavaria the difference between king and emperor had been in an important respect obliterated. At the famous declaration of Rhense in 1338 he denied the pope any say in the election of the king in

21

Germany. His protégé William of Ockham, the great philosopher, said there was only a verbal distinction between this king and the emperor. Even his opponent Pope John XXII spoke of *regnum seu imperium.*

From this time the term *regnum Alemanniae* began to fade out. If reference to the empire was required, 'German empire' or 'holy empire' were preferred. The notion was still found that the empire had four chief cities: Arles (for Burgundy), Aachen (for Germany), Milan (for Lombardy) and Rome (for the universal lordship over Christendom or, as it was even sometimes expressed, the world). But in German minds the dominance of Germany prevailed. The chroniclers Meisterlin and Schedel both wrote in the fifteenth century of the *Teutscher Kaiser,* and a pamphlet of 1500 declared that the Roman empire now resided in the German nation (*Der römische Reich soll iezt in deutscher Nation sein*).

The growing consciousness of German identity in language and political feeling which is argued in this book cannot be made to correspond with any strengthening of its kingship. The fundamental reason for this, if there is a single one, never ceases to exercise the mind. But a number of general and particular suggestions may be made here.

In the first place, history books suggest too glibly that the weakness of late medieval kingship in Germany was in a sort of direct contrast with an earlier strength. The opinion in its simplistic form depends upon comparing unlikes. The periods of 'strong' rule over loyal princes and churchmen in, say, the eleventh century, or a king's 'possession' of all the great duchies save Saxony and Lotharingia, occurred when political society itself was more primitive than it became in and after the thirteenth century, and belong to days when communications were even poorer, detailed and written administration most slight, royal treasure crudely distributable even when copious. Of course the king may have been stronger in relation to his subjects than he was later, just as Cnut was stronger than Henry VI of England. But the comparison is not illuminating.

A naive contrast between a strong early medieval monarchy and a weak late medieval one does not, however, explain away the ineffectiveness of German kingship at a period when the English and French monarchies were developing into centralized institutions. Attempts at explanation are still required.

German disadvantages are often rehearsed, and a list set down here more or less at random might run as follows: the size and regionalism of the country; the threats to security from east and west; the elective principle of kingship which impeded the formation of a distinct and continuing royal domain with a revenue and an administration capable of being expanded; the transformation of one-time royal servants in the localities into independent land-holders, no longer servile but noble in status; and the insubordination of great princely vassals who could take advantage of the kings' non-German preoccupation, not to mention papal hostility, to make themselves virtually independent.

The demerits are formidable and the list is doubtless incomplete, yet many have at some time been controverted, and they are difficult to arrange in an order of historical logic. If Germany was large and regional, so was France; other kings had rebellious vassals too; elective kingship can avoid dangerous minorities among heirs and can be operated (as indeed it often was in Germany) as a *de facto* heritable office; Italy could have been a source of wealth; and so on.

German royal weakness is best qualified by saying that it was neither a moral defect nor anywhere near total. It manifested itself in stages, with remissions, and although admittedly complex in origins appears to the present writer mainly a consequence of the Italian adventure. Certainly there were attractive reasons why Saxon, Salian and Staufen kings should seek fortune and fulfilment south of the Alps: cash-flow from 'imperial' towns, the sacred universalism of empire, the advantages of a more literate and ancient world, even at moments the prospect of an Italian kingdom. But the expeditions and the sojourns south of the Alps surely brought more ill experience than benefits: papal censures, military defeats, ruinous expenditures, royal deaths and, above all, absences of the king from the German homeland in the north for the sake of alluring southern regions too alien and too civilized to be absorbed.

In the matter of chronology, German kingship can be seen in trouble well before the time of Pope Innocent III, but papal policy thereafter compounded the destruction. The double election of 1198, the civil wars of the thirteenth century and the Interregnum of 1256–73 (see p.125) were main stages in the dissipation of royal resources. When the Staufen were gone and new dynasties came to dominate the later medieval German world, monarchs were still for the most part proudly conscious of the imperial character. But if Italy was no longer the deadliest deception, the empire remained an impediment. The Luxemburgs tried to make a secure base in Bohemia but much energy was spent on eastern Europe, schismatic popes, church councils and Turkish invaders. Bohemia blew up in their faces.

The Habsburgs who followed were pinned to the south-east of Europe for a number of compelling reasons. They had their Austrian problems to solve, as will be seen. The Turkish enemy was at hand and to resist him was not only a Habsburg need but a burden, half political and half religious, incurred when Frederick III (for good reason) supported Pope Eugenius IV against the Council of Basel and hence required to fight for the briefly reunited Greek and Latin churches. All this conspired to concentrate Habsburg efforts for a long time in Lower Danube regions.

There is more certainty in discussing the financial and administrative weakness of the monarchy.

In writing about royal wealth it is customary to make a distinction between what belonged to the king as his own family possession *(Hausgut)* and what belonged to the crown or the empire. (The difference between *Krongut* and *Reichsgut* is itself contentious and mirrors the increasing haziness between the offices of king and emperor, but the matter will not be further discussed here.)[7] The royal *Hausgut* fluctuated from king to king and time to time. There is a touching story about a question put to Rudolf of Habsburg by the knight Walter von Klingen:

'Lord, who is the keeper of your treasure?'

'God has looked after me up to now, and will go on doing so.'[8]

At the other extreme, Charles IV looked after himself, both in acquiring dynastic possessions and sometimes in employing skilled clerks to document them, as in the case of the Brandenburg *Landbuch*. There is more to be said, in its place, about the private fortunes of the kings, but in an account of the kingship's general nature the reader naturally wants to know about kingly income as such.

Probably there was no original distinction between the two. If the Saxon kings amassed properties and rights in the duchies they came to possess, some them Carolingian, and then died out in the direct line, it would not be strange for many of these to be aggregated with the possessions of the Salian house, clustered in the elbow of the Rhine south of its junction with the Main. In due course the succession of

Staufen to the empire would bring massive properties in Swabia to join their inheritance in Franconia and elsewhere.

The distinction between *Hausgut* and *Reichsgut* takes on a sharper meaning when the Staufen were annihilated in the male line and their properties exposed to plunder, and when new dynasties arrived on the scene with little but their *Hausmacht* to support them.

The surviving records of *Reichsgut* are very few indeed, but Dr Ernst Schubert adopted the ingenious technique of discovering something about it from documents recording royal gifts and pledges, especially in the fourteenth century.[9]

The most important royal income from the empire consisted of various kinds of tax levied on towns. These derived not from overall royal levies, as in England, but from historical circumstances particular to each case: demands for the support of campaigns, threats of penalty or of pledging if a demand were refused, gifts in recognition of royal honour *(Ehrung)* when a king was crowned or when he paid a visit to a city. There is a haphazard sense about these fiscal relations of towns to the emperor, a feeling less of consensual organization than of menaces mingled with flattery and based more on expediency than precedent. When Philip duke of Burgundy travelled in 1454 to the Diet of Regensburg the imperial cities gave him *Ehrungsgaben* 'as though he were the emperor'.[10] If a conspicuous display might awe a city into offering presents, the converse could happen too, in the sense that a newly elected king without continuous administration might not know the perquisites he could claim in recognition of honour.

More durable were the multiple rights possessed by emperors over the villages, forests, farmsteads, mills and other real property of certain districts, especially in south-western Germany. These were not extensions of city rights but more like royal manors in England, places where the king could stay on his constant journeyings. Generically they were called 'imperial districts' *(Reichsbereiche)* and bore local names tacked on to the word *Reich*. A king would be able to say: 'The court will be staying (without payment) in the *Kaiserslautener Reich* or the *Andernacher Reich*'. It was a sad reflection that by Sigismund's time so many of these had been lost that when in 1417 he stayed at Constance his chamberlain, Konrad von Weinsberg, had to dispense over 5,000 florins a day on the court's food alone where, in a district once thick with imperial estates, it would formerly have been supplied as of right.[11]

Other important possessions were the imperial forests like those round Nuremberg and Hagenau, preserved better than most assets from lasting pledging by the king, and the imperial abbeys, which were useful points of hospitality on the journeyings of kings and their employees. Sometimes this passing right over an imperial abbey had been greatly extended by the acquisition of imperial advocacy or stewardship *(Reichsvogtei)* over it. This involved farmsteads, courts, even villages. Such was the case at St Gall, over which the king possessed innumerable landed and incorporeal rights. These complex properties were valuable. Those of St Gall were ultimately sold off piecemeal by Lewis IV.

This is not a comprehensive list of imperial property-types, but allusion should be made to income from the Jewish communities in various royal cities, to fees for chancery and royal court work, and to the 'fines' so familiar in English history. It was a charge against Wenzel, as it was against his English brother-in-law Richard II, that he had summoned and arbitrarily fined too many people.

Accurate valuation of imperial property at any one time is impossible, though Dr Schubert has been willing to guess intelligently at an annual income in the earlier fourteenth century of some 100,000 florins. As a very rough comparison, the richest electors in the year 1500 were getting about 80,000 florins.[12] The best use one can make of vague aggregate figures is to observe how severe was the loss of *Reichsgut* between the death of Frederick II in 1250 and the time of Sigismund, who complained that he got only 13,000 florins from the empire.

But that is a time-span of some two hundred years. When, more precisely, was this imperial property lost? The answer to that question is bound to affect our judgement of kings. Again, it is impossible to be certain about details, but a generalized picture may be sketched.

A substantial proportion of the empire's property was probably usurped in the Interregnum and not recovered, despite efforts by Rudolf of Habsburg. Recent scholarship argues that most of the losses of that time went in pledges by kings for their political needs and support from territorial powers. To a prince or count, local pieces of imperial property were of much more individual importance in rounding out a domain than any particular estate would be to a king whose overall policy was on a vaster scale. In this way there was a leakage of *Reichsgut* from the beginning of the Interregnum onwards, especially in south-west and central Germany, and not slackening much as the fourteenth century proceeded. But, in E. Schubert's analysis, the great bulk of imperial pledging was done by Charles IV. Unlike his predecessors he acted not out of penury but ambition. He took huge sums from imperial assets in order to secure the election of his son Wenzel to the German and imperial throne without any charge upon the Bohemian kingdom that was the very basis of his dynasty. Whereas earlier royal beneficiaries had often been scattered local magnates and monasteries, such as the families of former Staufen burgraves, now in the mid-fourteenth century the alienations were more especially to the great, and especially to the Rhineland Electors.

It was in particular the birth of Wenzel in 1361 that loosed the torrent of Charles's imperial pledging. To pinpoint the moment proves the intention. Even Charles made efforts to redeem pledges after Wenzel's election, but it was too late. Too much had stuck to powerful fingers, and it was all made final as well as admitted in early sixteenth-century acts like the Electoral Agreement of 1519, which declared that princes should remain in undisturbed possession of their imperial pledged lands.

It will be obvious that by the fifteenth century the German monarchy possessed very little wealth or capacity for raising it beyond the family possessions any individual king might inherit or acquire. Why, then, did the empire not raise imperial taxes for imperial purposes, at least in their German context? The answer is that late in the day two methods were indeed tried, one in the end partly successful, the other hardly used at all.[13]

The urgency of royal poverty was brought home to others than the king by the Hussite wars of 1420–34. With the Luxemburg inheritance fragmented and Hungary needing resources, the violent Hussite eruptions and the mounting of five separate crusading campaigns posed appalling military and financial problems, not only for Sigismund but for Latin Christendom in general and numbers of terrified German princes in particular. The warfare called for continuous funding. In 1422 the Diet of Nuremberg agreed a monetary tax on all Germany of 1 per cent on governments, 1 per cent on individuals, and more on Jews. The same kind of levy was attempted in 1433–4 at the Diet of Basel, but the defeat of the extreme Hussites at Lipany removed the urgency and the whole fiscal device petered out. The failure had not been total and the scheme provided a model for the later Common Penny. The stiffest resistance seems to have come from the towns, which were afraid not so much of the immediate payments as of the imagined dangers of disclosing individual fortunes, and the humiliation of admitting regular taxability by a royal authority which might in any case pledge such an admitted right to others.

The second expedient had a longer history. It was to draw up a quota list, or *Matrikel*, of personages and bodies with the amounts they should pay. This too was launched in the *Reichstag* at Nuremberg in 1422, one list of relieve Karlstein Castle in Prague, the other for 'the daily expense of war'. Its further exploitation came at and after the end of the fifteenth century, and will be discussed briefly at the end of this chapter in the context of the Henneberg Reform movement. But it did not strengthen the German monarchy of the late middle ages, despite the empire's increasingly German self-consciousness. On the contrary, when used as it was in 1437 it proved not only a highly regressive tax but also one enforced locally by princely decree, and was hence one more instrument of German particularism.

A counterpart to royal poverty was the monarchy's lack of developed institutions of administration and law such as could be seen at more advanced stages in certain principalities, not to speak of the western kingdoms.

The most formed royal institution was the chancery. It was even more part of the court than in England, but represented the king and dealt with royal matters rather than purely territorial ones.[14] Frederick II had issued a copious charter-flow of miscellaneous content: royal castles, towns, peace-keeping and hawking.[15] This organization did not last. Lewis of Bavaria had to organize a chancery, and issued few documents and apparently no financial records. Charles IV's reorganization of the office is well-known and was referred to in Chapter 1. But the point should be made here that the chancery was now becoming more independent of the king's own daily business. It contained protonotaries and diplomats of high rank, and could function without evident disruption by the king's prolonged absence.

Professor Moraw goes rather further than this in seeing the tenuous construction of a royal chancery tradition from the time of Rudolf of Habsburg, in which the reign of Lewis of Bavaria is a period of obscurity and not necessarily of fracture.

It would be historically satisfying to trace through a chancery office, as seems possible, from the time of Charles IV to the end of the middle ages. But as many ages learn with bitterness, trained graduate colleagues do not necessarily make profit for their employers, and it seems that little revenue flowed from the typical chancery activity, in the fifteenth century, of confirming charters and privileges. The chancery could express power but not create or bestow it. Sigismund had a busy chancery under the famous Kaspar Schlick (taken over by the Habsburgs), but its voluminous issue of documents, what H. Koller excellently called its joy in writing *(Schreibfreudigkeit)*, did not further real administration so much as simply confirm rights and grants to please recipients and attract small payments.

The heart of the monarchy's patrimonial commonwealth was the court *(Hof)*, which journeyed about at need. The kingship is frequently and correctly noted for its failure to do justice adequately in its vast realm, but for all that there is something to say about its judicial aspect, the *Hofgericht*.

By the mid-fourteenth century most spiritual and secular princes and all imperial towns were free of external summons in cases concerning their subjects or citizens. But royal officialdom could still operate regionally for the king in hearing cases concerning the king's own lands. As assessors it could use laymen of knightly status or, on occasion, men of learning.[16] The body which did this, the *Hofgericht*, may have received Sicilian influences from the Staufen time, but from Rudolf of Habsburg's time certainly possessed a modest staff of judges and notaries, many still known by name and visible in operating across dynastic changes. For example, Lewis of Bavaria's *Hofrichter* of 1345 also held office under Charles IV, though the two kings were bitter enemies.

Demonstration of continuity, though not yet complete, brings the *Hofgericht* near to being an institution of government, but does not mean that it flourished. On the contrary, it appears to have declined in power in the fifteenth century, as the territorial jurisdictions grew more professional and bold, and to have disappeared altogether in 1451. Gregor of Heimburg spoke sardonically before the *Hofgericht* in Nuremberg on the futility of calling princes of the empire before it: 'And who could find a prince to serve, pour soul, as summoner? Money and goods, house and farm, wife and child, they'd rob you of the lot, for you cannot demand justice against them'.

But there was another court, used for certain needs, a far cry from an English summons to the king's council, yet not without some slight vestige of similarity. When councillors sitting by themselves gave a judgement rather than simply counsel to the king, and about some principle of royal privilege, there you had a Chamber Court *(Kammergericht)*. This was heard of under Sigismund, even by name and distinctly.[17] In 1425 he wrote to Basel of his *kuniglichen kamer- und hofgerichten*. The court played some part later in freeing certain cities from the Vehmic courts and functioned as the emperor's ultimate, personal administration of justice in cases otherwise protected by privilege. The subject-matter was usually fiscal, but unconfined by precisely laid-down boundaries. In some instances at least it sat under a Procurator-Fiscal, and its work was enlarged, as will be seen, in Frederick III's later years. A judgement of 1445 calls it *das höchst und obrist gericht.*[18] It met at need, frequently at Rottweil near Stuttgart, and although itself subject to delays, costs and inefficiency it was given new life by Maximilian.

These observations on the 'general nature' of the German kingship cannot but be defective, for the subject is both contentious and of great difficulty. The balance of detail and generality too is a matter of judgement. But if in the more narrative portion of this chapter which ensues, or indeed elsewhere in the book, there are repetitions, these are not always unintended. For the complexity of the German scene is such that patterns must reappear in the tapestry. And indeed, in any tapestry, for a picture to emerge at all, details must sometimes be omitted as well as reduplicated.

(b) *New dynasties*

Beginners in the study of history often assume that great political events are shaped either by the personalities of ruling individuals or, alternatively, by irresistible material forces. To these bold simplifications should be added another consideration, no more all-explanatory than the others, yet perhaps insufficiently grasped by young medievalists. This is the fact of the dynasty, or dominant family, which embodied government in remote times and has not even yet ceased to be without political significance.

The prolonged succession of father by son, as in Capetian France, was the biological vehicle of a success-story so impressive that we are easily beguiled into thinking of such genetic behaviour as a kind of norm, and a norm of moral worth into the bargain. But in reality medieval dynasties seem more often to have confounded themselves with too many children, sharing the patrimony, or else to have died out in the male line, than to have proceeded like the first chapter of St Matthew's Gospel.

In the two centuries which run approximately from 1250 to 1450 the political shape of Europe was fundamentally moulded by the extinction and new creation of dynasts.

In 1246 the ruling Austrian family of Babenberg died out. In 1254 the last Hohenstaufen king and emperor was killed. In 1301 the last Árpád king of Hungary died childless. In 1306 the Bohemian line of Přemsylids ended in a daughter. In 1370 the last Piast king of Poland, Casimir the Great, died without leaving a son.

In place of these, different families moved by marriage and war to the seats of rulership. Sometimes an ancient dynasty extended itself into fresh lands; more often a lesser house rose from modest possessions to great princely stature. The Angevins were one of the most impressive families of the medieval world and, having come to southern Italy from France, went thence to Hungary in 1308 by marriage and produced Louis the Great. By the time of his death in 1382 he was ruling both Hungary and Poland. There too the line ended with daughters, but they were daughters of whom one took the Hungarian crown and passed it to Sigismund and the other married a Lithuanian heathen to create an enlarged, Catholic and independent Poland.

These details are not irrelevant to the course of German society. Dynasty is not just a game for family historians. The family histories, even in outline, explain the importance to Germany of its eastern neighbours: why Hungary entered the Austrian imperial complex, where it stayed till the end of the Old Reich in 1806, and why Poland went a different way. The Piasts, among whom were dukes of Silesia as well as kings of Poland, could not prevent the Luxemburg acquisition of Silesia, though in some ways they resisted Germanization. As to the mixed German-Slav kingdom of Bohemia, that lay at the very heart of German royal politics and must receive some more attention in a moment. But in all the dynastic cases here cited, the ending of lines brought political thrusts from the German west.

The new dynasties which concern us most centrally here were those which provided the royal families of late medieval Germany: Habsburg, Wittelsbach and Luxemburg. Each began its political life in a small territory of western or south-western Germany, and each grew to royal status, acquiring vast dominions beyond its original home.

The Habsburgs stemmed from a fortress named 'the castle of the goshawk' *(Habichtsburg)*, between Basel and Zürich, built about 1020 by a bishop of Strassburg. The family was older still, fecund and ramified. The fortunes of the collateral lines need not concern us, but it is of interest to understand that the elder line was friendly with the thirteenth-century Hohenstaufen. It gained lands in the upper Rhineland, later known as the *Vorlande* in distinction from the renowned acquisitions in Austria. The Habsburgs illustrate the historical fact, familiar in Germany, that centre-stage catastrophe rarely obliterates the whole cast.

Count Rudolf of Habsburg was elected king in 1273 and began to bring the disorder of the Interregnum to an end. By diplomacy and warfare against King Ottokar of Bohemia he captured the territories of Upper and Lower Austria and of Styria. This nucleus of the great future duchy of Austria was Teutonic, colonized in the main from Bavaria but later also by Swabians. Upper and Lower Austria lay along the Danube and were divided by its tributary, the river Enns. Adjacent to the south, in slices like a layer-cake, were Styria *(Steiermark)*, Carinthia *(Kärnten)* and Carniola *(Krain)*. This last is now in Yugoslavia, but in our period the eastern boundaries of these provinces formed the frontier of the empire beyond which lay Hungary. Wedged in between Carniola and Carinthia from the Hungarian side was the important countship of Cilli. Away to the west was the Tyrol, separated from medieval Austria by the great archbishopric of Salzburg.

Austria proper had been held by the Babenbergs, who looked back to Barbarossa's creation of a duchy there recorded in a document of 1156 called the 'Lesser Privilege' *(Privilegium Minus)*. This had laid upon the dukes light obligations only. After the extinction of the Babenbergs in 1246 there was rivalry for possession between Slavs (Přemyslids), Hungarians and Habsburgs. Rudolf of Habsburg was victorious in 1278 and the whole of Austria soon fell into that family's lordship: Carinthia and Carniola were given in 1335 by Lewis IV Wittelsbach, then emperor, in return for Habsburg support, and the

Tyrol was acquired in 1363. By that time the Austrian Habsburgs had become one of the two most important German dynasties who were not electors. They had supplied another emperor in Albert I (1298–1308), the first to be formulated in a royal document as *Mehrer*, or 'enlarger', of the empire,[19] though the concept appears in the *Mirror of the Swabians* as part of the royal oath, and was to be repeated in the Golden Bull in 1356. A peak of success was reached by Duke Rudolf IV (1339–65), who possessed the whole duchy, crushed the Schaumberger, his strongest rivals, founded the University of Vienna and forged the Greater Privilege *(Privilegium Maius)* in 1358–9.[20] This was Austria's compensation for being left out of the circle of imperial electors by Rudolf's enemy, Charles IV. Like the royal residence in Vienna, Rudolf's university betrays a strong sense of rivalry with Luxemburg Prague.

After Rudolf's death without heirs the Habsburgs fell into complex partitions and the integral duchy was split between different branches until the Styrian duke Frederick was elected emperor in 1440. He will appear again in these pages, but the point ought to be made at once that although luck favoured him in bringing Austria together again he was always a conscious dynast, an admirer of his great-uncle Rudolf IV, and a deliberate continuator of what texts call 'the house or lordship of Austria'.

The Wittelsbachs too had small beginnings. They were counts of Scheyern, north-east of Augsburg, in the eleventh century, with possessions between the Lech and the Danube. Otto, sixth count, had been a follower of Barbarossa, who invested him with the duchy of Bavaria after the fall of Henry the Lion in 1180. This was the family's turning-point, for once a nobleman had been elevated and enriched he and his kin acquired a greater eligibility for valuable marriages. In a sense marriage was one of the 'political' sacraments.

At all events, the Wittelsbachs gained the Rhine Palatinate in this way in 1214. Their lordship in Bavaria was rapidly extended also by the natural extinction of many other families of the higher Bavarian nobility, until by the late thirteenth century they found themselves princes of the first rank. Their two serious defects were the fraternal partitioning of Bavaria and the hostility of the house of Luxemburg. Charles IV excluded Bavaria, like Austria, from the circle of imperial electors. His detestation of their house probably did more than anything to keep the Wittelsbachs in the second league of royalty.

They supplied the monarch twice only: Lewis IV, who died at war with Charles of Luxemburg, and Rupert, who was succeeded by another Luxemburg.

The third royal dynasty was, of course, Luxemburg itself. The family's lands were in the Ardennes, between Rhine and Maas, where they had been counts since about 1160. A marriage in 1293 gained them Brabant. A younger brother, Baldwin, became archbishop of Trier in 1307 at the age of twenty-two, with an electoral vote and a background of wealth sufficient to help his elder brother Henry to the throne in 1308. Thereafter, the rise of the dynasty was meteoric.

The Luxemburgs have been left until last in this review of new dynasties because their history is in many ways the most complex, and because the period covered by this book begins properly with Charles IV, the greatest of the house. But it is not a story that can start without explanations.

The Interregnum of 1256 to 1273 had been ended by the election of a Habsburg whose power and success were unexpected by princes eager for independence. After Rudolf I's death in 1291, the new king (Adolf of Nassau) had in an unprecedented move been deposed by the princes (1298), and his successor, another Habsburg, murdered in 1308. This man, Albert I, had been married to Elisabeth, half-sister of Conradin, a Hohenstaufen, and was sufficiently in their tradition to cause anxiety to some princes. During these years a strong rivalry had grown up between the Habsburgs, now of course possessors of much of Austria, and the house of Luxemburg, which had settled in Bohemia and was about to provide an emperor.

The times saw a strange mixture of old and new. The Hohenstaufen past was effectively finished, its territories in central and south-western Germany political debris, its *ministeriales* private feudatories. In its place new tensions threatened: Habsburg in Austria against Luxemburg in Bohemia against Wittelsbach in Bavaria and the Rhineland Palatinate. The papacy was just beginning its 'exile' in Avignon, but the Italian game of German kings had not yet been quite played out, for it still offered the lure of money and support and attracted groups in Italy (call them Ghibelline if you like) who thought they saw political stability from the north.

It will be convenient to leave this aside for the moment and turn to Bohemia, for Bohemia was as crucial as Austria in this era of new dynastic beginnings. If Austria was unambiguously Teuton, the crown lands of Bohemia were of mixed settlement: Slav in many villages, German in some villages and most towns; German strongly in the west, more Slav in the east. Colonization was still proceeding. It has been a contentious topic, but the German immigration was probably not yet as thick on the margins as it became in the seventeenth and eighteenth centuries.[21]

In any case, it was a country not only beautiful, rich in ore, agriculturally and (relatively) industrially productive, but also sufficiently bounded by mountains and defined by linguistic characters to give it a conscious identity. The old dynasty had been Czech. Moravia to the east was also Slav. The higher nobility was partly German and partly Slav, collectively strong, and aware of itself as a political and social body. Its tenure of land was barely feudal, and except for some emergency obligations to the king almost free (allodial). In its meetings it had the right to determine what was customary and therefore lawful. It had been given the right to elect its king in 1212 by Frederick II in reward for help.[22]

The kingdom also had economic problems in unusually marked inequalities of wealth. The plague seems to have spared the country more than most others; there was a rural poor and an urban one too, who were to give revolutionary edge to later discontents.

The Czech royal family of Přemyslid died out in 1306 except for the princess Elisabeth. Custom excluded women from succession, and the lords feared and disliked the Habsburgs. The other notable anti-Habsburgs were the members of the Luxemburg family, Francophile, on good terms with the papacy and, in the person of Henry, count of Luxemburg, possessed since 1308 of the empire. In Bohemia a good deal of influence was exercised by men of religion and especially by Cistercian abbots, whose estates were among the largest in the kingdom. It was in these circles that the plan was made that Elisabeth Přemyslid should marry John, the son of the Emperor Henry VII, and it was Abbot Konrad of the Bohemian monastery of Königssaal, who, in a secret interview in Prague Cathedral, won over the princess to the marriage.

The story sounds a romantic one. After a covert flight from Prague, Elisabeth married John of Luxemburg on 31 August 1310, when she was eighteen and he was fourteen. Many Bohemian nobles wanted John as king, and he was accepted and invested with a number of castles in his new country.

35

The reality was less glamorous. The couple did not match well, and John removed the children to be brought up in monasteries and married off to politically suitable spouses. He has been kindly handled by the legend-makers, cast as 'the wandering king', blind, and dying at Crécy in support of the French king, the Luxemburg ally. In fact, John was interested in building up royal power and began the great policy of acquisition by marriage and treaty continued by his own son Charles.

When Henry VII died his son was a candidate for the kingship, but the electors wanted an older man and one who would continue to keep the Habsburgs out. Their preference was Lewis Wittelsbach, duke of Bavaria, who in the double election of 1314 emerged successfully as Lewis IV. He was in fact the Luxemburg candidate, supported by the archbishops of Mainz and Trier, against Frederick of Habsburg.

It will now be apparent why some account of Lewis IV is needed as an explanation of Charles IV himself. Lewis was made king as a *tertium quid*, to keep the Habsburgs from the throne. But the election of Lewis gave the political world more than it had bargained for. He was a warrior and no man's puppet, least of all the pope's, and certainly not one of the Luxemburgs'. He defeated Frederick of Habsburg (who had wanted the crown) in a battle at Mühldorf in 1322, and in a gracious gesture offered him the hand of friendship. Short of money and territory, he was interested in Italy and thought he could master Lombardy. For this reason too he wanted the Tyrol as a base. In the north, he granted the vacant Mark of Brandenburg to his own elder son, also called Lewis, and befriended his original opponent Frederick, to whom he gave Carinthia.

Papal antagonism to Lewis IV has, not without reason, been seen as an opposition between old principles, but fundamentally it stemmed from the king's intervention in Lombardy, already in revolt, and not controllable by a pope in the presence of a hostile German king.[23] This consideration, rather than canonical theory, hardened Pope John XXII's insistence on the papal 'right' to approve 'the emperor or king of the Romans'. Lewis's reply in 1338 at the Diet of Rhense that no such approval was ever necessary may not have been a novelty, but it left nobody other than the electors with any claim to make or unmake the emperor.

(c) *Charles IV*

It was Clement VI, the most politically adept of the Avignon popes,

who decided to dispose of Lewis IV and to support Charles of
Luxemburg. On 11 July 1346 Charles was elected king, even though
some of the electors were uneasy in their minds about the deposition of
Lewis at papal behest. How the manoeuvre would have turned out if
Lewis had not died of a stroke during the subsequent campaigning is
impossible to conjecture. Charles's co-operation with the papacy, his
old friendship with Pierre Roger, now Clement VI, and his tiresome 'autobiography'[24] have marked him as a 'priests' emperor'
(Pfaffenkaiser), but this is a nickname oddly inappropriate to a man
who owed his success more to his political adroitness over a wide area
of Germany than to any clerical temper.

The hallmark of Charles IV's reign is the dynastic aggrandizement
of the Luxemburg family. Everything else appears subordinate. Even
the building up of Prague and the encouragement of cultural activity
subserved the end of glorifying his Bohemia and its widening crown
lands: *dulce solum natalis patrie.*[25] It was, of course, a Bohemia seen at
first through French-trained eyes, for Charles had been brought up in
France, habituated to love of the French Gothic which Matthew of
Arras created for him in St Vitus's Cathedral, and obliged to re-learn
Czech after he had grown up. Later he came to value and use his
German heritage, encouraging his German-speaking chancery staff
and accepting German bishops provided to his sees by Clement VI.
Nor should one deny his character as moralist and patron. But his
more private worlds seem, at a guess, directed, like his public displays
of coronations, progresses and Diets, to the goals of increasing
Bohemian crown territory and passing it on to his son. The
Autobiography itself betrays his sense of the Luxemburg right to rule.
'Lewis who calls himself emperor', he had written scathingly of the
man who appeared to have stolen his father's heritage. Indeed, he
began the book by referring to Henry VII, his grandfather, as
'emperor of the Romans' and pointing out how good marriages had
brought his house to the centre of power in Bohemia.

Charles's own first marriage, in 1324, was to Blanche of Valois,
sister of the French king who himself was Charles's uncle by marriage.
The ties formed by these early years help to explain the shock of fifty
years later when Charles's son Wenzel appeared, in his support of
Urban VI and his acceptance of the English king as brother-in-law, to
be repudiating the French connection.

In March 1349, after Blanche's death, Charles married Anne of the

Rhine Palatinate and gained thereby further support in the Rhineland and the towns of the south-west. In 1353 she was followed by Anna of Schweidenitz, niece of the king of Hungary, who brought him a portion of Silesia he still lacked. The birth to her of Wenzel in 1361 was an occasion for great rejoicing and the start of dynastic plans already described.

Lastly, in 1363, Charles married Elisabeth, daughter of the duke of Pomerania and granddaughter of Casimir the Great of Poland, heiress of the Piasts, mother of King Sigismund and hope of Luxemburg's eastern claims. The politics which preceded this marriage are complex and revolve round diplomatic mistakes made by Charles in his relationships with the Poles, Hungarians and Habsburgs. It was a marriage of reconciliation, and was followed by the first of the famous arrangements by which Luxemburg and Habsburg each agreed that if one of their lines failed the other should receive the inheritance.[26]

These marriages, it will be noted, carried Charles's dominions eastward. When he went to Rome for coronation in 1355 the Romans, who had looked for a new prosperity under a new Luxemburg, complained that he came more like a shop-keeper than an emperor (*'unkaiserlich, wie ein Krämer'*). They did not realize that the Staufen with their drilled squadrons were gone, and even the violent intentions of Henry VII were no more. Here was a new and northern schemer, half Slav by birth, French by upbringing, Bohemian in his centre of interest and eastward-looking when he considered the future. For him to avoid Italy was only prudence. P. Knoll has sketched Charles's attempt to make a peace-bloc with Poland and Hungary, and Ferdinand Seibt suggested that his ultimate goal was a German-Slav empire which might include also Lithuania and Rus.

Charles IV's dynastic policy had phases and variable options, some of them already referred to. An important one concerned Louis the Great, Angevin king of Hungary and lord of Poland, who left the two daughters Mary and Hedwig. In 1372 Charles arranged the betrothal of his own son Sigismund, then aged four, to Mary. His plans to get Poland for her failed, but she was in due course crowned Queen of Hungary and from her derived the claim of Sigismund and subsequently the Habsburgs. Hedwig (Jadwiga), on the other hand, was married in 1386 at the wish of the Polish nobles to Jagiello, Grand Duke of Lithuania, who turned Catholic, changed his name to Vladimir, and kept his huge new realm free from imperial absorption.

Despite the displacement of Luxemburg (and ultimately Habsburg) power to the south-east instead of its engulfment of the north-east as well, Bohemia remained central. Charles's court and council were centred in Prague, though he drew numbers of their members from southern and south-western Germany, took them on long journeys, and saw that they worked regionally alongside his provincial officials in other parts of his domains. The Luxemburger crown lands came to dominate central Europe. To Bohemia and Moravia were added Silesia, Lusatia, Bautzen, Görlitz and in 1373 the Mark of Brandenburg, which saw the Wittelsbachs no more.

In Prague the New Town was large and of great beauty. The city, a European jewel, housed skilled administrators and received eloquent preachers whom the king invited first from Austria and later from his own country. Yet there is a paradox about the political structure Charles created. In some ways the newly acquired Bohemian crown lands to the north and east were more securely governed for his dynasty than was Bohemia itself, in whose forests, farms, townships and fortified houses of gentlemen the name of Přemyslid was remembered more warmly than that of Luxemburg. With hindsight we know of the revolution that was to devastate the country in the next century. But even in his own lifetime Charles lacked a certain acceptance. His great law-book, the so-called *Majestas Carolina*, was intended partly to strengthen kingly power against the high Bohemian nobility, but at the Bohemian Diet of 1355 his nobles refused to accept it. In its very nature as a written code it was suspected by them as a threat to their customary role as a law-interpreting body. The written administration in the acquired territories of Silesia and Brandenburg was more successful. Luxemburg territorial policy in this sense had a soft centre.

On the other hand, the Golden Bull of 1356, which has been held as the great consecration of imperial federalism, even to have 'licensed anarchy', may be regarded as an extraordinary monument to Luxemburg dynastic interest, the more so as the solemn instrument for electing the emperor by great princes was adroitly followed by their guided choice of Charles's son, Wenzel.

In January 1356 Charles IV summoned an imperial Diet to Nuremberg, where the Golden Bull was promulgated as a document of twenty-three sections. A further eight sections were issued the next Christmas at another meeting, held at Metz.[27] The Bull owes much of its fame to its rarity value as a constitutional law of the empire as a whole. It has been rightly said that it was the end of a process of definition, not the beginning. It has also been argued that the particular electors chosen were the most important of a currently rather small estate of princes, of whom not many had come to the fore since the fall of Henry the Lion in 1180. On the other hand, by 1356 the kingdom of Bohemia still overshadowed others in size and potential resources, and the composition of the Electors' College seems undoubtedly in the Bohemian interest, not only positively, in the princes chosen, but negatively in the omission of Wittelsbach Bavaria and Habsburg Austria.

The Bull began by referring to Charles IV as 'enlarger' of the empire, an idea that goes back at least to the thirteenth-century precept, appearing in the *Mirror of the Swabians* that the king must swear to enrich and not impoverish his realm; and it is heard of again in 1400 in the accusations that Wenzel had done just that.

After laying a curse on the forces of disunity the Bull prescribes the process of the election and the persons of the electors. They were to be the king of Bohemia, the archbishops of Mainz, Cologne and Trier, the count palatine of the Rhine, the duke of Saxony and the margrave of Brandenburg. After taking the oath in the vernacular, administered by the archbishop of Mainz, to choose an honest ruler, they were to conduct the election of the king by a simple majority in the cathedral church of St Bartholomew, Frankfurt-am-Main. No elector was to leave the city until the choice had been made of this 'secular lord of the world which is Christendom'. No mention was made of any papal right to assent or have part in the election.

The Bull confirmed the privileges and political integrity of the electoral princes, who were described as 'pillars and bulwarks of the empire'. The lay electors were to enjoy hereditary succession by primogeniture within their own particular princedoms. If a line died out, the emperor had the right to enfeoff whom he liked, though the Bohemians were to continue the enjoyment of their right to choose their own king.

The electors were to meet once a year in an imperial city. Their lordship over their own subjects was confirmed and reinforced by the clause forbidding such subjects to take up part-time residence in towns in order to acquire citizenship and thus escape the jurisdiction of their former princely master. These were the people described as *Pfahlbürger,* literally 'suburban citizens', but bearing a contemptuous meaning. The struggle of princes against cities for jurisdiction was not something new in 1388, let alone at the end of the fifteenth century.

There were some clauses of interest in the literal sense, but in reality of idealistic character. Such were the regulations for private warfare, not the first nor the last of their kind and an incident in the Public Peace movement rather than a novelty. Such too was the exhortation of the lay electors to have their young heirs taught other languages according to their ability: not only their native German but Italian, Czech and Latin, either by sending the boys to appropriate places for instruction or arranging tutors or playmates for them at home. The reader is reminded of Charles's own polyglot upbringing, though the Bull, written at a time when the queen was a Silesian, interestingly makes no reference to French.

The Golden Bull is flattering in its words to the electors, but it is not easy to see it as an electors' triumph. As observed, it was in the Bohemian crown (or Luxemburg) interest. The Rhineland archbishops had prescriptive expectations to be among their number, but they were also Luxemburg allies. Even if the count palatine was of the hated Wittelsbach family, he was a rival to his Bavarian cousins; the margrave of Brandenburg was also at that moment a Wittelsbach but Charles had plans to supplant him, and his nomination in 1356 as an elector would confer the electoral right on a principality which was to be a key one in the Luxemburg structure, and would soften the omission of the originally Wittelsbach Bavaria. The duke of Saxony-Wittenberg was Charles's dependant.

Nor do the Bull's phrases strengthening electoral princely power seem to have been in themselves effective. Partition continued to afflict greater princely dynasties as well as lesser ones. Proper primogeniture was not established in the Palatinate until Frederick I's 'Arrogation' of 1452, while Brandenburg and Saxony remained notorious for fragmentation. Württemberg achieved primogeniture in 1482, Bavaria in 1506, Brandenburg in 1599, the Habsburg German territories in 1621. The towns went on accepting *Pfahlbürger* when it suited the interests of the king. The later decline of royal power must be ascribed to a complex series of misfortunes, not to a constitutional document.

(d) *Wenzel IV*

Wenzel was born in 1361 in Nuremberg to Anna of Schweidenitz, Charles's third wife, and ceremoniously baptized in the imperial city which Charles had favoured and the son was to neglect.

But the birth of his first son was an event of joy to the king, who at once began to reverse the royal policy of redeeming imperial property to raise the money necessary to get the child elected as his successor. This activity was evidently thought out exactly enough to confirm the historian's sense of Charles IV's political consistency. The slow diminishment of the Wittelsbach dominions, the cultivation of princely friends, the selective use of towns, all have marks of deliberation. So too now in the raising of money. The Strassburg chronicler Twinger called Charles the richest emperor for many hundred years, but it was imperial not house property he was going to pledge and spend. He had no intention of touching the Bohemian crown lands which he was augmenting to form a secure and permanent base for the Luxemburg monarchy. Even some contemporaries criticized him as an emperor who gave the electors great wealth to buy the kingdom.[28]

In the short run, of course, Charles succeeded, and the triumph was remarkable. Electors close to him, like Trier and Cologne, had determined to resist any election during the king's lifetime, but they were bought. Charles himself possessed Bohemia and, since 1373, Brandenburg also, and the Palatinate and Saxony were not hard to win over. Charles went to the trouble of getting consent from important non-electoral princes who would support him against papal objections. He did not suffer from the arrogance that brushes aside details. So Wenzel was elected, and crowned at Aachen on 6 July 1376, over two years before his father's death.

But the death of Charles IV in November 1378 showed how frail a merely family polity can be. Charles left numerous male kinsmen, of whom the most important politically were his three sons, Wenzel, Sigismund and John, and two of his nephews, Jost and Prokop. The text of the Golden Bull spoke of the indivisibility of electoral principalities, admittedly only in their heartlands, but it shows at least that Charles understood the significance of primogeniture. But he lived in a world of partibility and (without departing from the letter of the Bull) he shared out the huge Luxemburg territories in a manner which suggests that he cannot have regarded his approval of primogeniture and his belief in the supreme importance of the dynasty as contradictory. If the object had been to prevent family quarrels, the division failed. To Wenzel, already elected successor, went the Bohemian crown lands but not Moravia; that was to be shared by Jost and Prokop. Sigismund had Brandenburg and his expectations in Hungary. To John went the duchy of Görlitz.

Disaster was not immediate. Wenzel inherited experienced councillors and court officials. His own Bohemian chancellor, John of Jenstein, also became chancellor of the empire and an important administrator, and he was made archbishop of Prague by Pope Urban VI. The royal territories too look impressive at first glance.

Matters began to go wrong in 1384. There was a quarrel with Jenstein about a new archbishopric Wenzel wanted in western Bohemia, and the vicar-general of Prague, called Nepomuk, was subjected to a trial and somehow got drowned in the Moldau. The events were recalled later in the articles of Wenzel's deposition which alluded to his cruelty. Nepomuk became a Czech hero and Wenzel was cast unjustly in the role of an anti-Slav.

At this time also numerous men entered the royal council and chancery, many of them said to be the king's friends, foreigners, commoners and amenable to bribes. The motives behind the changes are obscure, but the higher nobility clearly resented the newcomers, and the imposition of a 'fiscal feudalism', demand for monetary 'dues' on their privileged class hitherto almost free from royal burdens, angered the sufferers. A satire called *The New Council* was written by Smil Flaška of Pardubitz, a nephew of the archbishop[29] and an educated nobleman who had been made to pay.

Ill-feelings were strengthened and complicated by the Luxemburg kinsmen's struggle against each other for possessions and power. King Wenzel himself could rely only on limited crown domains, castles and townships in Bohemia, where the higher nobility were hostile to him. Silesia was a more productive part of Wenzel's inheritance.

Sigismund got embroiled in warfare for his Hungarian bride and her crown, and consequently found himself in the state of debt which became his chronic condition. All the Luxemburgers dissipated their inheritances by pledging. None of them had sons, and their sense of rivalry with each other for possible succession became very bitter.

In Bohemia the gainers from these family quarrels were the nobility. They alone could make some show of enforcing public peace, and in the end it was their agents who took over offices in court and country, and the land was ruled by the strongest of them, barons like the anti-Hussite Henry of Rožinberk, and the more radical Čeněk of Vartemberk.

Beyond Bohemia and the Luxemburg family quarrels the wider world suffered from worsening disorder. Here again, the reasons are complex and cannot be reduced to a simple formulation.

The Great Schism had broken out in September 1378 and the next year Wenzel made a league with the Rhineland electors in favour of the Roman pope, Urban VI. Urban could hardly do enough to reward Wenzel, and it was his legate, Cardinal Pileus, who helped arrange the marriage of Wenzel's sister Anne to Richard II of England. But Germany was not unanimous even in papal politics. There were princely supporters in western Germany for the Avignonese pope, who of course had the French behind him, and the new diplomatic alliance between Wenzel, Rome and England was a reversal of the old friendship between France and the house of Luxemburg when it became a royal dynasty. Even so, Wenzel did not bother to organize an imperial coronation, which might have helped him, possibly even to the extent of averting his deposition. His political activity in Italy involved a deal with Milan in which money changed hands, and its ruler, Giangaleazzo Visconti, was granted the imperial title of duke. For this his deposers were later able to accuse him of 'dilapidating' the empire instead of enlarging it.

In Germany itself there was a link between the decline of public order and a sharper hostility between nobilities and the towns. It is suggested below (Chapter 3) that Wenzel's own character had some bearing on his failure to encourage the Public Peace movement as his father had done. At the same time, the later fourteenth century witnessed even tenser relations both within cities themselves and between city and noble territories. The merchant oligarchies felt increasingly threatened by aristocratic attacks, both physical and fiscal. Their need to defend themselves against princely powers from without called for taxation, which in turn stimulated town rebellions. For their part, princes were often short of money, irritated by the towns' attractiveness to their subjects, and eager to exploit what towns could be made to yield in revenue and juridical obedience. An active and skilful king like Charles IV could often hold the balance. Under Wenzel, defeat had to be avoided through self-help by towns acting on their own or, more often now, in alliance. Among the town archives from this time 'feud-books' multiply, in which aggravations, leagues and campaigns were logged to memorialize insults and improve defences. The Swabian League of towns under Ulm's leadership dates from 1376, and the movement spread over southern and western Germany.

Towns needed the king's permission to form leagues; princes wanted them dissolved. Wenzel did what he could but was really successful only in causing offence. He was more inclined to favour towns than other kings had been, yet his neglect of the powerful imperial city of Nuremberg shows a lack of coherent policy. He sent an official, Conrad of Geisenheim, bishop of Lübeck, on peace-making missions between towns and princes. In 1384 a four-year agreement at Heidelberg (the *Heidelberger Stallung*) patched up a peace between the princes and the towns whose leagues were for the first time actually recognized. In 1388, however, the towns were defeated in battle and forbidden by the princely victors, led by the Rhineland archbishops, to form such leagues in the future.

To sum up, Wenzel had been faced by at least nine problems, none of which he could solve. He lacked sufficient income and angered his subjects, especially in Bohemia, by summoning them and trying to extract revenue by arbitrary fines *(Achtlösungen);* he was enmeshed in bitter rivalry with members of his own family of Luxemburg; he made enemies amongst Bohemian ecclesiastics, a powerful and landed class; he promoted councillors unwelcome to the Bohemian nobility; he conspicuously failed to maintain peace either in Bohemia or in Germany; he failed to heal the Schism and even to remain constant to one side; he failed to achieve imperial coronation but sold an imperial princedom to Visconti of Milan; he fell foul of the princes, especially Rhinelanders and south Germans, for supporting urban aspirations, yet without backing the towns effectively.

The actual deposition of Wenzel was brought about when a rebellion of his Bohemian nobles, in intermittent alliance with some of the Luxemburgers, was escalated by the Rhineland princes. At the centre of this conspiracy was the count palatine (a Wittelsbach) and the archbishop of Mainz, John of Nassau. Their propaganda won over others. Early in 1398 Wenzel met the princes for the first time in ten years and, there in Frankfurt, was forced to receive a list of grievances. It was a clever schedule, containing something for everyone, and corresponding approximately to the problems listed above.

At the end, the deposition of Wenzel from the empire was not without its difficulties. There was a precedent in Adolf of Nassau (1298), and it is not impossible, though unprovable, that the very recent deposition of Richard II of England, Wenzel's brother-in-law, may have suggested that what had proved possible and acceptable in one realm might also appear legitimate elsewhere.[30] At the imperial election of 1411, a jurist said that in the whole civil law there was nothing on the matter, but in the canon law they had the decretal *Per Venerabilem* which touched it. But papalist ideas about approving the emperor had been abrogated at Rhense in 1338. Furthermore, Rhense implied that king and emperor were now in reality the same thing. So it had been argued under the first Wittelsbach; so it was implied after the death of the second. It is not odd, therefore, that if *Venerabilem* was irrelevant in 1400, the only deposers possible were the electors, who had made both king and emperor by their choice; and their reasons or excuses for unmaking him might well be not just the remembrance that they had been paid for their votes — that would suggest consciences too tender to be credible — but the multiple insufficiency he had shown in fulfilling his coronation oath, and in general in acting as the 'enlarger' of the empire bidden him in the Golden Bull. The *Schwabenspiegel* had said: 'the king swears always to make the empire greater and not poorer' (*daz riche alle zit mere und niht erme* [*mache*]).[31] For this failure the Strassburg chronicler too, and at the time, specifically denounced Wenzel.

The practical sequel was undramatic. After some months of dispute about a successor, the Rhenish electors gave Wenzel a day to appear at Lahnstein in the Palatinate to justify himself. He refused to come, sitting in Prague, as an unkind observer put it, 'like a pig in a sty'. Next day, on 20 August 1400, Rupert III, count palatine, was elected, and with him the Wittelsbachs made their last return to the throne.

(e) *Rupert of Wittelsbach*

In 1400 the empire had become habituated to half a century of Luxemburg rule, and there were still enough members of the dynasty alive and active to create an expectancy that one or other might be elected, then or later. But the conspiracy had been principally a Rhenish one, and the choice of the Wittelsbach count palatine is not surprising.

Rupert — 'Klem' as they called him — was a man of forty-eight, with experience of government in the Palatinate, where he had shared rule with his great-uncle and his father. Like his predecessor, he was a man of some education, and one of the increasingly common type of German prince who promoted professors to be among their councillors.

His reign has two sides. On the one must be seen political weakness, failure and brevity; on the other, even now being reassessed by German scholars like Peter Moraw, is the continued and noteworthy building-up of a royal administration which was not merely a princely household team made to serve its master while he held the kingship, but the beginning of a specialized bureaucracy drawn in some cases from beyond the principality and put to serve the monarchy rather than just the prince.

We may look first at the gloomy side. King Rupert had a moderate inheritance, but a numerous family to provide for and supporters who expected rewards. His election had not been a universal acclamation. Furthermore, the Luxemburgers obstinately refused to recognize him. They even kept the crown jewels (more important politically then than now) locked up in Karlstein Castle for the duration of his reign. Rupert was also made to feel the hostility of the imperial cities of Frankfurt and Aachen, and had himself crowned at Cologne. He never was crowned in Rome, and although he mounted an Italian expedition it brought him no military or financial gain. He was in fact too poor, not only on account of the bribes he had had to pay towards his election but as a continuing consequence of the Luxemburgers' copious disposal of the imperial income, to which reference has already been made.

Even those who had elected Rupert were disillusioned after three years. The failure of the Italian expedition in 1402 was less important than the king's inability to build power in the north. But Wenzel was still king in Bohemia and its great crown territories, and Sigismund was now king of Hungary and had renewed his succession treaty with the Habsburgs. Rupert was not in this league of leading rulers.

The diminished stature of the monarch was made obvious in Germany by an association of princes in 1405 called the League of

Marbach, which went far in expressing the idea that the electors did not merely make the king but continued to share power with him and might oppose him if they agreed he was negligent.

So Rupert's political marks were mainly negative. He even lost Brabant and Luxemburg county to Burgundy, and he died in 1410 after a year's illness.

On the other hand, the reign witnessed a kind of royal institutional strength. It may be by chance that modern research has lighted on Rupert's reign and shown developments then which had already long begun, but that does not alter the fact that Rupert had ability in handling an administration and making friends in towns.[32] He had contacts outside his own principality in Hungary and south Germany. Ulrich Kammerer of Buda was, with the Medici, a financier of Rupert's Italian expedition.[33] He had supporters in Nuremberg. During his reign councillors appear in his service from outside his own territory, often from south Germany, sometimes from noble families, and sometimes too men who had served Wenzel and would go on to serve Sigismund. A list of their names would perhaps be out of proportion here, but it is worth noting that they included Hohenzollern. The historic rise of that family did not begin from the friendship with Sigismund.

There are two general lessons here. One is that an ineffective German king did not mean that there were no effective Germans in public life. This is developed in Chapter 5 (c) below. The other is that Rupert's reign evidently saw a further institutional development of the royal chancery, which can be observed dealing with specifically royal matters, like Italian policy, rather than Palatinate ones. P. Moraw noted this increasingly 'royal' chancery and suggested that it was largely the work of Raban von Helmstatt who, with other university graduates in civil law, was forming a professional élite.

(f) *Sigismund*

After Rupert's death there was nearly an imperial schism. A few people thought that Wenzel automatically became king again, but the real contention was between the Luxemburg cousins, Sigismund and Jost. The Rhineland electors were divided, except in their resolve not to have Wenzel back. The most interesting figure was Frederick of Hohenzollern, burgrave of Nuremberg and friend of the late King

Rupert. He argued with ingenuity that as he was, by request, representing the absent Sigismund, he was thereby in possession of the Brandenburg vote. Theory apart, Frederick played an important part in persuading Trier and the Palatinate to vote for Sigismund. The autumn of 1410 saw an undignified double election in Frankfurt, and Jost got a narrow majority. But he died soon afterwards and Sigismund was then accepted without dispute.

Sigismund's original royal lordship was the kingdom of Hungary, which he held as a separate kingdom for fifty years. He also had a temperament which brought him as a duty to work for the healing of the Latin Church's schism (1378–1417). This was connected with the need he perceived for a united Christian front against the Turks. Though the Council of Constance was summoned by John XXIII, the current pope of the Pisan line, he did so at the instance of Sigismund in order to get help against Ladislas of Naples. It is also true that John XXIII's crusade against King Ladislas of Naples and his sale of indulgences in this cause was the occasion of Hus's violent denunciation and consequent disorders in Prague.

There is hence an element of paradox in Sigismund's reign. He behaved like an emperor in struggling to reunite the church at the great council in the imperial city of Constance. At the same time Constance took up his energy and, of course, destroyed Hus and was thus indirectly responsible for depriving Sigismund of his Bohemian kingdom and convulsing Germany.

These great themes — the 'Conciliar Movement' and the Hussite wars — are central to the history of the age. But in a book on Germany it will be more appropriate to turn attention to more specific developments there.

Most important, the balance of power amongst the princes began to change. In some principalities political and institutional powers were strengthened and more orderly government was achieved. In Germany as a whole there was if anything more violence, not within but between territorial lordships. The position of the king was politically weakened. But reflection on monarchy and political rule was stimulated and schemes for reform were discussed among men of intelligence.

We may first look briefly at princely politics. At the beginning of his reign Sigismund granted the Mark of Brandenburg to Frederick of Hohenzollern, burgrave of Nuremberg, in return for payment and political support. The Hohenzollern had already done German kings good service, and were to do them more, especially in the conduct of the Hussite wars. As everyone knows, the coming of the Hohenzollern to north Germany was full of consequence for the future, but the immediate contemporary considerations are less clear. Richental's *Chronicle* of the Council of Constance illustrated the enfeoffment of Frederick with Brandenburg pictorially, but more as a piece of daily news than the memorial of a great event. The words on the page make Sigismund say: 'Burgrave Frederick, I hereby invest you with the inheritance of my cousin, the Mark of Brandenburg, and wish you good fortune and sufficient war and opposition.' He got what was offered, and had paid well for it with money raised from Swabian cities. Brandenburg was a pauper's paradise, properties and inheritances waiting to be bought, so one could in a sense say that Sigismund's enfeoffment of Frederick signified one aspect of south Germany's purchase of the north. But it was not long before Frederick was glad to get back to the south and leave Brandenburg to his son.

A second important change in princely geography was when the Ascanian dukes of Saxony (Wittenberg) died out in 1422, and Sigismund gave this electoral duchy to the family of Wettin. The effect on Saxony will be considered later. In this context, the advancement of the Wettiner strengthened the electoral princes against the monarchy.

This was not at all what Sigismund had had in mind. His objects were, of course, to heal the schism and defend Christendom, but also to reorganize political relationships in Germany in order to gain more authority for the monarchy itself. Yet the reverse happened. Cruel experience of warfare and feud, together with positive opportunities for territorial gain and princely organization, were teaching lords of territories to look to themselves for help. As Sigismund became more and more involved with Bohemia after the Council of Constance, princes felt able to oppose his schemes for royal reform more strongly. In 1424 they combined to protect their own privileges in an electoral alliance named after Bingen in the Rhine Palatinate, where it was arranged *(Binger Kurverein)*. Several times during these years they refused to come to the king when he summoned them, claimed to be co-rulers, and threatened to depose him.[34] This phase of electoral solidarity did not last beyond 1429, but Sigismund's contemporary plans for a new royal order, based in Swabia and built up of his direct lordship over knights and towns, were just as ineffective.

Sigismund's reign was an age of unfulfilled plans. Of course this is a sign of political weakness. But it is not a mark of stupidity. The balance of conflicting interests may make people think harder rather than hit harder. In Germany intelligent men were showing themselves conscious of German interests and beginning slowly to debate the reform of German imperial institutions. Their ideas were rarely novel and quite often they had been stimulated by similar problems in the church, especially that of the pope's relationship with the cardinals and the church as a whole. It is not always remembered that some of the most important church reformers were Germans, like Dietrich of Niem and Henry of Langenstein. They had counterparts in the imperial reforming thinkers.

A pamphlet written at the time of Constance[35] suggested that just as the pope had his College of Cardinals, so the emperor should have at his side an elected council to help him improve and administer justice, and that it should limit the emperor's power by making certain matters, like the levying of taxation, depend upon a majority vote.

At the time of Basel, probably in 1438, a famous outline plan called 'the Emperor Sigismund's Reformation'[36] was drawn up. Its authorship is contentious. It has been called the work of 'a circle of clever reformers including the young Cusa and Johann Schele, bishop of Lübeck'. More recent research, on the other hand, argues that the author remains unknown, and that he expressed views contrary to those of Cusa.

It was a much studied document, for it survives in some seventeen manuscripts and eight printings between 1476 and 1522. It expressed the deep and strengthening desire that the monarch be obeyed. The writer was not alone among fifteenth-century Germans in feeling that the past had been better than the present, that once there had been 'good old imperial laws', that papal exactions had been less, and that Venice had not been the centre of a commercial dominance harmful to Germany.

Nicholas of Cusa, too, in his *Concordantia Catholicon* of 1433, anticipated proposals for a council of regency formed by the Estates of the empire which ought to meet all the year round in Frankfurt. They ought to include the electoral princes with their noblemen and councillors, and representatives from larger towns. Most reformers now expected an important part to be played by the cities.

Another idea taken up by Cusa but not invented by him was to divide Germany up into fairly large administrative districts called Circles *(Kreise)*. More was heard of this and other proposals later, especially at the end of the century.

So Sigismund did not lack articulate advice. Voices all round him spoke of orderly administration, a good court structure, an honest chancery, secure finances and the guarding of the peace.

It would be less than fair to blame Sigismund for negligence. He was not an incompetent, and showed that in fact he took financial reform seriously when in 1415 he gave over great power to the hereditary chamberlain, Konrad von Weinsberg, in the very style of the reforming literature, in order to organize the royal income. His weakness was not in paucity of ideas but in lack of money, not in shortage of competent officials but in lack of a secure base or capital from which to administer.

His political life had certainly not been wholly negative. He had presided over the reunification of the Latin church at Constance. He had defended Hungary and regained some authority in Bohemia. He had attended, like a good Luxemburg, to the fate of his dynasty.

When Sigismund was dying in 1437 he was preoccupied with the desire that his son-in-law should succeed him. This was Duke Albert V of Austria. Sigismund's heiress Elisabeth had married this man in 1421. It was an act of political importance that can hardly be exaggerated, for it ensured that the Luxemburg inheritance should pass to the house of Habsburg. This is what the Luxemburgs had come to foresee and desire as their own line failed. It is how the Austro-Hungarian Empire was created.

(g) *Albert II*

On an earlier page of this chapter it was explained that the duchy of Austria had fallen into complex partitions after the death without children of Duke Rudolf IV in 1365. Rule was shared by his brothers Albert and Leopold, but in 1379 they partitioned their huge inheritance so that it became convenient to talk about the Albertine and the Leopoldine lines. In general the Albertines had the Danubian lands (Upper and Lower Austria) and the Leopoldines had the more southern portions, including Styria, as well as the Tyrol.

A terrible disaster happened to the Leopoldines in 1386, when their army was cut to pieces by the Swiss at Sempach, just north of Lucerne, and Duke Leopold himself was killed. After this the Leopoldine line was itself divided into the Styrian and the Tyrolese branches.

All this sounds like another serious fragmentation, but in fact the Habsburg 'House of Austria', often divided by quarrels, never ceased to consider itself a single princely house.

It was the Albertine duke who was chosen king and emperor by the electors in Frankfurt as soon as Sigismund was dead. The election was on 18 March 1438, and after a short hesitation he accepted and became Albert II.

Readers of these pages may think it odd that the old fourteenth-century enmity between Luxemburg and Habsburg should turn out like this. But Sigismund had needed the Habsburgs, and especially the Albertines, who had rich tolls on the Danube, and who could help against the Turks by raising money in their *Landtag* and against the Hussites by sending soldiers. Albert had already in 1422 been made margrave of Moravia by Sigismund, his new father-in-law. The Bohemians did not like him and of course one cannot say what would have happened had he lived. But for the first time the Austrian duchy was joined with the Bohemian, Hungarian and German crowns.

Albert's short reign makes him a shadowy figure, but his combination of personal effort with misfortune is enough to excite a certain pity. He continued Konrad von Weinsberg in his office of hereditary chamberlain, but without being able to do much to improve the royal Chamber Court. As an Austrian he was geographically at the edge of empire but by the same token at the frontier of Christendom. The times too were evil for him, for the Council of Basel, the union of Latin and Greek churches, however fleeting, and the Ottoman threat itself imposed upon Albert a crusade which he seems to have regarded as a duty. It is not surprising that he failed to build up a detailed administration, and the fact that he attempted to take his chancery with him to the wars suggests a very rudimentary organization. Administration slackened off in Austria and little got done in Hungary and Bohemia.

In Germany itself the electors continued to become more dominant. Meeting in Nuremberg, they tried to arrange some form of electoral co-rule, also to mediatize the cities and to establish four Circles, each under a princely captain with full power to protect the peace. Albert himself suggested these captains be chosen by their Circles and that Bohemia and Austria be exempted from the scheme. But neither princes nor towns would accept his proposals.

There was little time for further initiatives. In 1439 Albert II flung back a Turkish attack in Hungary but became ill and died on the campaign.

(h) *Frederick III*

The death of Albert II in 1439 left a complex situation in Habsburg Austria. His widow was pregnant, so there was for the moment no heir to the 'Albertine' lands. The Tyrolese branch was represented by a boy, Sigismund. The Styrian duke was Frederick, who had the legal custody of young Sigismund of the Tyrol.

On 22 February 1440 Elisabeth, widow of Albert II, gave birth to the son known to history as Ladislas Postumus. Frederick of Styria was therefore the only grown-up Habsburg duke (he was twenty-five), and it was natural enough that the Estates gave him the custody of the baby Ladislas also. In this way, Frederick of Styria held in his hands for the time being the whole of Austria — Albertine, Tyrolese and his own Styria — and so was in possession of all that belonged to the House of Habsburg.

Albert II had been able to make a testament before he died and insisted that Austria, Bohemia and Hungary be held together. For all that, neither Bohemians nor Hungarians wanted a Habsburg ruler, though they claimed custody of Ladislas. To anticipate for a moment the child's future, Ladislas was chosen king of Bohemia, though George of Podiebrady became regent and then king when Ladislas died of the plague in 1457. In Hungary Ladislas was recognized as king in 1445 but John Hunyadi, father of Corvinus, was appointed regent.

In Germany everyone could see that Frederick of Styria was in legitimate possession of all the Austrian provinces. He was regarded as the only possible choice as king by the great Rhineland archbishop-electors. In addition, most electors were anxious to avoid the elevation of Hohenzollern, who had contested Bohemia and was a power in the land. Frederick of Styria was hence elected without trouble on 6 April 1440 and crowned that summer at Aachen.

The young man who now became king was the son of Duke Ernst of

Styria, a big man, dark-skinned and with sparkling eyes, Italianate like his Visconti mother.[37] Frederick's mother, however, was the princess Czimbarka from the Polish province of Masovia, said to possess a simple Catholic piety and a startling physical strength. There are several portraits of Frederick different enough from each other, even allowing for artistic interpretations, to illustrate his varied physical and personal inheritances. The imperial portrait in the Styrian monastery of Lauwitz presents heavy features and hooded, introverted eyes. The Italian portrait of him in 1452, now in the Uffizi Gallery in Florence, shows a man of thirty-seven in full-length profile, straight-backed and blond, reminding the world that this Habsburg emperor was half-Slav.[38]

Both his parents had died by the time Frederick was fourteen and he was brought up by his uncle, Frederick duke of Tyrol, after whom he had been named. Mocked in youth as 'empty-pockets', this Tyrolese proved a good guardian to his nephew, and even a man of business who encouraged his ward's lifelong habit of meticulous attention to detail.

There are contrasting sides to Frederick's nature. In the middle of the Council of Basel, when he was a young man, Frederick decided to go on crusade to the Holy Land in imitation of his own father's pilgrimage. Typically, it was a small expedition, and turned into a shopping spree. He took more money than he needed, to buy in Venice on his way back the silks and brocades which he knew would cost more in Austria. In the east he visited bazaars in disguise in order not to be recognized and over-charged.

On the other hand, Frederick was moody and withdrawn. Contemptuous legends have accumulated round him, some of them demolished by Lhotsky. Labelled as a passive 'archsleepyhead', he has been equally derided for obsession with the motto AEIOU, interpreted as meaning Austria was lord of the whole world. But this was only a cabbalistic sign favoured by Frederick before there was question of his kingship, and not even used by Maximilian later.

From early manhood Frederick had had to struggle for his independence and to secure his treasures and archives left by his father in 1424. His political style was carefully to assert his rights and to expect double-dealing in others. If anxious and diffident and unhappy in assemblies, he showed within his own lands a talent for administration, a familiarity with finance, and a grasp of detail better than that possessed by some emperors more usually admired.

Frederick III studied the past of his own dynasty with a concentration which derived partly from a proud sense of family and partly from a desire to claim the castles and political rights that were his own by inheritance. If he had a hero it was Duke Rudolf IV, already met in these pages, who had been a principal creator of undivided Austria. The unofficial *Privilegium Maius* of 1358–9 had expressed the concept of a great independent duchy, and to this document Frederick, recently crowned emperor, gave in 1453 the authority of imperial enactment. Ultimately, fortune brought Frederick the whole of Austria and gave him the satisfaction and justification that has often been withheld from him.

It was years before substantial success could be envisaged. Better than Austria as 'lord of the world', today's historians might borrow a harder motto from Rilke, another great Austrian:

Who speaks of victory
When to endure is all...?[39]

The most serious and immediate problem at Frederick's election was the wardship of Ladislas. His custody was of political value, however little his Habsburg origin was esteemed. The Austrian Estates joined an alliance against Frederick to get hold of Ladislas, for as the 'Albertine' heir he could be said to belong to 'Austria' proper. Nor was Frederick III's administration liked in these Danube lands. To many Austrians Frederick was merely 'the Styrian', and this unfriendly view was something Frederick complained of bitterly and with justice. On their side, northern Austrians did not see why their money should be spent on Styrian towns like Wiener Neustadt and Graz and why Frederick should hold on to the treasures and archives of Vienna Castle.

At about this time Frederick found political and diplomatic help from Aeneas Sylvius Piccolomini. The Sienese humanist met Frederick and his chancellor, Schlick, at Basel and struck up a friendship. The king offered him work. He became Frederick III's secretary in 1442 and a priest in about 1447, when he was also created bishop of Trieste.

Piccolomini was no uncritical admirer of Frederick III, let alone Austria. He once described the king as 'rather stupid', though perhaps this judgement says more about the speaker than the subject. In

Austria Piccolomini thought he had a mission to bring letters and taste to northern barbarians. No one doubts he was intelligent, with a keen political sense, and in this context he guessed that the Habsburgs had a future. He had already been quickly on the spot to advise Frederick's predecessor Albert to accept the empire, hinting subtly at the chances of heritability. His new service with Frederick was worth discomfort to his sensibilities. 'Like Ovid exiled among the Goths', he reflected in a letter, and the comments about the Austrian wine, women, Jews and monks, characteristic of a certain kind of academic humanist, cease rather quickly to be amusing.

All this stood in interesting contrast with his master's style. It is said that when Frederick went to Rome the beau monde smirked at the unmodish Austrian style we see in the Uffizi portrait. True or not, there were juxtaposed styles at the centres of fifteenth-century power which must arouse lively interest in the historian. Whether he looks at Rome, Vienna, Graz, Basel, indeed almost anywhere a diplomat might need to visit, the student sees how Teuton, Slav and Latin mingle. Nor was the mixture simply racial. There were many intellectual hybrids, part humanist, part scholastic, burghers and noblemen too, not always quite distinct. Much is epitomized in Frederick III, who married a delicate Portuguese in Rome but preferred in later life to brood behind barred doors, guarded from smooth orators by Czech mercenaries whose chatter the court could not understand.

The political story leads now to 1446 when Kaspar Schlick, the chancellor, and Frederick III recognized the supremacy of the pope over the council. At this, Piccolomini renounced his neutrality, wrote his justifications, and helped Frederick persuade the German princes to the same conclusion.

A sequel and a reward was Frederick's imperial coronation in Rome. He had heard about the Portuguese princess Eleanore at the Burgundian court in 1447, and decided to marry her after carefully considering the good of his House. So in 1452 Frederick set off for Rome taking with him Ladislas his ward, now aged twelve. He arranged to meet Eleanore in Siena. When she appeared, fragile and black-haired, bystanders said Frederick went pale. She quickly won his care and regard.

The new pope, Nicholas V, was a personal friend of Frederick and paid for the expedition. Frederick freely performed the marshal's service of holding the pope's stirrup. The coronation impoverished no one. There was no army, and no claim on Italian soil: 'love for all and no one hostile'.[40]

On their return to Austria there was uproar. The Austrian League, together with Hungarians, Bohemians and various south German allies, besieged Frederick in his palace at Wiener Neustadt. Letters of defiance were sent to Frederick even by Austrian lords. Some of this trouble had been brewed for Frederick by Sigismund in earlier anti-Habsburg manoeuvres, when the then emperor had created new imperial princes out of landed Austrian families like the Cilli, Montfort, Kraiger and Wallsee. Frederick had never accepted these acts. But he now behaved with dignity, and gave up Ladislas, which is what his enemies wanted. The Austrians are said to have put the lad into a bath to wash everything Styrian off him. In his notebook Frederick observed: 'the greatest happiness is to forget what cannot be recovered'.[41]

It will be readily understood why Frederick spent twenty-seven years of his reign (1444–71) almost entirely in his dynastic Austrian lands. Yet even in the 1450s matters began to improve for him, though the changes were indirect and slow.

In Hungary Hunyadi had been the emperor's representative in the crusading army in 1456 when the Turks stood before Belgrade, but he died there. Hunyadi's two sons, one of whom is better known to history as Matthias Corvinus, murdered von Cilli in order to get hold of Ladislas. The deed ended the Cilli line, and after some fighting most of the seventy Cilli lordships in the Austrian provinces passed to the Habsburg emperor.

The death of Ladislas Postumus from the plague in 1457 was not so much the removal of another obstacle as the occasion of new complexities, but even these were after a fashion weathered by the Habsburgs. The disappearance of Ladislas meant that the bonds between Austria on the one hand and Bohemia and Hungary on the other were ruptured. Podiebrady and Corvinus, regents of these two kingdoms respectively, seized the crowns and were prudently recognized by Frederick III. The two new kings were doubly related by marriage but different in many respects from each other. Although German chroniclers considered both with hatred to be usurpers,[42] Frederick had more trouble from Corvinus that from King George, the moderate Bohemian gentleman. Corvinus was a potential crusader, orthodox, recognized by Jagellion Poland, regarded with some favour in the papal curia, and unhindered by tiresome Estates grumbling about money. No doubt he was a jumped-up provincial from Wallachia, but a humanist and Italianizer also, a man of mark. For these reasons it was all the more an achievement for Frederick III and his son Maximilian to withstand in the end the claims and attacks of Corvinus, to get him out of Austria and Vienna itself, and to cement a Habsburg lordship which would last for four hundred years.

So Frederick III's acceptance of 1457 was no supine act, even at the time. At the Peace of Ödenburg Frederick reserved the Hungarian title *de jure* and was granted the succession if Corvinus should die without an heir. The Crown of St Stephen, politically sacred to Hungarians, was sold by Frederick to Corvinus for 80,000 Hungarian florins. The sequel only came later, when Maximilian recovered the part of Austria taken by Corvinus and indeed secured the whole of Hungary for himself; but since Maximilian was in almost every sense Frederick III's creation the triumph too was prophetically partly his.

In Germany the emperor's prolonged absence brought its own dangers. A conspiracy led by the Wittelsbachs to depose Frederick and replace him by King George Podiebrady of Bohemia was opposed by Albert Achilles, Hohenzollern margrave of Brandenburg (1458–61). This is a highly abbreviated statement of a complex situation in which private war between princes flourished, town leagues attempted to defend themselves against mediatization or even conquest by princes, and large regions like Franconia remained fragmented.

It was this shifting formation of princely parties which gave significance to the ambitions of Charles the Bold, duke of Burgundy. There were those, like Podiebrady, who thought in the late 1460s that Charles might be made king of the Romans. Brandenburg, frightened of Podiebrady, the Wittelsbachs and their allies, supported the emperor but also at one moment considered that Charles the Bold might share royal rule by a kingship west of the Rhine. Nor was Burgundian interest in imperial power over Germany a novel idea of Charles; Philip the Good himself had revolved such thoughts when he married a Portuguese to move closer to the Habsburg family network.[43] Charles's military and political plans were hence not absurd fantasies but constructive, if grandiose, plans laid in a feuding world deprived of clear leadership. If, as seems possible, more

Germans were frightened by Charles than by the Turks, they had, in their time and places, some reason to be so.

The more familiar part of this story is Charles the Bold's attempt in the 1470s to be named as co-ruler with Frederick and to become his successor by marrying off his daughter and heiress Maria to Maximilian, Frederick III's son. Negotiations ran through a variety of proposals. Frederick was inclined to listen because, among other reasons, he needed Burgundian military help in Austria and elsewhere. Charles declared that if named imperial successor he would ensure the subsequent election of his desired son-in-law, Maximilian.

Frederick was in such deep trouble that with all his caution he agreed to a personal discussion with Charles. It is easy to smile at the contrasting personal magnificence of Charles and the poverty of Frederick, who lacked even a suitable wardrobe. But the problem of clothes is symbolic. Once Frederick had bargained in Venice for good cloth; at his Roman coronation he had clad himself as best he could but not avoided scorn. Now he had to meet Charles of Burgundy, a European trend-setter, if the phrase be permitted, and Frederick in his necessity was given help in Augsburg by one Ulrich Fugger, who could accommodate him with silks and the like in return for ennoblement.[44]

The meeting between Frederick of Habsburg and Charles of Valois took place in September 1473 at Trier on the Mosel, amidst a gathering of anxious princes. It was stage-managed by Charles, who wanted his daughter Maria betrothed to Maximilian and the succession for himself, or at the very least a kingship over Burgundy. It seems that Charles overplayed the scene both in his demands and in his manner. On 25 November Frederick made off from Trier at night and was miles down the Mosel when Charles discovered his absence.

Charles the Bold was killed at Nancy in 1477 and in the same year Maximilian married Maria. But of course it was he who profited and Burgundy that joined the empire.

In 1486 Frederick III was superseded as king by Maximilian while continuing to retain his own title. This move was proposed by the new and reforming archbishop of Mainz, Berthold von Henneberg, but it was not an act of force. Frederick, now about seventy, worked gladly for the transition. Much of Austria, including Vienna, was in the hands of Corvinus, who had made a truce with the Turks. Frederick wanted to be rescued from the situation.

Maximilian, in the prime of life, wanted to secure Burgundy from France and to succeed to the empire, and he might well have been able in this way to assemble enough power to deal with the Austro-Hungarian situation. Not without difficulty, but ultimately in triumph, Maximilian was elected in Frankfurt. He succeeded as emperor in 1493 on his father's death.

Maximilian's election as king had been a timely and extraordinary victory for Frederick and a great setback to Corvinus. In Austria the inhabitants were learning, in Frederick's words, 'the difference between a tyrant and a good lord'. In Germany the reforming movement grew out of the change of kings.

Rather than the evils of particularism, so vivid to modern critics, it was threats from outside Germany that impelled the emperor and the princes in their different ways to attempt a clearer and more effective structure for monarchical government. To Maximilian the need for reform seemed more urgent than it had done to Frederick III because Habsburg policies had rapidly become more far-reaching and required military and therefore fiscal support on a larger scale. Princely interest, on the other hand, viewed imperial reform in a more sectional way: prepared to consider a national tax and accept the existence of national institutions, but less enthusiastic about strengthening the royal house.

Initiative lay with one of the most impressive princes of the age, Berthold von Henneberg, archbishop of Mainz (1484–1504). He understood the need to strengthen central judicial authority independently of the emperor's immediate whereabouts, and was no less concerned to protect Habsburg interests from Magyars and Turks in the east. Henneberg also took a gloomy view of the separation of Silesia and Moravia from the empire by Corvinus.

It has been argued that the later medieval shift of princely power from west to east gave impetus to a Rhineland drive to restore monarchical influence, not only for its own sake but also for the political sake of the rich but fragmented Rhineland, in the midst of which lay 'golden Mainz', the seat of this arch-chancellor of the empire. According to this line of debate, Henneberg has been held up as a 'good German' and Maximilian as a 'hybrid foreigner'.[45]

It is an argument so far without a solution. Henneberg wanted an electoral college of princes, but great secular princes like Hohenzollern of Brandenburg, Wettin of Saxony or Wittelsbach of

Bavaria had good hopes of taking care of themselves and were anyhow reluctant to spend money regularly on journeys to assemblies. The debate remains. Yet it seems reasonable to suppose that the Rhenish archbishops and the count palatine of the Rhine were men of political awareness and anxious about the fate of Old Germany. Taking into account the generations of feuding in the fragmented west, the memory of Wenzel's deficiencies, the recent scare over Charles of Burgundy and the serious Habsburg preoccupations in the distant east, there is no need for a theory that Henneberg wanted an enlarged Rhenish state.

The first major efforts at reform were made at the Frankfurt Diet of 1486, after Maximilian's election as co-ruler with his father. Maximilian needed to establish peace in Germany, and the active promotion of imperial reform was in his own interests. The plan was effective prohibition of private war, improvement in imperial justice, the construction of an imperial army paid for by an imperial tax, and it also included a scheme to bring a share of imperial rule to the Estates. Henneberg worked at details, hoping for practical results, not the victory of any one sectional interest.

But the reforming movement did not work out well. For example, full power to bind towns to the tax-decisions of a remote assembly at which they might not have a representative was simply not achieved. Nor was there any success in incorporating the lower nobility into a monarchical framework of consensual government, as Edward I of England had done in the 1280s.

The great princes were naturally unenthusiastic about royal competition with their own taxative and judicial powers. Everyone superficially wanted peace, but the political oppositions were too deep for reconciliation. For Maximilian money and soldiers were priorities. For princes it was good to be left alone. Their problems were various and by no means entirely excuses for mindless egoism. Those who see quite accurately the development in places of princely 'states' may with equally good judgement realize that some lords disposed of very little government and some quite eminent princes were in fact very poor. In 1498 the elector of Saxony, no less, complained that personal attendance at an imperial Diet normally cost him half his annual income.

The Reichstag at Worms in 1495 is a modest monument to imperial unity and may mark a convenient end to the present political outline.

It made a new Ordinance for the Imperial Chamber Court and brought into being some of the proposals which had been made by Frederick III, especially the provision that this court should have a permanent location and possess its own authority to impose penalties wherever the king might be at the moment. It did not, of course, make inroads on princely justice.

By this time the old king had died. His last years rouse again the kind of admiration due to endurance: *überstehn ist alles.* Corvinus had been anything but content with the agreement of Ödenburg, least of all with Frederick's refusal of his daughter's hand, and as the Hungarian, ensconced in Vienna's *Hofburg,* began to call himself archduke of Austria, Frederick made ready to flee to Innsbruck and thence into Germany, with his forty-two carts, his daughter Kunigunde, his chancery, archives and personal treas ... He could only beg Corvinus to take care of the trees and animals in the castle garden at Wiener Neustadt.

But Frederick's morale survived. The capture of Maximilian in Bruges in 1488 goaded the old emperor to collect an army and release his son personally. Soon he got a peace with Bavaria, and in July 1492 a Venetian embassy found him at Linz. They came to congratulate him and to mediate a settlement with France, and they found him weak but in control. A gangrenous foot was amputated but his only complaint was that the Roman empire must now move on one leg.[46] He died on 19 August 1493.

3

Instruments of Rule and Misrule

Historians sometimes write that the princely territories of late medieval Germany make a truer comparison with the western monarchies of the time than does the empire itself.[1] What kind of political existence these territories enjoyed will be the subject of the next chapter. But of Germany itself, as a whole, more must be said here. For although it is hardly possible to write a continuous political history away from the monarchical theme, there were certain institutions which may be termed instruments of rule. These were the German nobility, the practice of private war, the leagues of knights, the periodic organization of Public Peace *(Landfriede),* the so-called Vehmic courts of Westphalia, and the general scheme of ordinary judicial courts. Towns are treated in a separate chapter. The present topics are chosen as characteristic of Germany in general, and as instruments by which attempts were made to operate political power over wide areas. In the absence of a strong monarchy, men naturally strove to apply and widen such powers as they themselves possessed. If they failed, if their efforts seem to have turned into misrule, it may well be because they were too weak to act other than defensively. The nobility was not united by any great common cause; its political cohesion was even less than that of the towns. It was by its very nature a large collection of families, mostly local in a vast country, but some with a much longer reach than others. The first aim of these families was to secure themselves. Not being subjected to a general royal law, their expedients were necessarily temporary and often violent.

(a) *Nobilities*

Pre-industrial, feudal societies were ruled by nobilities, and these are historically the first instruments of rule. Nobilities were groups of families which had once proved their strength by seizing and dominating land. In early Teutonic society there was no real distinction between the man who was noble and the man who was free. There were men who found themselves with enough landed property and warlike strength to live as they wished, under the natural constraints only of family, terrain and neighbours like themselves. Of course, there were others too, poorer, weaker, and hence settled in subjection, compelled to perform the will of their rulers in all kinds of ways, from building walls and tilling fields to attending courts of jurisdiction. The man who was free in early Germanic society was in a sense noble. The man who had to do what he was told in such a detailed and regular way that his tasks ultimately got written down in custumals was not free. The German word for nobleman and nobility is *Adel,* of which there is no plural. It denoted a condition. Originally it meant the patrimonial estate, legitimately inherited from generation to generation, but soon it came to be applied to the family or kin of such estate-holders. No doubt these were once such as the chosen war-leaders of whom Tacitus wrote, whose dominance brought them their land, and whose 'yes' gave the earliest force to law. Supreme among them was the commanding general, the duke *(Herzog),* set over a whole tribal group to lead its army *(Heer)* in warfare constant enough to be hardly distinguishable from the operation of normal government. From among the dukes the king was chosen, and till after the end of the middle ages 'duke' remained the highest specific title, to be awarded by the emperor alone.

The number of dukes was relatively small. Originally the rank had been confined to the rulers of the tribal or stem-duchies: Lotharingia, Swabia, Saxony, Franconia and Bavaria. In the course of time these were either split up or absorbed into the royal house, so that the ducal title was either multiplied or lost, while other duchies, both great and small, were created by the king. The Austrian duchy of 1156 was a fairly early new creation. Luxemburg was raised to ducal rank in 1354 by Charles IV. Württemberg in 1495 was the last medieval creation. There were some others in between.

The other specific noble title in Germany was *Graf,* which is perhaps best translated as 'count', but certainly not as 'earl', since English earls were much more homogeneous a group in wealth and status than the German *Grafen.* A count had once been a Carolingian officer with delegated responsibility for ruling locally in the king's name. In the course of time count-ships became mediatized, that is, held of others than of the king; or they got partitioned, and new ones also were created or even assumed. By way of example, the province of Franconia saw many new count-ships spring into existence between the eleventh and the fourteenth century. It had been a duchy early in royal hands but then politically fragmented with the end of Staufen power. *Ministeriales* who served king or lords were given the title of count; some acquired it prescriptively through exercising jurisdiction over newly colonized land, others indeed just started calling themselves counts, like the Truhendigen during the Interregnum (1250–73). It became a land of small count-ships: Graisbach, Hirschberg, Leuchtenberg, Wertheim, Rieneck, Henneberg, Castell, Schlüsselberg and Heideck.[2]

By the end of the middle ages there were nearly a hundred count-ships in the German-speaking lands, but these were very unequal in size and importance, for they ranged from minor landholders up to major princes of the empire. The most important often had honourable prefixes to their titles, like the count palatine *(Pfalzgraf)* of the Rhine, whose style signified a once-important Frankish official and counsellor, or the margrave *(Markgraf)* of Brandenburg, whose prefix denoted a frontier principality. Both these by our period were electors, but there were others, of almost the same status, who were not electors, like the margrave of Meissen, the landgrave of Hesse, and the burgrave of Nuremberg, who was supposed to rule that ancient imperial city from his castle there.

All these and others besides were 'princes' of the empire. The term 'prince' *(Fürst; princeps)* meant not so much a specific rank as a man who held a major fief as direct vassal of the king. A great nobleman like this had larger territorial possessions and a superior political position to those who were not princes. The development of the imperial princely status is obscure, but by 1180 there were ninety spiritual and sixteen secular princes. Later the number increased. They were enfeoffed by the king with the sceptre if they were churchmen and the standard *(Fahne)* if they were secular.[3] Princes were sharers *(Teilhaber)* in the empire. The chronicler Otto of Freising (d.1158), who was a maternal uncle of Frederick Barbarossa, wrote [4] of *principes* who elect the emperor. But he also alluded to dukes who served in the army under 'the prince', meaning the emperor, so his use of the word is imprecise, though it obviously meant a magnate of royal status.

Berthold of Zähringen, whose family became extinct in the male line in 1218, was, according to Otto, 'one of the noblest princes of the realm' but 'usurped the duchy of Swabia', and in Otto's mind a duke without one of the great old duchies was but the holder of an empty title.

These men of exalted rank, dukes and counts, some of whom were princes, formed only the apex of German noble society. From earliest times Teutonic nobility was heritable, and in the absence of primogenitary custom the class was large and diverse in economic fortune. But sons naturally took precedence over servants and retainers, and a primitive aristocracy of birth was formed. *Adel* has the same root as the Anglo-Saxon *aetheling* and denotes what modern English people may call 'blue blood'. The metaphor is good because it expresses the double meaning of something which is both biological and extraordinary. Such was the nobility, which in Germany included most of the high clergy, often younger sons of blue-blooded families.

In the course of time the structure of the German nobility became more complicated. Leading families, princely as well as royal, required the help of administrators and counsellors, lay as well as clerical, and the highly-placed servants who got appointed secured for themselves not only protection from outside attack and safety from the arbitrary will of the lords who were their friends, but lands of their own, peasants on the lands, and personal retainers. So the expansion of society engendered a new kind of nobility, that of service. To the old nobility of birth *(Geburtsadel, Uradel)* was added the new nobility *(Dienstadel, Jungadel)*. These *ministeriales*, originally unfree like all other non-noble persons, were rapidly becoming knightly and noble in the twelfth century.[5] These men mostly did not live continuously in their masters' households but on their own lands, from which they could be called when necessary. It is an unremarkable development, traceable in many societies. Students of English history are quite familiar with the early nobility of *gesithkund* men which was reinforced and altered by thegns, who might be self-made; likewise the nobility after the Norman Conquest was ultimately changed by reinforcement from the ranks of the king's servants. There seems to be a third stage, when the king overtly created a nobleman by letters patent in virtue of what that man would in future do, have and be. This was in the later fourteenth century, when exactly the same process was at work in the court of the Emperor

Charles IV at Prague. The English barony by patent is paralleled by the imperial nobility by letter *(Briefadel)*.

In later medieval Germany these nobilities had become more or less indistinguishable. Most of the higher nobility sprang from older families. This included all the dukes and many of the counts, free by birth to the limit of family memories; *edelfrei*, as they would say, which is the nearest equivalent to *gentil* or the slightly later English *gentle*. But they had been joined by their one-time upper servants. History has given their Latin description of *ministerialis* a more exalted connotation than *Dienstmann*. But local property and power transformed them. Acts of mass forgetfulness permitted them the noble status which follows material acquisition. At moments the fog lifts to reveal the process. Barbarossa's Constitution against Arsonists (1186) happens to exclude from knightly status all who were not the sons of knights, and elsewhere makes a distinction between those whose parents were legitimately knights and others who were spurious knights. Laws against *arrivistes* are a sure sign of social mobility. In the thirteenth century imperial judges in Italy began to say that admission to knighthood was something which required their leave, and that they made knights just as they made notaries and judges. This was a teaching of the law-schools, which saw both knights and lawyers as defenders of the empire, instruments of rule. A more explicit development came in 1231, in Frederick II's Constitution on the making of knights. 'Henceforth', the emperor ordered, 'no one shall receive the honourable grade of knighthood unless he comes from a knightly family.' Here again is a clear sign that what was being forbidden had been happening. The Staufen themselves had been creating a vigorous class of new men to serve them in their Swabian and Franconian lands, and everyone was now demonstrating the sharpened consciousness of status which accompanies rapid social mobility. So in Germany the myth that a gentleman is born and not made continued to be authoritatively mouthed even as satisfied thugs or pompous jacks-in-office were accepting the girdle and sword. Ready as always to believe the French more *gentil* than other peoples, the Germans, like the English, changed this ceremonial girdling in the fourteenth century to the French-style dubbing of knights, the *adoubement* on the shoulders with the flat of the sword. The principle was the same. Knights in Germany were lower nobility, and new noblemen were being created to bear rule in an aristocratic society, just as we have seen (in Chapter 2) some old but modest nobility climbing into the rank of kings.

We must return to our knights, for much of late medieval Germany was their land. In one way they still thought of themselves as beyond nation in relation to other knights, as certain old-fashioned German officers still did in the early twentieth-century wars. The effigy of a mailed knight in Magdeburg Cathedral, dating from about 1250, is of a Moor. As late as the fifteenth century western knights were welcomed by the Teutonic Order in Prussia when they went for a season's crusading against the heathen Lithuanians, and even if there were touchy incidents, the ceremonial dining at a Round Table was regularly held.

In another way German knighthood was in danger of getting seedy when it was not taken up and used constructively by rulers. Castles multiplied unwarrantably, especially during the Interregnum. By 1300 there were perhaps more than 10,000 in Germany. Their holders and tenants, often simple knights, formed a lower nobility which operated with a handful of retainers, perhaps a toll-station, even a gallows. But they had not much of a function without either an employer or a thriving military skill. In 1302 at Courtrai and in 1315 at Morgarten in Switzerland, plebeian and peasant infantry fighting with pikes in defence of their homes had hacked to pieces their chivalric enemies. The defeat of mounted knights was becoming a common experience: at Bannockburn, Crécy, Sempach, Nikopolis and Tannenberg. If pikes and missiles threatened them in the field, gunpowder was about to threaten them at home. Almost worse, mercantile townsmen, who were richer than they, were aping the style and even the title of knighthood, securing arms and insignia from kings in return for money and service, and actually taking part in tourneys, though usually with blunted lances. It was little wonder that real knights of the late medieval period who found no useful work with an archbishop of Trier or a count of Württemberg (of whom more later) went on the rampage as professional bandits against soft merchant convoys, or formed leagues to protect themselves against each other and the harsh world outside their circle.

The interesting fact is that a few of them were intelligent and survived to write or dictate their memoirs in old age. They have left a legend of ferocity. On his deathbed the fading faculties of Wilhelm von Henneberg in 1480 confused the pious candle thrust into his hand with the lance he had been accustomed to hold. Likewise, Wilwolt von Schaumburg cried out at the last against hallucinatory devils whom he saw as the adversaries he had run down during his active life.

Three of these 'robber-knights' may illustrate their kind. There was Oskar von Wolkenstein from the southern Tyrol, who died in 1445. An accident in youth had deprived him of his right eye, and a painting of him made in 1432 and now at Innsbruck University shows him with the new artistic realism of the age, the hollow socket set in the heavy, serious face. The figure is aristocratic: long, orderly hair under a fur cap, tunic with fur collar and ornately patterned with a goblet-motif, and sash with the same. Here is a *Raubritter* from the upper end of the market, so to say, friend of the Emperor Sigismund, poet, knight-errant (or mobile mercenary) for fourteen years and with a patrimonial inheritance to return to.

Another well-connected but working adventurer was the Swabian Jörg von Ehingen (1428–1508), trained as a knight in the Austrian archduke's household at Innsbruck, furnished with three horses by his loving father, and lured by the need for a living to foreign parts. He went to Prague, Rhodes and thence the Holy Land, where he was ransomed from the Turks with money he had prudently brought with him; thence to Alexandria, Cyprus and back to Austria. Later he travelled from court to court in France, Anjou, Navarre, Portugal, Castile, Fez, England and Scotland. He even served the count of Württemberg as high steward *(Obervogt)* of Tübingen before he retired to write his memoirs at the age of eighty.

Götz von Berlichingen was a real robber, and even if he falls slightly outside our period (1481 to 1562) he remains an archetype.[6] He was a friend of Franz von Sickingen, Luther's backer, and in due course inspired a play by Goethe, who romanticized him. To historians he is known by his artless but circumstantial memoirs. Von Berlichingen came from one of the many fragmented parts of Germany, just to the east of Heidelberg. He belonged to a knightly family without much substance, preferred horses to school, and became a professional retainer. He was often employed by the margrave of Brandenburg, but joined in anything he thought profitable. In 1504 he lost a hand, but acquired an artificial one of iron which enhanced his fearsome reputation. In 1516 he gained a large ransom from the capture of Count Philip von Waldeck, and used the money to build Schloss Hornberg, where he died forty-six years later. He was exactly the sort of person the Swabian League of 1488 had tried to put down, but he was treated with unaccountable leniency even after leading the Odenwald peasants in the War of 1525. Later he redeemed his reputation somewhat by fighting for Charles V against both French and Turks, and his last eighteen years were uneventful. At the end of his life he dictated his memoirs. They are the ramblings of an octogenarian, ignorant of political or intellectual affairs, adventurous incidents mostly prefaced by *'Volgt...'* ('Then...'). He wore a helmet crested with the device of a wolf's head, and his nature is epitomized in his own story of seeing some wolves worrying a sheep as he rode by, and of his passing shout, 'Good luck, brothers!' Far from being romantic the character emerges as egotistical and violent, typical of the criminals who plagued so much of Germany.

(b)   *Private war*

Whatever the later elaborations of the German knighthood, its slow military obsolescence, the spread of military trappings into the households of burghers, and the settlement of noblemen in various places into the peaceful service of princes, it remains generally true that large numbers of German knights and their followers spent their time fighting. War between private parties *(Fehde)* went on being an accepted instrument of politics and law. There were supposed to be conditions under which it took place, and there were continuous efforts to regulate it. But private war remained acceptable throughout the German middle ages, and its most distinguished historical exponent of modern times has given it a kind of institutional respectability.[7]

In its origins private war was blood-feud, capable of being dressed up in the mystical language of honour. Men in primitive societies feel that some injuries cannot be compensated by mere payment: in Icelandic saga a man remarks that he does not carry his father in his purse *(seinen Vater nicht im Beutel trägt)*. In German-speaking lands the practice continued, obviously, because no one could prevent it, and it got extended for the same reason. Probably the murder of a close kinsman was quite a rare occasion for starting a campaign, though kinship was much in people's minds as the stuff of security and alliance. In 1461 Duke Sigmund of the Tyrol and Duke Ludwig of Bavaria-Landshut made a pact with words which declared that true

71

kinship and blood were the basis of their love, friendship and duty.[8] More often the *casus belli* was debt, real or imagined, territorial claim following a partitioned inheritance, a marriage or an ambiguous grant, or simply the friction between neighbours, especially where mercantile wealth was in some way open to plunder.

By late medieval times private war was differentiated from public war in which the prince or emperor might engage. But even if *Fehde* was not *Krieg,* it could be serious. It could involve a campaign or expedition *(Zug).* It could be carried over provincial boundaries so that the defier became the enemy of the whole province *(Land)* in which his opponent lived. It could be levied by men in common against their lord, and by towns against their feudal master or against other towns. Town archives contain both documents about particular campaigns and also complete feud-books. At times the conceptual boundaries were blurred. Nuremberg's strike against some threatening knightly castles was a *Zug,* but its conflict with the margrave of Brandenburg was *Krieg.*

At the other end of the scale private war was distinguished from riot or murder by conforming to the customary rules of publicity. Time and again it was proclaimed in Public Peace announcements that a defiance must always be given with due warning of hostilities to follow. Three days was the minimum, symbolic threats like the strewing of ashes should precede the reality, letters of defiance *(Absagebrief)* should be sent. Deep reproach was felt against those who rose in unceremonious insurrection, like the Tyrolean peasants against Neustift Abbey near Brixen in 1525: 'a cruel, frightful and inhuman rising of the common peasantry', complained the lords.[9] Clergy and cities were held to be immune, as were those not in the retinue or protection of the conflicting parties.

The most obvious reflection prompted by this state of affairs is on the weakness of German society's consituent elements. Anarchy is perpetuated if no one has overmastering strength. An example of this is the major Westphalian feud from 1442 to 1447 between the archbishop of Cologne and the rather insignificant town of Soest. The archbishop was Dietrich von Mörs, member of a powerful and ambitious family, anxious to dominate the region. Soest was allied with the duke of Cleves-Mark. The region had been badly disturbed since the thirteenth century. Nobody was strong enough to win. Even the archbishop's hired force of several thousand Saxons and

Bohemians could not break the town's resistance, the archbishop ran out of money, and many of his mercenaries took themselves off. At one point he had captured a couple of castles and the immediate reaction was an abject obeisance of the neighbourhood to him, with promises to be true subjects to the archbishop 'for ever' (reserving their good, old customs!). But such victories were rarely pursued to a conclusion, partly for lack of money and partly because local knights who served as mercenary captains were incompetent and, most interestingly, sometimes related to their opponents.[10]

Private war was a more frequent and natural condition in those numerous parts of Germany which were politically fragmented. These will be considered from a different viewpoint in Chapter 4, but it must not escape notice here that much of old, or western and central, Germany was in this condition. The disappearance of the Hohenstaufen, the Interregnum, and the rivalry of Habsburg, Wittelsbach and Luxemburg left many areas unsubjected, or not yet subjected, to higher nobility, with the consequences that there were innumerable occasions for dispute and many men able to eke a living by taking sides. This is where the *Raubritter* had their heartlands, where they lived in their country castles or fortified houses, sometimes in conditions of poverty.[11] When bound in companies or leagues for banditry, self-help or hire as mercenaries they took some collective name and wore uniform or insignia: the red sleeves of the Lahn-Rhine countryside, the crowns, horns, stars or wolves of other societies, with knights distinguished by gold trimmings, the esquires *(Knechte)* by silver.

It must be said again that this knightly capacity to organize for feuding and self-protection, this insecurity, was a consequence of the German realm's frontier character as much as of anything else, and with frontiers, that is to say, which were internal, shifting, uncertain. The Hussite catastrophe aggravated the situation enormously, spilling fanatical armies over central Europe and leaving their debris about to be hired for war even when the fanaticism had evaporated. The nervousness spread by these events is caught exactly in a tax-return of 1474 made to the Chamber of Electoral Saxony from a minor nobleman called Seiffard von Lüttichau who had property in Kmehlen, on the borders of Lusatia and Bohemia.[12] Amongst his necessary expenses like ploughs, maidservants and the rest, he claimed 'for two esquires to ride with me at £5 each, that makes

£10...and for two watchmen whom I must have as I live on the Bohemian frontier, £4.'

(c)   *The knightly League of St George*

The sense of political insecurity was unusually strong at the time of King Wenzel's accession in 1378, and it was from this point that the leagues of knights began to flourish. The knights in Germany regarded themselves as lower nobility and behaved as such. Yet their position was anomalous. They did not wish to be subject to the local prince; and although some noble families entered towns and became patricians, still less did most knights wish to be subject to burghers, whose wealth they envied while despising their unmilitary preoccupations. Above all, princes and towns were at a point of intense competition, for independence, territory, and jurisdiction over potential tax-payers and able-bodied men, wherever they might live. Knights therefore were caught in the middle, too poor for comfort, unacceptable to greater lords or to towns, and at best able to sell their military skills by engaging on one side or the other in private wars. In this climate the leagues began to flourish: the League of the Horn in Hesse; of the Lion from the Wetterau up the Rhine to the Alps and down-Rhine to the Low Countries, and even eastwards into Thuringia; and in South Germany the Leagues of St William and of St George.

The League of St George is a good example of a sectional association formed for mutual protection.[13] It was a confederation of lesser Swabian nobility called into being in the midst of an unpleasant local war between the great abbey of St Gall and its peasants. This was the Appenzell War of 1403–11. The knights were aware of the need to protect themselves both from internal feuding and attacks from outside. They had modest livelihoods to defend and potential military contracts from magnates and cities who might hire them. The documents which survive show also that the knights had a certain *esprit de corps* and political ideals of an old-fashioned sort.

The League was constituted for limited periods and operated by a series of agreed renewals, at first often of three years' duration, later in the fifteenth century somewhat longer. As each period drew to its end, one of the captains would send out letters *(Bundbriefe)* to members and others who seemed suitable and likely to join. This procedure was quite difficult, as the clerical work was done by scribes who had to be accommodated in the captain's house or at least nearby. There was no fixed centre and the archives and cash, such as they were, moved around as captains and scribes changed. In 1438 an arbitrating captain in Nuremberg had to excuse himself for not being able to find certain treaties, as the Society's scribe had just died.[14] It was all rather makeshift. Each *Bundbrief,* sealed by the members, created in effect a new Society, held together by freshly taken oaths of loyalty to the elected captains, though the patronage of St George maintained a titular and emotional link through time. Policy and activity naturally varied in accordance with changing events. In theory the members should have met every two months, but this was difficult to keep up even though they all came from Swabia. Meeting-places changed and were determined by the availability of lodging and the identity of the summoning captain. At the meeting the financial subscriptions were payable on pain of a fine, membership was discussed, members sworn in, and arbitrations and campaigns arranged. Although these independent knights are usually spoken of as poor, the problem of the League of St George seems to have been less poverty than distance and the administrative vagueness of untrained gentlemen. In 1442 they were said by Ulm to be a rich company *(eine riche ritterschafft),* and in 1488 the *Bundbrief,* referring to the principal difficulty, described the province of Swabia as 'wide and broad.'[15]

In the earlier fifteenth century King Sigismund, for whom Swabia was so important, would have liked the Society to have formed a league with the Swabian imperial cities as a counterbalance to the power of the great princes. This was not successful, and the Society remained essentially one for the benefit of its knightly members, who might or might not enjoy the protection of powerful noble families or membership of a city.

It was possible to do deals with cities by providing mercenaries, or with higher nobles by getting them to join the Society in return for support against other important nobles who were excluded. In such a way the Count von Werdenberg was helped against the Count Eberhard von Klingenberg in 1463. Klingenberg tried to recruit help in Lucerne, but to no avail. His castles were besieged and he had to give in. True, cities and nobility never formed as homogeneous a political society as in England, but they could get deeply involved in each other's feuds and trade problems. Another example is the help given by the knights of St George to Puppelin von Ellerbach, one of their important members, against Walter von Freyberg, who was a servant of Duke Albrecht of Bavaria-Munich but a non-member. The object of the quarrel was ridiculously small: the advowson of the church of Holzschwang. But Freyberg refused to submit to arbitration. He had a brother who was a canon of Augsburg and a ducal master who was going to protect him, so he felt quite confident in waging private war against Puppelin and his supporters. In doing so, however, he lost a good deal of public sympathy for neglecting the provincial law of Swabia which required the declaration *(Absage)* to be made by day and before witnesses; after much negotiation through the Society's captain and potential arbitrators like one of the counts of Württemberg, it seems that Freyberg was at last brought to compromise. This is the stuff of medieval German politics. There were rules about everything, but nearly always some important person was not prepared to keep them. In this case, advowson, the right to present a clergyman to a parish church, was considered a feudal right and properly dealt with by the relevant jurisdictional lord or in a provincial court. But when ordinary courts were refused and men were being killed and cattle distrained, a good arbitrator was welcome, whether arranged through a knightly Society or through a local Public Peace.

Fundamentally, the members of the Society of St George, doubtless like their counterparts elsewhere in Germany, believed that they were standing up against unfair aggression[16] and that the ultimate remedy lay with the empire of which they were an organic part. As the *Bundbrief* of 1424 put it: 'And most especially should we remain together true to the holy empire'.

At the end of the century the emperor himself, Frederick III, gave expression to this assumption when he wrote, on 5 February 1488, that the province of Swabia had no princes of its own other than himself as Roman emperor. Though he was often far away, he gave leave for Societies of this kind to exist, in the belief or at least the hope that they would continue the injunction of their *Bundbrief* of 1426 'to praise God, our dear Lady and the holy knight St George, and to honour the Holy Roman Empire'.

(d) *Public Peace*

Of all the arrangements which were designed to bring public order to later medieval Germany, that of the Public Peace, or *Landfriede,* was the most widely and frequently used. It is doubtful whether it can properly be described as an institution. It was neither a royal law nor a continuous system of courts, but an *ad hoc* agreement, rather like a treaty, between varying combinations of princes, lords and towns within a given region, to keep the public peace and suppress certain categories of serious violence for a defined period. In some ways it was rather like a Society of knights but on a bigger scale and with a wider membership. Usually, but not quite always, it was initiated by the king. A Public Peace was discussed, agreed and proclaimed at a certain place for a certain length of time, and was intended to operate by means of officials appointed for the occasion by the contracting parties. Normally there was an officially constituted committee with competence over a particular region under a captain. The captain was often an imperial official and called *Hauptmann* or *Obmann.* The public was warned to abstain from violent crimes or suffer the consequences. If it worked well, subordinate officials, rather like mounted police and provided by the local lords who had sealed the document of Peace, would seize malefactors and bring them before the special judges. Men who committed serious crimes and were caught red-handed might sometimes be executed on the spot, and on occasion bandits and highway robbers, the typical scourge of Germany, could be chased across territorial frontiers in 'hot pursuit' *(Nacheile).* Cases concerned with ordinary civil matters or feudal relationships were supposed to be excluded from the Public Peace and dealt with by the ordinary courts of the local jurisdictional lord. But it will easily be seen that there was ample scope for disagreement about the substance and the working of the Public Peace. In any case, the movement underwent some changes of political emphasis in the course of the fourteenth and fifteenth centuries. There is continuing debate about its effectiveness.[17]

Agreements between great men to try and limit crime and private war are not historical surprises. There is a continuing likeness between them across the ages. Under the Carolingians the king's *missi* called assemblies to keep the king's peace. From about 990 onwards the southern French nobility and the abbots of Cluny started the Peace of God movement. German kings proclaimed Public Peace. So the search for precedents is not likely to be particularly enlightening, though historical continuity is clear. In the early twelfth century there were local agreements in Germany, such as Henry IV's Peace of Mainz in 1103, but an early, if not the first, general one was that made under Barbarossa at the Diet of Roncaglia in 1158. The Peace Constitution of that year actually forbade private war altogether, but this was ignored, and the Constitution against Arsonists of 1186 at the Diet of Nuremberg set certain conditions for the conduct of feuds. A further clear early example of *Landfriede* in Germany comes from 1235, when Frederick II proclaimed peace at Mainz in an attempt to strengthen royal authority, forbidding private war and appointing a justiciar to try disputes between magnates.

In the second half of the thirteenth century, when the Hohenstaufen had been destroyed, this kind of superior peace-keeping authority was the most the king could exercise. It was, as H. Angermeier put it, 'an inheritance that must be ever earned anew'. On the one hand it was deeply desired, especially by the towns whose life depended upon peace. On the other hand it was opposed by powers, especially the nobilities, who feared loss of wealth and jurisdiction and looked to the arbitrament of war. The ultimate failure of towns and nobility to co-operate and the king to overmaster their private wills led to the failure of the Peace movement and the dislocation of German politics till the day of Prussian hegemony and, at the extreme realization of the State, of the National Socialist *Gleichschaltung* of early 1933.

These griefs began centuries earlier. Some have argued that a universal royal peace for Germany was crippled by Frederick II's well-known grants of jurisdiction to the princes of 1220 and 1232. It is doubtful whether any one period was dramatically decisive. The monarchy failed in stages: the double election of Otto of Saxony and Philip of Swabia, the failure of the young King Henry, Frederick II's son, the Interregnum of 1250–73, the inutility of King Wenzel between 1378 and 1400, and the deflection of royal interest into south-eastern Europe from 1439, all these spun the plot. At no period was the monarchy wholly lost, even if it was reduced almost to brave words alone. But the monarchy's credibility was lowest precisely when it neglected the *Landfriede* and hence failed to produce conditions of public order. It was in large measure for this neglect that the two depositions of the later middle ages, those of Adolf of Nassau (1298) and of Wenzel of Luxemburg (1400) were carried out, and that Frederick III was nearly supplanted in 1459–61.

The 'peace' which during these times was thought of as the task ultimately of the king was hardly different from that desired by English kings like Henry II: to get rid of those who committed murder, robbery and arson and those who harboured such wrongdoers. The list might be extended according to the circumstances of the *Landfriede* to include those who took unjust tolls, pledges and forage. Even though civil wrongs and feudal disputes were excluded, it was common for apparently trivial matters to flare into violence in a land where feuding was part of the accepted order, and this is reflected in the prohibition of 'unjust defiance' in many Public Peace treaties. Indeed, all crimes were more likely to be committed when private war occurred, so the Public Peace was the theoretical ideal antidote. Only private war itself was never explicitly and totally banned between 1235 and the so-called Eternal Public Peace of 1495.

The more detailed attempts to secure Public Peace start, naturally enough, with the Interregnum. After 1250 royal power was destroyed and, in what one German historian has described as a 'building-boom', private men of power constructed some ten thousand castles. In these years it is less correct to talk about the annihilation of jurisdiction than its dissemination among miniature polities. The consequent difficulty in creating any large peace-keeping institution is clear. The best that could be done was to create leagues, like that of the Rhenish towns in 1254–7, and to exercise leadership like that of the margrave Heinrich of Thuringia, who called a disunited area to some sort of order.

After more stable monarchy had been restored, the responsibility of local lords for maintaining peace continued to be recognized. King Lewis declared in 1323 at Nuremberg that every prince, count, lord and city shall 'pacify the roads and protect all men on water and land as best each may in his territory and courts'.[18]

During the fourteenth century Public Peace was sought not only by this sort of appeal of the king to individual lords of jurisdictions but through confederations *(Einungen)* of princes, regions and even towns. These were usually achieved through the negotiations of local powers, encouraged but not necessarily organized by the king. The reason for these local initiatives is plain enough. Much of the century was occupied with conflict between the great royal dynasties of Wittelsbach, Luxemburg and Habsburg, so that peace organizations tended to be set up in particular regions. Royal interests were involved, but they tended to be regionalized. Numerous agreements came from the Rhineland. Lewis of Bavaria formed a peace organization in 1315 in Alsace with the count palatine and the Swiss. He abolished certain Rhine tolls, to the detriment of the pro-Habsburg archbishop of Cologne, and set up others, so-called 'peace tolls', at Coblenz and Remagen. In doing this he got the agreement of the archbishop of Mainz 'for the sake of better general conditions and peace'. In fact, all though the 1320s and 1330s the great Rhenish archbishops and their satellites were the effective agents of public peace in the region. Further afield it was other local authorities that acted effectively. The Swiss gave a striking example of a working *Landfriede* after Morgarten in 1315, in the treaty between the three forest cantons which was both political and judicial. In Thuringia the power of the landgrave became all-important in dealing with violence and unauthorized tolls and mints. In north Germany royal power was lacking and public order was administered either through princely courts or through *ad hoc* courts set up by leagues of nobles and towns.

In the reign of Charles IV it looked as though the kingship was going to survive as an effective peace-keeping force. Political success may look like luck, and be measured by tangible winnings, yet a strong and affable personality is usually to be felt behind the recording documents. The Luxemburg family lands were extended by Charles's marriages. He travelled extensively. The Magdeburg Chronicle relates how on one occasion at Mainz the emperor, surrounded by magnates, declared that what the princes advised him was more important to him than any mere town law.[19] Whether he visited a region or not, he used deputies and vicars whom he treated with a politic mixture of friendship and authority: the archbishop of Cologne in Westphalia, the archbishop of Trier in the Mosel land, the burgomaster of Lübeck in the north, bishops and the burgrave of Nuremberg in Franconia, which was on his side anyway. This was how he defeated the Wittelsbachs, and this was how he reinforced courts in an area infested with criminous knights. In 1349 everyone in Franconia had to swear an oath against those 'who acted against us and the Public Peace' *(der tut wider uns und den lantfrit).*[20] The king could even order people to join a Public Peace, as he did in 1357 to the archbishops of Trier and Mainz by his direct command: *iussu et mandato.*[21] The Golden Bull itself consecrated the idea of a general royal peace which made it high treason to molest an elector on his way to help choose the new king. Only in Wittelsbach Bavaria was Charles IV's Peace movement overshadowed by dynastic hostility, so that crime was fought there more by the efforts of its own courts and *vigilantes*.

The dissolution of peace took place under Charles's son Wenzel. The politics of this disastrous reign have already been discussed. But the failure of the *Landfriede* was the failure of a personality as much as of an institution. Just as Charles had built up agreements through affable authority, so Wenzel let them go because he could not make friends. He pursued peace politics through formal Diets, and issued grand, overall directives. If one points to the Peace of Eger of 1389, that great and comprehensive effort to put down every kind of disorder, even the hooliganism of lordless men and attacks on people going to courts, it must be answered that this was a princely programme, not a royal one, and it did not now exclude collaboration even against the king, whose passivity was complete. One of the articles of Wenzel's deposition document said that he had allowed wars, robberies, murders and arsons in the German lands, and had in that sense been, as the Strassburg chronicler put it, a diminisher of the empire and not the enlarger which the Golden Bull bade him be.

Public Peace history in the fifteenth century was a logical continuation of Wenzel's failure. The deposition was no more forgotten than were those of Edward II and Richard II in England, and the fall of Wenzel from the kingship of the Romans put an end in the minds of political men to the king's exclusive claim to be the origin and supreme guardian of peace. King Rupert possessed little influence in these matters, and the Public Peace of Franconia (1403), once so loyal to the Luxemburgs, was organized by princes. Agreements like that of Marbach which were now being made excluded the king and resolved to use the ordinary courts. To that extent they were in effect leagues rather than *Landfrieden*, the more so as warfare levied even against the king was envisaged.

Sigismund's reign, for all its noisy personal publicity, was a difficult time for Public Peace policy. The new king tried to use the Estates and especially the towns as agents of order, but he was too occupied with the Hussite wars and extra-German affairs to be effective. The reality of peace-keeping passed more into the hands of the four great Rhenish electors. The day was gone when the king had good hopes of welding the princely and town Estates together, and the knights were now more clearly aligned with the princes. What was new was the idea (and not just the practical expedient) that the electors rather than the king might control the public peace, and that they might do so by dividing Germany into distinct geographical regions or 'Circles'. The scheme was that each of these should be set under a captain who would adminster a truly public and permanent law in respect of peace and order. In theory it was impressive. It was suggested that the king might nominate the captains. Yet from far-away Austria he had not the power or organization to make such courts work; so the fifteenth century reached the halfway mark in a condition of public disorder comparable with that of the Interregnum.

In this respect the reign of Frederick III is paradoxical. He was quite aware that the problem of peace existed, and that it was the responsibility of himself and not of lesser men. The barrier to effective action was his need to remain in Austria, not sloth. True, he was not happy with assemblies and meetings which called for the gifts of personal persuasion. When the archbishop of Trier asked for a Public Peace and requested an imperial vicar to supervise it, Frederick replied that he would hold an imperial Diet as soon as possible but meanwhile ordered the establishment of a new imperial Chamber Court at Rottweil near Stuttgart to settle infractions of the peace. This was Frederick's style. When petitioned by his towns in Swabia about the wild private wars of the region, he referred them to his regular jurisdiction. When pestered by the Vehmic courts, as we shall see, he pointed to Rottweil or alluded to his supreme jurisdiction. If seignorial courts failed to act he just issued simple orders to do so or else accept a named arbitrator. Frederick III was good at announcing his imperial supremacy, and there is something magnificent about the continued assertions even if they were not very effective.

There is a historical development half-concealed behind these problems of Frederick III. Older writers have seen simply a Germany fuller than ever of vagrant criminals and have raised routine lamentations about 'general disorder'. H. Angermeier, on the other hand, argued that this was not wholly so. His view seemed to be that despite the king's deep belief in the empire as the best guarantee of peace and justice on earth, he in fact relinquished the maintenance of law and order increasingly to territorial princes. In consequence, from about the mid-fifteenth century a better peace was being kept, but only *within* princely territories and in accordance with princely aims of strengthening their rule. On the darker side, there was a remarkable amount of warfare between princes themselves. For Angermeier the fifteenth century was an age of peace within and war between the lordships of the land. As to the first, one may look at orderly Württemberg under Eberhard, or at ducal Alsace, where mounted police on Burgundian pay kept order in the streets and inns under the command of the hated *Landvogt,* Peter von Hagenbach. As to the second, one can pick almost at random on the Soest feud, the Münster feud, the wars of Franconian aggrandizement in the interests of Albert Achilles, or the public aggressions of Charles the Bold which set western Europe by the ears.

Frederick III never relinquished his belief in the competence of his own royal courts, and he had a good deal to be pleased about in his accord with the papacy, the basic support from such princely houses as Brandenburg, Saxony, Württemberg and Baden, and the modest successes achieved by the imperial Chamber and its procurator-fiscal in punishing law-breakers. Archbishop Adolf of Mainz was his Chamber judge from 1470 to 1475, and this provides another instance of the bonds between Frederick III and Mainz as against the evil genius of fifteenth-century Cologne, whose archbishop in his pride had used the Vehmic courts. Problems of imperial jurisdiction were nowhere near settled, and the Public Peace movement never again offered the hopes envisaged and partly realized under Charles IV. But it had served a turn.

(e)   *The Vehmic courts of Westphalia*

A more eccentric attempt to impose law and order on Germany than the Public Peace movement was the so-called *Veme* or *Feme,* the Vehmic courts of Westphalia. These have received more detailed attention elsewhere,[22] but they illustrate the consequences of political decentralization too well to be altogether omitted in this context.

For about a century a number of obscure court-holders calling themselves 'free counts' purported with some success from their small German province to administer royal justice in the empire's name all over Germany, in cases of serious crime or where justice in civil causes had been withheld by other courts. There appear to be three main reasons why this local assumption of supreme authority was possible.

First, the archbishop of Cologne, who had also become duke of Westphalia, was a dominant figure in fourteenth- and fifteenth-century German politics and the Peace-keeping movement. Secondly, the kings of the Luxemburg dynasty, Charles IV, Wenzel and Sigismund, relied heavily on their great neighbours, the Rhenish archbishops, to maintain their policy of public order. Thirdly, Westphalia itself was a region troubled by violent disturbances yet inhabited by significant numbers of prospering men, anxious not only for peace but also for further self-advancement. These were in a unique position to develop an existing court jurisdiction, make it their own with the blessing of authority, and extend it audaciously far over Germany.

In 1353 the archbishop of Cologne claimed that he had the right to supervise these 'free courts' which by then had sprung obscurely into life. The 'counts' themselves, who took their titles mostly from unimportant villages in the area of Dortmund in south-eastern Westphalia, were themselves claiming to have received authority from the king, and before long the king had indeed granted the archbishop the privilege of creating and supervising the 'free counts'. It seems there are two crucial moments in this history: 1372, when a Westphalian Public Peace was proclaimed by Charles IV, and the bishop of Paderborn, close servant of the archbishop of Cologne, arranged to use these local courts to apply the Public Peace; and 1385, when the first summons was issued from one of these courts to a defendant outside Westphalia. In 1386 the city of Ulm in Swabia wrote a famous letter to Speyer saying that certain princes and lords had sworn a Public Peace called *Faim* which was making wide claims, and that secretly appointed counts *(Femegrafen)* were pledged to hang those condemned for their guilt and refusal to answer. By 1392 the courts were everywhere known as 'the Westphalian courts' and their jurisdiction was practised intermittently, and sometimes dramatically, far afield in Germany and even against magnates and towns. The organization, deliberately secret, operated through sworn and undercover members, not unlike a Mafia. It was sustained by the wish of kings for peace (sometimes to the point of urging subjects to join), by the archbishop-elector's desire for power, and by the greed and self-importance of a class of Westphalian *arrivistes*. Undoubtedly, some cases were settled and some rough justice done. The work cannot yet, if ever, be safely quantified, but it is interestingly clear that both very exalted and quite humble people were at times involved, as accusers, defendants and possibly juror-executioners.

The decline of the Vehmic courts came after the 1430s, when German cities began to resist. Bern took steps to improve its own courts, and the stirrings of conservative outrage brought harsh measures against Vehmic agents and litigants in north, central and south Germany. Knightly Societies insured their members against Vehmic process. Ultimately, the emperor himself, none less than the oft-despised Frederick III, repudiated the Westphalian jurisdictions so impudently invoked in his name. On 19 August 1488 Basel received a letter from the emperor expressly saying that if the city courts were incompetent, appeal should be made to the emperor himself or to the imperial chamber court which he had just set up at Rottweil.

Historians are rightly suspicious of dramatizations. Most change is in slow-motion to the observing eye. Goethe and Kleist, who romanticized the *Veme*, need not be reproved as writers; the historian may be content again to note the mingling of rule and misrule in a land which longed for constituted authority.

(f) *Ordinary justice*

But what were the consituted authorities in distinction from the extraordinary ones which have been occupying attention? If the 'ordinary' courts were of such limited effectiveness that they required constant attempts to provide peace and justice by other means, we should still not remain blind to the fact that ordinary courts existed, in the great cities, in principalities, in little seignorial territories and in villages too.

The jurisdictional patchwork was obviously very complicated, but an attempt at generalization need not be over-bold if it is remembered that local practices were divergent.

The Carolingians had created over much of what later became Germany a network of counties in which the count, or *Graf*, exercised high and low jurisdiction on behalf of the monarch. Colonization, shifts and failures in the royal power, and other processes of decentralization meant that the count-ships became mediatized, or granted to intermediate lords. By the thirteenth century the king of the moment had his courts like any other prince in his own dynastic lands, and he retained some vestigial royal rights. In theory he could take cognizance of cases by calling them up to himself in some instances *(ius evocandi)* and he could receive appeals *(ius appellandi)* on the initiative of subjects unless even these rights had been renounced. As he journeyed about, the court constituted by his royal household *(Hofgericht)* superseded the local jurisdiction where he happened to be; but this practice too tended to disappear as the princes acquired high territorial justice. Princes and imperial towns in the later middle ages were always quoting their privileges of immunity *(de non evocando)*, and the complete freedom from royal jurisdiction given to the electors in the Golden Bull of 1356 was subsequently demanded by the other imperial princes, most imperial towns and innumerable church foundations.

Attempts to provide a supreme imperial court, competent to hear appeals from all subjects even in the absence of the emperor, were a development of the fifteenth century and not very successful.

Within the principalities and towns were courts which exercised the highest jurisdiction in civil and criminal matters. They had power of life and death, often gruesomely illustrated by artists of the time. In country settlements lesser courts were administered by the lord's agents in co-operation with leading villagers. Local divisions in Germany went under different names and were liable to change as lordships changed. In place of the English hundred and wapentake we hear of the *Gau, Zent* or *Hundert*. The jurisdiction exercised in these might belong to a great lord or a minor one, and the lord might or might not also be the local landlord with his own free or unfree peasants. Records of local customs which survive show great variation in the details of relationships, obligations and privileges.

Yet beneath the diversity there are generic likenesses in German local justice, and there are also signs from the thirteenth century at the latest that perceptive men wanted a more centralized and royally originated law. To take the last point first: in the thirteenth century, at the very time when centralization was collapsing, law-books were being written in the make-believe that an overall law still existed. Pre-eminently, there was the *Mirror of the Saxons (Sachsenspiegel)*, compiled between 1220 and 1235 by Eike von Repgow. He was himself an East Saxon and patriotic in a royalist sense: he made out that at least some of the old tribal duchies, like his own Saxony, had been kingdoms. There was also the *German Mirror (Deutschenspiegel)* of about 1260 by a priest from Augsburg who tried to formulate the body of law for the whole German people; and there was the *Mirror of the Swabians (Schwabenspiegel)*, a popular adaptation of the *German Mirror* produced some ten years later, also by a priest and probably in eastern Franconia, that is, near Nuremberg.

The idea that high justice comes from the king is dominant in books like these. It was what people believed was true, and it was being reformulated in case it was forgotten in a land increasingly dominated by lords other than the king.

If we glance for a moment at a German locality where everyday judicial work was carried on in later medieval times we should probably see one or more professional judges, known as the *Richter*, working under the lord with a local group of substantial free men called jurors or *Schöffen*. If the judge was exercising high jurisdiction delegated by king or prince he might be called *Vogt*, perhaps best rendered as 'steward'. The village judge was sometimes appointed by the lord and given land, but had the delicate task of acting also in village interests. In ancient German law judgements were given by the jury of village elders, the *Schöffen,* and the judge *(Richter)* was simply their mouthpiece and executive officer. In the course of time the judge probably came much more often to act on his own under control of the jurisdictional lord, until he was thought of as possessing an office *(Amt)* and being an official *(Beamte)*. The word *Richter* is a general one. In many cases he was the same as the village mayor or head man, called *Schulze* in German and *Starost* in Polish. On the other hand a considerable local lord, like Seiffard von Lüttichau of Kmehlen in Saxony in the later fifteenth century, had a *Richter* in each of his villages.[23]

Judicial courts often met thrice yearly. In about 1340 the free men who came and settled among the other tenants of the monastery of Tennenbach in the Rhineland were told they must go like others to court three times a year, in February, May and August.[24] Anyone who wanted to depart might do so but only by day and in sunshine. An offender might be banished to the other side of the Rhine or into the Black Forest. In 1355 the landgrave of Hesse acknowledged that the peasants of the village of Schlierbach had taken him as their jurisdictional lord. The forty peasants are named and the court was declared to sit on three Mondays during the year, when small money penalties could be inflicted and the men organized to protect the village with timber defences.[25] This preoccupation with security is a constant motif. The abbess and chapter of the imperial convent at Essen proclaimed an 'assize of arms' about 1331 and declared what weapons and armour should be possessed by each of their free and unfree tenants, according to their wealth.[26] The reason given was 'danger from local invaders'.

In the eastern colonial lands it is possible to watch new courts being created from the beginning. For example, in 1418 the Marshal of the Teutonic Order ratified the recent foundation of a village near Königsberg under the law of Kulm. A local German magnate got four *Hufen* [a *Hufe* was generally between 60 and 100 acres] of land in inheritance and a third of the profits from the greater and lesser courts, though jurisdiction over native Prussians was reserved to the Order itself.[27] In the commandery of Marienburg on the Vistula delta the German settler-managers called *locatores* themselves became hereditary village mayors *(Schulzen)* with about ten per cent of the village land for themselves, rent-free, and a right to the office which could be passed on in inheritance or sold. Problems arose with partition of the office or inheritance by a child. But only one person could possess the court. This village official was Janus-faced: he had authority over the lives and work of villagers yet might be excluded from political assemblies like the Diet of Elbing along with 'inn-keepers, Tartars, Samlanders and peasants'.

In towns the institutions of ordinary justice were obviously more complex. As in England, older and more important cities often became a model for the organization of their colony-towns. A newly-enfranchised town in England would receive a 'filiation' charter granting it the customs of its mother-town and saying that future disputes should be settled according to the customs and rules of the mother-town. So too in Germany there were a few great families of town law *(Stadtrecht)*, stemming from Cologne, Magdeburg, Speyer, Lübeck and so on, each spreading out to govern towns founded in the vicinity.[28]

Leading citizens still thought in terms of royal origins. For one thing they were glad if they could claim direct subjection to the emperor, for that meant freedom from local princes; for another, their town law, influenced by Roman civil law, harked back to the Carolingian privileges granted to merchants; or again, a great city like Nuremberg, which had its own customary law, found it based on the

Mirror of the Swabians, where the king features prominently.

But city law was subject to piecemeal changes by the councillors, or *Schöffen,* year by year. Merchants began to need greater clarity and authority in their mercantile law, and men trained in Roman law were there to help. The reception of Roman law in fifteenth-century Germany was not universal, and it is a contentious topic. But the adoption of Roman procedures and the adaptation of customary law in many places is undeniable.

In Nuremberg, codification began in 1477 by a committee of the city council helped by jurists, 'men of dignity, permitted to wear garments with gold borders and to carry swords'. Such was Gregor Heimburg, enemy of the papacy, trained in Padua, who joined Nuremberg in 1435. Their draft was ratified by the council in 1479, priests were told to read it from pulpits, and a printed version was prepared by Anton Koberger. This was the first printed publication of a town law-code in Germany.

Special interest attaches to codification in later medieval Germany, quite apart from the debated question of whether it led to the more successful oppression of the peasantry and the political development of princely rule. Better written law was needed by a growing economy of contract, debt and property transactions, not to speak of the problems of military procurement. The *Richter* and his *Schöffen* could not manage the world for ever. Procedures began to change as these old-fashioned judges and juries were replaced by jurists trained in academies, and this was not merely because princes thought a Romanist professor would serve them better politically but because litigants preferred advocates who had been to university, whether in Italy or Germany. Popular judges were easily puzzled by complex cases and were happy to call in more educated arbitrators who could comprehend technical writing and produce a written opinion behind the scenes.[29]

So a physical separation occurred between litigants who once faced each other in court and expected a judgement from the consciences of their fellows. Experts sat in rooms and wrote for their clients. If an authoritarianism appeared, it was because the litigants who used the courts wanted it. It was an authoritarianism supported, for example, by the duke of Jülich 'for the sake of impartiality and the poor' as well as of his prerogative. Other princes, and towns too, wanted like improvements in their courts, councils and chancelleries. To put it a different way, Roman law did not enter as an alien substantive law from outside, for Germans did not need that. They lived in a world where there was general habitual agreement about the right order of society, however ill that order was kept and however acrimonious the conflicts about rights. What Germans required was intellectual order. A good Roman lawyer thought conceptually and divided his subject-matter analytically, as he had been trained to do. But he adapted his concepts to the facts before him. Hence the importance in his mental world of the Distinction, the Gloss and the Commentary, which were concerned with particular instances fitted into a whole conceptual framework. This was better than reverting to quasi-magical oaths of accusation and disclaimer. Never mind if 'humanists' disliked the empiricism of glossed texts, and continued their querulous search for texts which were 'pure'. In the field of law this was donnishness at its most remote and ineffectual. German law by the end of our period had been put into better order and gone a long way towards coping with new economic and legal problems. It was not being refashioned as a weapon to cow the peasantry or increase their burdens. If that was being done it was by the hands of extremely German potentates, not their literate advisers;[30] serfdom, which will need to be examined later, was a creation of territorial lords, not of academics and not of the German towns of that age.

4

Principalities and Powers

(a) *From stem-duchies to territories*

A student who leafs through a German historical atlas might be
forgiven for supposing that between the early tenth and the late
thirteenth century western and central Germany had crumbled from a
great political federation of huge duchies into mere fragments. The
reader's bewilderment at so complex a German dissolution might at
the same time be relieved at the greater historical simplicity of the
substantial new colonial territories stretching away from the eastern
margins of the old lands: Austria, Brandenburg, Silesia, Prussia.

Historical understanding is hard to acquire just from maps,
especially the older, simplified ones which label large,
undifferentiated land-masses as 'duchies'. The labels suggest that
here were great political units under the more or less detailed control
of exalted noblemen. So it needs a written text too to explain the
realities of politics: that property could inhere in rights as well as
fields, that boundaries changed on account of fears or ambitions, that
dynasty is fundamentally beyond the map-maker when it comes to
portraying the genesis and distribution of sturdy families with
marriageable children or territories riven with dispute and lacking
governance. Few maps can be more difficult and innocently
misleading than those of medieval Germany and, urgently as we need
to know the location of places and features, much has to be explained
in words. 'This is no mean task', wrote Georg Sante in 1964, 'in an age
that yearns for a definite historical picture if it is not to take refuge in a
mere weariness with history.'[1]

After the collapse of the Carolingian empire in the ninth century,
the whole area of 'old' Germany, conquered by Frankish tribes, was
composed of the so-called stem-duchies: Lotharingia, Franconia,

91

Saxony, Swabia and Bavaria. The dukes had a warlike mode of life and a more or less king-like status, but actual kings of Germany were elected, styled king of the Romans, and usually crowned emperor subsequently by the pope.

The kings had ways of trying to weaken the duchies, though they could not simply abolish them. Kings could take over duchies themselves, give them to their relations, depose dukes, import foreigners as dukes or partition a duchy. Carinthia was cut off Bavaria in 976, to take a single example. When Conrad, the first Salian (or Franconian) king, was elected in 1024 he was himself in possession of Franconia, which was henceforth always under royal overlordship. He made his son Henry duke of both Bavaria and Swabia, and margrave of Carinthia, so that by then the Lotharingian and Saxon duchies were the only ones held by independent princes.

The twelfth century saw the end of the stem-duchies and the beginning of territorial ones. Kings, especially the Hohenstaufen, who got the throne for five generations, created numbers of new duchies under territorial dukes, like Austria and the County Palatine of the Rhine in 1156 or Würzburg in 1168. The most shattering event, full of consequence for the future, was the ruin of Henry the Lion, Welf duke of Saxony and Bavaria, by the Emperor Frederick I (Barbarossa) in 1180. The old dukedom of Saxony was shared out between the archbishop of Cologne, the Ascanians and others, and Bavaria came into the hands of the up-and-coming family of Wittelsbach.

These twelfth-century concussions look like the beginning of the notorious German political fragmentation. But we must be careful. Having accused historical atlases of baby-talk we must not fall into the same simplifications by imagining the old duchies as political monoliths. For instance, the admirable historical atlas published by the Bayerischer Schulbuch-Verlag in its medieval volume shows clearly that important noble dynasties had hereditary properties in particular parts of Germany within one duchy or another, and sometimes more than one, so that when a man of particular dynasty became king his hereditary lands would be added to whatever royal possessions might be available to him.[2] The Carolingians were strong in the Rhine-Main region, the Ottos in Saxony and in Bavaria, the Salians over the stretch of Rhineland round Speyer and Worms, and the Staufen in Swabia, Alsace and Franconia.

This property did not consist of huge ranches divided by

geometrical frontiers, but of land, people and rights strewn about in an almost endless variety of combination and density: villages, fields, forests, rents, tolls, monasteries, judicial courts and other forms of income or value natural to agrarian society. Maps can only show ingenious conventional symbols, clustered or scattered; but if the eye imposes several sets of such symbols over a given region, to show the property of several lords, then the political complexity of even an early duchy will be understood. This multiplicity of proprietorship suggests that 'fragmentation' was not the sudden and disastrous catastrophe of text-book Germany so much as the natural condition of human societies unwelded by concentrated politico-administrative power.

Late medieval Germany was fragmented in a different sense from the earlier land only because there were more human beings on the ground, more noblemen, more organization, yet no overmastering force to seize major princedoms and control the proliferation of lesser ruling families by political and legal means, as an Edward I of England would have done. A strong monarchy would doubtless have brought slow cohesion, as in the western kingdoms. A weak one permitted continued fragmentation but had not created it.

The thirteenth century saw further severe shocks in Germany: the double election of 1198 which brought destructive civil war; the embroilment with the papacy and the failure of the Hohenstaufen in Italy and Germany; and the terrible Interregnum of 1256 to 1273. The failure of a strong kingship to emerge during and after this time meant naturally that princes and lords continued to strive for local mastery in a world where local rearmament and fortification were increasing, but no power or authority appeared effectively to serve the office of king. The double process of regional power-politics and demographic boom produced the political kaleidoscope of princely Germany, but this dynastic geography is not as bewildering as first sight suggests.

The territories of late medieval Germany are too numerous to name usefully in a general book: there are adequate reference works. But it is important to set them in some sort of proportion with each other and explain the nature and style of territorial government before giving some examples to show the diversities.

Leaving aside the cities, discussed in Chapter 5, there were the electoral principalities (seven), other major principalities (about twenty-five secular ones and some ninety archbishoprics, bishoprics and abbeys), over a hundred count-ships, though of very unequal importance, and a mass of lesser lordships.[3] This vast web of seignorial rights had evolved out of particular circumstances, not just sprung into being from great permissive statutes like those of Frederick II. Many ecclesiastical foundations were very old and in enjoyment of immunity, expertise and prestige. The eastern principalities, on the other hand, were new. It is much easier to see the historical construction of a territory in the east than in the west where, apart from the extraordinary convoluted political geography, the historical foundations of many territories are not just acts of conquest or frontier settlement, but a combination of historical elements in many permutations: landlordship over tenants owing rents and/or services, landlordship over domains bearing crops and flocks directly for the lord, juridical lordship over men (mediated ultimately from royal authority, created in colonized regions, or simply seized), not to mention the existence of completely free land (allod) whose holder owed no one anything.

To complicate the scene, territories could change their shape, their name, even their location. Sometimes they were bonded together through a marriage, sometimes increased by purchase, unredeemed pledges, grant or conquest. In secular territories fertile marriages of princes were great dividers, for the partibility of rulership began to be seriously challenged only from the middle of the fifteenth century onwards.

To return for a moment to the problem of historical cartography, there seems to be one historical truth inadequately taught from maps of late medieval Germany, and this is the preponderance of political fragments. The bright, confident colours of famous princedoms like Bavaria attract the eye away from undifferentiated areas which in aggregate must have been larger than those of the major territories. In Germany tiny lordships abounded. A quick tour should make this clear.

Old Saxony, spreading south-westwards from the lower Elbe, was an area of lesser principalities, fragmented without system. There were some church territories, like Paderborn, the abbey of Corvey and the bishoprics of Minden and Hildesheim, out also numerous small lay lordships on the middle and upper Weser, like the countships of Plesse and Everstein, mostly enclosed within lands belonging to the great house of Welf, which will be discussed below.

The lower Rhineland was also split up amongst numerous families of small nobility, some of whom had gained in riches since the thirteenth century by their appointment as 'advocates' or stewards *(Vögte)* of church estates. The most successful of these were the four counties, later duchies, of Jülich, Mark, Berg and Cleves: they had broken free of the archbishopric of Cologne in 1288 after the Battle of Worringen, and they retained their identity despite repeated divisions of lands and the feuds with which the surrounding countrysides were racked.

Although west central Germany was occupied by some important and fairly stable principalities, in their interstices were a myriad fragments, like the scattered possessions of the abbey of Prüm. Southward again were the strewn properties of the bishopric of Metz and a host of little lordships stretching down to the Saarland.

Hesse was an important lordship and contained some prominent noble families, like Waldeck, Ziegenhain and Katzenelnbogen, but other local comital families fell apart into numerous collateral lines and became poor. Nearby Thuringia after the mid-thirteenth century offered the spectacle of intense fragmentation into small lordships which had not been absorbed at the end of the medieval period by the greater surrounding powers of Mainz, Brunswick, Meissen or Electoral Saxony.

Perhaps south-western Germany was the most dramatically fragmented region of all. Homeland of great families — Zähringer, Hohenstaufen, Habsburg, Hohenzollern — it showed during our period a friability almost into political dust. Even rural holdings were partible.[4] Leaving aside the exceptional Württemberg, of which more later, the area was covered with a multiplicity of dwarf states and town republics, forming and re-forming into leagues. The Austrian possessions on either side of the Black Forest were almost the only continuing political structure, but they were attached loosely to the distant Habsburg power. The margraviate of Baden had developed out of possessions once belonging to the Zähringer, to whom the rulers were collaterally related, but theirs was a territory made up more of jurisdictional than landed rights and was often partitioned. Likewise the lordship of Fürstenberg was a composite mass of lesser ones, direct or enfeoffed, many of these also descending from the Zähringer. Most interesting of all perhaps are the Zollern lordships, not only by reason of their majestic future in Franconia, Brandenburg and Prussia, but for the miniature dynastic presence signified to this day by the fairy-tale castle at Hechingen and the railway line beside it running down to Sigmaringen on which the coaches themselves bear the legend 'Hohenzollern'.

Of the south-western lordships which endured, some were traceable at least back to the eleventh century, like Zollern, others were of more recent beginnings, sometimes as the property of *ministerialis* families like Waldburg-Wolfegg, and a few were most unusual in being Fugger lordships, like Kirchberg an der Iller or Weissenhorn, and thus in an odd sense feudal creations of capitalist enterprise. But the local south-western lordships were often very small indeed, even the church ones. Their baroque interiors of a later day bear witness to little more than a grandeur of the imagination.

Examples like this could be multiplied, but there is no need to emphasize the general truth in that way: late medieval Germany was a sea of political fragments in which some larger pieces floated. Even some of the more important polities were themselves of a cellular or sponge-like composition. Such were the archbishopric of Mainz and the County Palatine of the Rhine, both electoral principalities, centred in the Rhine-Main region, but made up of numerous estates and rights scattered and intermixed with those of others.

Fragmentation could take another interesting form. Instead of the possessions of a locally dominant prince being thickly scattered over an area but interspersed with those of other lords, you could have some outlying possessions of a strong and centralized principality which was far away. A west German example is of the property belonging to the Teutonic Knights, rulers of Prussia. The Order possessed many pieces elsewhere: the Grand Master had a private bailiwick at Coblenz, and there was a honeycomb of commanderies near the junction of the Rhine and Main. These lordships obviously exercised influence in the neighbourhood.[5]

Two other types of fragment are of interest in an analysis of political Germany. One is the existence of areas given over to knightly estates which were in reality independent of a prince and even, till the sixteenth century, of the emperor. The other is what for lack of a better term must be called 'peasant states'.

The Kraichgau is a region on the east bank of the Rhine, between Heidelberg and Heilbronn, fertile in character. In the sixteenth century it contained seventy-two estates belonging to men of knightly rank,[6] and earlier much the same. The counts palatine had been trying since the earlier fourteenth century to acquire rights there, and when Rupert I became emperor in 1400 these knights began to serve him in various offices. But the connection did not last. The Palatinate failed to absorb the Kraichgau at that time, and the hostility between Palatinate and Württemberg gave the knights opportunity for independence. For a considerable period they existed as one of the knightly leagues discussed in Chapter 3, in this case the Society of the Donkey. The name seems not inapt. The illiteracy of the knights made them of limited use to an administering prince, and no doubt everybody suffered from the existence of a poor, uneducated but noble society under its *Hauptmann,* not yet absorbed and disciplined by proper political rule.

Little political communities which were able to enjoy a prolonged life unsubdued by king or noble can hardly be imagined in England, and in Germany were evidently possible only in lands of alpine remoteness or deeply isolated on the marshes by the North Sea.[7] Two seem specially worth singling out. Friesland had become a community set apart since the ninth century through inning from the sea and the local ability to defend itself from invaders who probably did not really want it anyway. The holdings were small and not greatly differentiated in size. The inhabitants did no military service to outsiders, and it was an understood convention that anyone who helped a foreign overlord would be thrown into the North Sea. They applied their own law in their own vernacular and appointed their own village priests. A sworn council seems to have acted as collective judge and tribal administrator and to have been in possession of a seal inscribed *Universitas Frisonum.*

Dithmarschen lay at the extremity of the Elbe on the right bank, abutting on to Holstein but virtually an island. Attempts of powerful outsiders to rule ended in bloodshed and failure. By 1283 texts speak of *Universitas terrae Dithmarciae,* and during the fourteenth and fifteenth centuries ruling was done by an elected council which met in a market-place on Saturdays. Leading families emerged, grown rich on their share of Hanseatic trade and proud of believing themselves to be at once noble and peasant. Their written customs show the community deeply suspicious of outsiders, especially prelates. Defeat and incorporation into the county of Holstein came only in 1559.

The structure of territorial Germany during the later middle ages is more than a subject for mere description or even for the typology which has been sketched. The variations are so great that realities can be presented only in detail, so more examples will follow. But two or three questions are insistent enough to be voiced here, though they cannot be answered immediately in any satisfying way.

The first is the physical matter of frontiers. In an enormous landmass divided up by proprietorship or political dominance according to the shifting decisions of war, marriage or whatever, it is perplexing to know what the significance of a frontier might be, how it was marked, and who took notice of it. Here it is a question of general knowledge, common sense and guesswork. Natural frontiers like rivers, sea, forest-edge, or occasionally a line of hills provide the visual frames of reference. There remain the questions of a frontier's utility. Against incursions of war and banditry the answer of course was fortification and garrison, and this will be observed later in this book, as when for instance the Wittelsbachs or the Luxemburgs built fortified chains of posts along acquired frontiers.[8] From such stone settlements troops could issue forth at need or, more usually, officials could operate, in the saddle or in office-chamber. Another use of a frontier is as a place of toll, and in that context toll-houses or structures were erected, barriers placed to halt travellers, and at least some kind of guard or garrison placed on call. There are enough jokes about enterprising free-lances setting up their own toll-booths before being found out to suggest that many travellers were circumspect or even jumpy enough to pay and be off. But as a generality, and in cases of major trading convoys, it was in the interest of princes to keep safe the ways as well as take their tolls, so the institution of *Geleit* was usual. This was escort-duty, performed by a lord's men detailed for the duty, and with the corollary that merchants and travellers were expected to follow the routes thus authorized and guarded. Locally contested frontiers might be marked in some way in order to make the point, and in an illiterate society this was by agreed ditch-lines or the marking of trees. Finally, the imagination of a frontier must settle on the rural inhabitants themselves, wondering how they knew where they were politically, as they must have done, and whither they might or must go. This would appear in the discharge of service and the serving of jurisdictions. If work for a lord is owing, if a family is justiciable in a given lord's court, if rents are to be paid regularly, then it follows that officials will be habituated to travelling round and giving instructions to individual cottages and their dwellers. Such mundane matters are glimpsed in the *Weistümer*. What other kinds of frontier are thinkable in the shifting world we are contemplating?

The second generality about territorial Germany at this epoch is surely its weakness, as a whole and in its many parts. The number of troops the emperor could raise at any one time was small. The failures of the Turks to assimilate more of Europe and of the Hussites to set up a powerful principality were due to the various weaknesses of the aggressors rather than the power of imperial armies. Some principalities developed military forces, as will be seen, but on a small scale. Testimony to German weakness is all about us in these years, in the failure of feuds, and the better success of arbitrations. Lasting success of arms was demonstrated only at the outskirts of empire: the westward movement of Poland against Teutonic Knights 'betrayed by what was false within' and the victories of the Swiss, who would soon not be exclusively German and not imperial at all, against Charles the Bold, terror of the German world.

The third general reflection which cannot be evaded is the question of statehood. German historians even of the living generation somtimes write that the origin of modern statehood is to be found in the German principalities of the late middle ages. In discounting the political force of the empire it is easy for such words to slip out in one form or another, and a general book like this should not make a fuss about the *obiter dicta* of experts. But there is a real point here, and one which perhaps seems of higher importance to continental than to English scholars. Can we see in the late medieval territories any forerunners of the 'modern state' and *a fortiori* what could this mean?

No answer other than a sceptical one can be given by the present writer. Most generally, in the first place, 'the modern state' is a creature no living historian should heedlessly consider fully evolved and ready for the text-book. Leviathan, that mortal God, left our fathers at least some privacy. Modernity tends to take new meanings as time goes by. To anyone who remembers the *Gleichschaltung* in Germany between January and May 1933, even Bismarck's Prussia might seem to have retained areas of individual identity. As we age and technologies advance the structure of politics seems sometimes to take on possible new meanings, and consequently the 'state' to dispose potentially of ever more refined modes of surveillance, recording and manipulation. The intention here is not to offer a personal, idiosyncratic view of terror but to play down the organization of late medieval government.

In Germany as elsewhere, various princes were finding trained lawers useful and were encouraging such men to study in local German as well as the more famous Italian universities. Likewise, some princes were appointing permanent officials over districts, and were rounding out territorial claims. The word 'subject' *(Untertan)* was appearing as a general replacement for 'man' or 'vassal'.

But the change of scenery was gradual and the arenas of political activity small. In any one territory there were still multiple courts of jurisdiction. Law professors enjoyed patronage but not a tenure bestowed after competitive entry, and it is dubious if they could have written expositions of sovereignty. In matters of finance there was still room for doubt whether officials were serving the lord or the territory or both. Professor G. Droege thinks there was no conscious separation between the financial administration of the court and of the *Land*.[9]

Political forms too were often backward-looking: feudal service, feudal dependence and feudal forms of law were still widely used.[10] The problem of the partible inheritance of the princedom had only just begun to be faced. There was not much talk of abstract bodies politic. Above all, the very word 'state' in any modern sense was not used even in Prussia, as will be seen in Section (v) below.

It will be more useful from this point to look briefly at a few examples of principalities. The selection could not be made without misgivings. There were considerations of space, diversity and the availability of suitable material. Bavaria is a conscious but regretted omission. The Rhine Palatinate has been treated in English in a masterly fashion by Dr H.J. Cohn. Therefore a few territories have been chosen to illustrate diversity as well as to take advantage of scholarly work done on them in recent times.

(b) *Some examples*

(i)   Trier: an electoral archbishopric[11]

Ecclesiastical principalities enjoyed some advantages over secular ones in the maintenance of political stability. True, bishops and abbots could be involved in bitter conflict with their townsmen and their tenants and could act the feuding magnate no less than their secular cousins. But there were levels of abjection below which a church prince could hardly fall, if not by the sacrosanctity of the patron saint's endowment, then at least by reason of a prelate's freedom from wives and legitimate children to importune him for customary shares. Further, though usually of princely stock, bishops were not unlikely to be men of intelligence and education.

Trier was in such ways exceptionally favoured. The city had been a Roman imperial and an early Christian centre and maintained a stable bishopric through the Merovingian and Carolingian periods. Charlemagne made it an archbishopric, and the great men who held the office were electors of the emperor from the twelfth century.

As an important territory Trier began to develop in the thirteenth century. It lay along the River Mosel, one of Germany's 'golden arteries' of profitable trade. Once the lordship had doubtless offered little more than tolls and hunting rights in the hilly forests along the river banks. Frederick II's famous privileges to princes permitted fortifications and other initiatives of government which Trier exercised better than most, and the Interregnum speeded the process. It is no intended slight towards his most able predecessors to hurry on to Archbishop Baldwin of Luxemburg, one of medieval Germany's greatest men, under whom the principality reached political maturity. When he was elected in 1307 by the Chapter of Trier Baldwin was already their provost, though only twenty-two, and a handsome, clever student in Paris. The next year, as an imperial elector, he helped vote his brother Henry count of Luxemburg on to the imperial throne, and received large sums from him. Yet the prince-archbishopric of Trier did not turn into a prosperous and well-organized territory through the effortless magic of a fairy-tale but through the hard work of its prince and his servants. Perhaps above all Baldwin was a financial expert. He used Jewish bankers at a time when they were often rejected in the west, secured credit on the tolls of Koblenz and elsewhere, and became famous enough in such ways to be consulted financially by Mainz, Worms and Speyer. By 1340 he had acquired 103 castles where in 1210 the see had possessed only seven, and these now became nodal points of an administration managed by paid officials who might otherwise have become or remained robber-knights. The division of the territory into administrative districts (*Ämter*) was probably copied from Baldwin's Luxemburg homeland, and the system proved good enough to last until the French occupation in 1794.

Revenue and administration are of course complementary: the rents, taxes and borrowings would have been less productive without Baldwin's insistence on a high standard of written record. The charters or title-deeds were ordered to be triplicated in about 1330 and rearranged according to grantors in what one scribe called 'an almost hopeless task' *(opus quasi desperatum)*,[12] and Baldwin always took a hand-cartulary with him on his journeys to prove with writing what other princes might have found more natural to assert with swords.

By the end of his life in 1354 Baldwin had nearly doubled his principality and made it into a geographically manageable whole. A summary sounds too peaceful, and the process was not without strife against both nobles and townsmen. But the work was continued without serious alteration of course by another fourteenth-century archbishop, Kuno von Falkenstein, who came from a family of imperial *ministeriales*. He too became very rich and was able to leave 150,000 guilders in 1374 to his nephew, Archbishop Frederick of Cologne, with whose see he had formed close monetary bonds.

Despite episodes of failure and archbishops of lesser luck or ability, the evidence of financial skills and co-operation indicates why the Rhineland electors were of such special power and importance in late medieval Germany. Their power is manifest through the fifteenth century too, in the Trier Archbishop Jakob von Sierck and the famous Berthold von Henneberg, archbishop of Mainz. This is another, more ordered, side to German territorial life from the routine severities attributed by so many students of the Reformation to the epoch leading up to it.

(ii)   Württemberg: a 'successor' territory[13]

When the destruction of the Hohenstaufen left south-western Germany a mass of fragments after 1250, Württemberg was already a considerable area, and was built up subsequently into a leading principality, till in 1495 its count became a duke and in 1805, thanks to Napoleon, a king.

Württemberg was not a successor to the Staufen in a dynastic sense but in a geographical one. Indeed, the Konrad of Wirtemberg who first appears to history in 1081 as a Swabian nobleman possessed some property which was allodial, which meant held quite freely and of no feudal superior. To that extent these Württemberg princes, surrounded though they were by Staufen and then by Wittlesbach and Habsburg centres of power, were anciently rooted by comparison with many others.

But as a solid princedom Württemberg developed relatively late. It had begun with many of the classic disadvantages of German political life: powerful and intermittently hostile neighbours, like Bavaria, Baden and the Rhine Palatinate; the custom of princely partible inheritance, and a lack of special natural wealth.

Its good features were that the county was enlarged by inheritance and purchase and enriched by profitable trade-routes between Ulm, the Palatinate and the Frankfurt Fair. These biannual waves of commerce provided spring and autumn influxes of income for the purchase of new lordships and the redemption of pledged ones. The steady, modest flow of wealth provided a basis for political consolidation.

It was a region of small towns, small holdings, and an unusual lack of social and political differentiation between town and country, anyhow in respect of the better-off people. The nobility were not very rich; they and the better-off townsmen were both regarded as 'worshipful' *(Ehrbar)* in public status. The local administration of courts was organized from the prince's towns, which provided the headquarters of his administrative districts *(Ämter)*, and these were officered by townsmen and noblemen who took the count's pay. The count received rents and taxes from his towns and villages and exercised equal jurisdiction over them through his authority *(Landeshoheit)*, which he came to extend skilfully and piecemeal over a bewildering collection of little lordships. This again may sound too peaceful. There was undoubted resentment as the fifteenth century wore on from peasants who disliked the townsman's law. But in Württemberg one might suggest that over-government rather than under-government was the predominating tendency.

The most dangerous political threat was to internal unity by reason of the count-ship's partibility between brothers. Multiple heirs were the ruin of German principalities elsewhere, and the hard decisions to exclude youngers sons were only beginning to be taken in the fifteenth century, whatever the high-flown sentiments of the Golden Bull. In Württemberg the crucial conflict between Ulrich of Stuttgart and his brother Eberhard of Urach began in 1459. Details are out of scale here, but the Treaty of Münsinger of 1482 decreed, in Eberhard's favour, the impartibility of the territory and its future acquisitions. Stuttgart was to be the capital, though Tübingen remained the university city Eberhard had made it in 1477.

A memorial tablet of 1496 on the choir wall of Tübingen's collegiate church depicts Duke Eberhard the Bearded standing armed but with hands joined in prayer while receiving commemoration as founder of the *studium*. To fight, to pray, to study: it stands as a symbol of the little realm Eberhard did so much to shape. He was a man who was not only a successful political ruler but truly believed in the value of learning. For this 'passionate autodidact' intellectual achievement was not just a mark of fashion or status. He enjoyed tournaments yet surrounded himself with counsellors who were learned as well as those who were noble. In a remarkable passage, Professor Ernst observed how important was the diplomatic corps of counsellors built up by princes over Germany, for they were the men who knew each other all over the empire and were at times positioned to decide independently among themselves matters concerning their masters. 'They largely made the politics of their lords.'[14]

Furthermore, a prestigious lord like Eberhard, well organized and full of good sense, was asked to arbitrate quite often in other people's quarrels; naturally he could not know everything himself, and so relied to a good extent on men like Hans von Bubenhofen, his chief judge *(Landhofmeister)* from 1461 to 1481. Yet in the last resort Württemberg was not an oligarchy but a principality. It was the count who made the decisions.[15]

If wars of partition had been on a larger scale, or if Eberhard had allowed himself to be drawn physically outside his own realm in his support of the emperor in the complex struggles of his region, then his financial state might have been bad or ruinous, or the Estates might have played a bigger part in bailing him out, as they had to do elsewhere. With respect to his biographer Ernst, the Württemberg Estates do not seem to have been very important in the fifteenth century and were certainly more backward than those of Bavaria. Their function was to guarantee credit and help make treaties, not to wield significant political power. 'Parliament day is pay-up day' *(Landtag ist Geldtag)* seems an appropriate epitome. The court ruled, the nobles lent, lesser folk paid. The rough aphorism may be worth considering later in a context of peasant unrest.

What, then, was being paid for? Military adventures? The luxuries of an effete court? Surely no such things. Württemberg seems characterized by a sort of good order which arouses admiration or doubt according to the political temperament of the student. Two illustrations may be offered.

First, there was a firm understanding between the count, his officers and his townsmen. Some will say that the townsmen of the small Württemberg boroughs were little more than peasants. On the other hand, they were also not much different from the local nobility. For decades the Tübingen town seals bore legends such as 'Seal of the burghers of the Count N. of Tübingen'.[16] At one time the count of Tübingen had to sell his town to the rich abbey of Bebenhausen, half an hour's walk to the north, but the new seal simply changed to 'Seal of the citizens of Tübingen', and the count rapidly bought the place back. There was not much trouble. If for the moment we leave aside the peasantry with a question-mark against them, it was a land of social peace.

The other illustration also helps to clarify 'good order', for it concerns the military forces in the pay of the count. They were economical, well-trained and unsquandered. As in other German territories of the time there was a knightly cavalry element and an infantry levy of subjects. The latter became of unusual importance. Lists of all able-bodied men were made. They were trained on regular exercises and on occasion by lending them under suitable conditions to neighbouring powers. After 1480 the more skilful troops were selected for special training and equipment with hand-guns; these numbered not more than 800 out of a maximum of 3500 infantry, smaller numbers apparently than available in Brandenburg, but a considerable force if used with discretion. Pay was regular, brown uniforms were provided, and a reserve was created. Sunday practice in shooting was decreed in Eberhard's Württemberg, with instruction for all participants and prizes for the best. Military power was occasionally used against robber-knights who took advantage of their private castles, and when this happened the inhabitants of the danger area might be evacuated for the time being to the nearest market town whilst order was restored.

This was the Württemberg which was the heart of the Swabian League and provider of one of the best military forces in Germany. At the reforming Reichstag at Worms Eberhard appeared with a glittering retinue, anxious to play a leading part in imperial affairs.

(iii) Saxony: a territory which moved

Before the fall of Henry the Lion in 1180 his duchy of Saxony was a huge north German province lying mainly west of the Elbe.[17] But from the moment Barbarossa began to distribute it to others, Saxony began to signify different regions, usually qualified by the name of the dynasty in possession of the portion in question. With some simplification we may say that Saxony as the province of the Elbe tended to move upstream; with another simplification it can be said that from 1180 to 1423 there were two Saxonies, one poor and one rich, and later still an even more complex division.

After Henry the Lion's defeat his great family of Welf were allowed to keep some of their allodial lands in the heathy country west of the Elbe, and this became the duchy of Brunswick-Lüneburg in 1235 by grace of the Emperor Frederick II. These were the Welf territories.

On the Elbe itself, partly on the lower reaches but mainly in the middle course of the river, important regions were given to an Ascanian prince, Bernhard count of Anhalt, younger son of the great colonizer, Albert the Bear. This mass became Electoral Saxony, centred first at Lauenburg (downriver, near Hamburg), but by 1356 at Wittenberg, much further south.

In 1423 the Ascanians died out and the emperor gave the electoral duchy, centred at Wittenberg, to the family of Wettin. This was in the person of Frederick, margrave of Meissen. So the old frontier principality of Meissen joined Wettin Saxony, a region rich in silver mines, and Meissen counted as Saxon.

The reader who can hardly be bothered with these dynastic details should think again. They are not complex and, apart from the fact that the medieval world is unintelligible without acquaintanceship with dynasties, the facts packaged here hold a store of historical meaning for a Briton or indeed any European. The German of Meissen and Wittenberg formed the speech of Luther. Corn-barns near Hanover may still be seen bearing the royal arms of the king of Hanover who also, of course, wore another crown. And Lüneburg Heath holds solemn memories for soldiers still alive.

The Welf family survived its disasters, but its princely history was not a happy one. Subject to fragmentation by partitions and desperate to rebuild their territories, the Welf princes found themselves constantly poor and became one of the most notorious feuding clans of the age. Otto of Göttingen would send out defiances on the slightest pretext and even opened a self-destructive feud with his own capital of Göttingen in 1387 which gave occasion for the townscribe to start a feud-book. In the end the duke's castle was razed and peace arbitrated through the archbishop of Mainz. Three other Welf dynasts had to leave their residences after conflict with their burghers.

Feuds cost money, and the debt into which the Welfs fell meant that they had to resort to pledging their property. In the long run it was the towns which gained. The feud-book which Brunswick had had to start keeping before long took second place to its pledge-book. Castles with their appurtenant villages were the most usual type of gage, and when a settlement was pledged the administration and the courts of the local Welf stewards passed into town use. The desperate drive for income led Welf princes also both to compete for tenants as a source of rents and dues and to share their lordship with lesser noblemen and burghers. So there was a growing contrast in this area between princely weakness, aggressive in character, and an urban strength, nourished by Brunswick's Hanseatic connections and fortified by a sense of solidarity between Brunswick, Lüneburg and the built-up suburbs along the left bank of the Elbe and in the districts between the Aller and the Weser. These, not the territorial princes, were the local forces of peace and order.

Charles IV and the Luxemburg kings clearly disliked the Welfs and took away both Lüneburg and all their claim to the electorship of Saxony. (One might even speculate that the contrast between Welf lawlessness and the sense of law in neighbouring Westphalia played some part in the Luxemburgs' mild support for the Vehmic courts.) In any case the electorship went to Wettin Saxony, a less wretched place in the fourteenth century. Its rulers disposed of mineral wealth, their line was more continuous, and their possessions greater than those of Welf or Brandenburg.

Even this part of the Saxon sky did not remain unclouded, for feuds, decline in silver production and the Hussite irruptions brought ducal weakness and impoverishment in the fifteenth century. If the towns, like Leipzig and Zwickau, became relatively prosperous, the principality itself weakened again at the partition of 1485 between Ernest and Albert. The Ernestine line resided at Wittenberg and held the electorship. Frederick the Wise (1486–1525) complained, honestly or not, that he was too poor to go to Maximilian's Reichstag in 1498, but he made Wittenberg a centre of learning and, as the world knows, protected Luther.

(iv)   Brandenburg: a colony for sale

'Branibor' chief settlement of the tribe of Havelli, was captured in 928 by the Saxon king Henry the Fowler, but the real founder both of Brandenburg and its ruling Ascanian dynasty was Albert I (the Bear), margrave in about 1140. At a time when political structures in Old Germany were failing to cohere into large-scale administrative order, Brandenburg might have become a new-style colonial territory *par excellence*. The Mark had been pushed to the Oder by 1250. Indeed, those great historical estate-agents called *locatores,* free and unfree but united in colonial enterprise, had by the thirteenth century Germanized a thinly-settled Slav land and formed what were to be called the three major territorial divisions of the Old Mark, the Middle Mark and the New Mark. (The actual names were only used later: Altmark from 1304: Mittelmark and Neumark created 1260 but only called thus in 1402.)[18]

The margrave was an elector by 1235 at the latest, at a time of its prosperity and before it was partitioned. The principality was among the earliest deliberately formed territories where the new lord was served by unfree stewards who fulfilled the functions of government and replaced any existing hereditary nobilities. People settled by the *locatores* paid rents, and the land generated a fairly impressive money income, which is shown in Charles IV's Land Book of 1375–6, made for Brandenburg after he had bought it from the Wittelsbachs. From such beginnings the political life of Brandenburg ought to have been simple.

Unfortunately, the freedom of the prince was spoiled and trammelled by political weakness and poverty. The old idea that a margrave was a royal officer disappeared along with effective kingship in the thirteenth century. The margraves began to think, and were allowed to think, that they had a piece of property which could be inherited and sold.[19] In this colonial territory landlordship quickly came, in the absence of central political direction, to be conceived in money terms, as though political rulers were merely men of commerce. It is not surprising that these rulers multiplied through partitions and sales. Already by 1290 there were said to be nineteen living Ascanian margraves. Then in 1319, by one of those biological catastrophes which come at times to the help of human societies, the local Ascanian family failed, and the territory passed for a time (1323–73) into the hands of the Wittelsbachs. It was another of the Wittelsbach efforts to prove that they were of imperial quality, for this north-eastern territory was an electorate, a source of subjects and income, and well-placed to help the dynasty, already in Bavaria and the Rhine Palatinate, bestride Germany.

Wittelsbach Brandenburg did not last long either. By 1373 Charles IV had acquired it with money paid by the Swabian cities as a punishment for refusing their military aid. So Brandenburg joined the Luxemburg dynastic empire for a while and provided Charles with another electoral vote.

Even this did not create a solid and lasting Brandenburg. The territory was cursed by the inability of its dynastic lords to steer a middle course between having too many children and having none. The Luxemburgs drifted into partition and then died out. One of them sold New Mark to the Teutonic Order and another, Sigismund, performed a greater act than he knew when, as we have seen, he finally enfeoffed Frederick of Hohenzollern in 1417 as margrave and elector.

Frederick's task was of great difficulty. He had to restore order in a province riven by feuds and dominated by a nobility hostile to him. His subjugation of important families like the Quetzow was carried out piecemeal and with the use of artillery against castles thought impregnable. This was only the beginning of the Hohenzollern struggle for rule. The nobles were not in the medieval period wholly reduced to order, though the towns, as Professor Carsten has shown, were dominated and brought to a condition of torpor.[20]

The historian must not hasten to conclusions. Knowing what we do of later Brandenburg-Prussia, the sandy parade grounds, the professional ranks of grenadiers, we must not suppose that all this had been set in train by south German princelings on the make. But there was a beginning in the fifteenth century of more ordered ideas of succession. The Hohenzollern, like some others of the time, were not blind to the damage done by unconsidered partibility or rule-sharing among sons. Nor were these early Hohenzollern mere military fools. The Margrave Albert Achilles (1470–86) was by all accounts a remarkable man: a prince who could speak well in public and who proclaimed the importance of justice, good currency, and the public peace.[21] He was also a ruler who left a reasonably well-ordered economy and, most importantly, an arrangement, short of complete primogeniture, but aimed at preventing wild competition for Brandenburg territory between his sons. His successor, John Cicero (1486-99), continued to concentrate on making Brandenburg the centre of his interest and a governable whole.

(v) Prussia: the 'Order-state'

Without question this huge territory, now mostly engulfed in the Soviet Union, has a remote history sufficient to excite the medievalist by reason of the detail which has survived and the achievements which seem extraordinary. The disciplined organization which created great quantities of records has been matched by the miracle which has preserved them.[22]

Among the political dragons which sit at the entrance to our enquiries is one called *Ordensstaat*, the name by which the jurisdiction of the Teutonic Knights in north-west Europe is commonly known, which is transliterated above in the subtitle, and which offers the reader a tempting cue to imply that here, if anywhere in Germania, perhaps even in medieval Europe, was a political being appropriate to that term.

In 1220 Pope Honorius III issued a privilege making the Master and Brethren of the Teutonic Order free of all fealty except to the papal curia. In 1226 the Emperor Frederick II published the Golden Bull of Rimini which took the Order *and its acquisitions* into his protection, made it an imperial prince, and gave it 'jurisdiction and power'. These acts certainly gave the Order freedom to do what it liked in its conquered lands, and as historical fact there was a unitary lordship (of the Order) present from the beginning of the settlement.

The question of statehood is not so easily decided, whether or no it is more than a matter of semantics. R. Wenskus[23] alludes to the absence of private war till the fifteenth century, the juridical unity of lordship, the absence of any development of a polity out of pre-existing lordships, and the immediate imposition on the territory of administrative districts *(Ämter)*. On the other hand, he points out that the word *Staat* in the German language is met for the first time (in

1355) in this Prussian context, and it had then no different meaning from that which it bore at that epoch in west European languages: that is to say, it meant condition, position *(Zustand, Lage).*

At present the matter must rest here. It does not seem likely that a great lordship, even if the lord was the Order, or the Grand Master with or without his Great Council, formed any polity otherwise anachronistic to the medieval world. It was based on monastic vows, not on legislative abstraction. Though to others it was known as 'the territory of Prussia', to itself it was a plural: *terrae Prussiae.* It had no unitary court structure despite the single juridical being of the Order: there were different courts for different groups of inhabitants. Again, there is the question of a 'capital city', which presumably a sovereign state must have in which to embody its abstraction geographically. In 1309 the headquarters of the Order was moved from Venice to Marienburg and the Grand Master transferred himself thither with a good deal of pomp to supervise the work of the other great officers. Professor Thielen writes than this was 'the first deliberately founded capital for a head of state.'[24] It is difficult to accept the non-circularity of this argument. It was a deliberate foundation of a head house. But it was only a capital of a state if Prussia was already a state; the building of Marienburg hardly made it one. The military bustle beguiles us into Napoleonic illusions. Swords make states, but not all organized soldiers form states. If they are under vow of celibacy and obedience to Christ and the Roman Church it is more likely that they form an Order, however elaborate, even paradoxical. What we see at Marienburg is surely something more like Cîteaux than like Prague or Paris. One might add that Grand Masters were still then bound by their chapters more than was the Benedictine abbot.

In time all this changed, but it is not the present intent to write of the post-secularization days after 1525. The reservation made in this book is that one cannot find 'the state' in medieval Christendom, least of all in Germany, not even in Prussia, so the term should be avoided. But the reservation does not make the Order's princedom any less remarkable.

The first German knight crossed the Vistula in 1231, and for two hundred years thereafter a territory was built up, divided in a complex way into bishoprics for the cure of souls, but for the Order's own military and adminstrative purposes into commanderies within the Baltic lands, with scatterings of bailiwicks and other properties elsewhere in Germany. Administration of all this was assigned at the highest level to a small staff of obedientiary-officers. Under these were the knights and priests, full members of the Order also, who were assigned to convents but responsible not only for campaigns of attempted conquest against the Baltic non-Christians but also for managing the material affairs of convents and territories. Almost every vowed man in a house of the Order had also his external duties to perform.

The land settlements of Prussia were authorized by written documents called *Handfesten*. A *Handfeste* specified to the local entrepreneur *(locator)* which land exactly was being leased out and what rights and rents the lord required. German villages were set up under local bailiffs called *Schulzen* who had powers to administer and in certain cases to judge, who had preferentially large holdings, yet who seem to have remained 'peasants' (if that is the right word) and, like all men and women in that position, with hearts divided in loyalty between their lord and their fellow-villagers.

Castles were built against the unconquered heathen and the Order's enemies. Increasingly these enemies appeared to be not pagans but Catholic Poles, resurgent in the fourteenth century, and united since 1386 with the Lithuanians, whose conversion to Catholicism now proceeded by less martial means.

The fifteenth century was an age of paradox amounting to shame. For good or ill, the Order's reason for existence was to conquer and thereby convert the heathen for the religion of Christ. The course of time has demonstrated that this work was more lastingly accomplished by the Poles. The Order's achievements were in some ways greater if one measures them in technical terms of medieval communications, the making of inventories, the keeping of punctual times and, very different but by far the greatest, the physical endurance, year in and year out in a vile terrain, of life without wives and children and without even that sense of family which a peaceful and commonsensical Benedictine abbot can create about him.

But the Order was given up to war. Its efficiency compounded the cruelty its mode of life instilled. The efficiency in literate reporting even laid the cruelties bare: the private enrichments, the villages raided, defenders killed, survivors dragged to baptism. Enmities made with other ecclesiastics brought the matter to the Council of Constance, which declared with interesting modernity that heathen

112

do indeed have rights of their own; but it is doubtful if the full implications of this opinion sank into the minds of knights who, on occasion appealed to on the grounds of basic legality, shouted back: 'What is Culmic Law? We are your law!'

During its last medieval century the Order's territory of Prussia experienced triumphs and reverses. In 1402 New Mark was acquired and thus brought the Order to its widest expansion. In 1410 came the defeat at Tannenberg by the Poles in alliance with certain rebels from within the Order, and the Peace of Thorn (1411) condemned the Order to severe reparations. Demands for money stimulated effort. The Great Rent Book (1414–38) represents an administrative leap forward. Even if the tale is of lost rents and villages deserted, it is told not only in great reference works but in many kinds of inventory, instruction and questionary. These forms of written communication are undoubtedly more sophisticated than anything done at that time by non-Italian Europeans: timed letters, post-boys following regular routes with the stages logged by duty-officers with access to clocks.

In the last generations the Order seems, for all its defects, to have retained both the sentiments and the utility of a dying empire, certainly in the eyes of families with sons who aspired to careers. Still and perhaps always a frontier, Prussia attracted young men whose intention was to go for a time and return with a more impressive curriculum vitae. These were not the vowed men but a penumbra, as Thielen calls them, of young and unstable followers, joined to the Order by some lesser vow or tie, perhaps followers of an important officer who would see to his protégé's knightly training and future prospects. Not just soldiers trod that way, but diplomats and, one supposes on a lower road, lawyers, physicians and masons.

But it was not an empire, nor a state, and it fell apart much more conclusively through dissensions between Germans themselves than through local mutinies or Slavic invasions. In 1439 the 'Low German' convents of Königsberg, Balga and Brandenburg revolted against the Upper German favouritism of the Rhineland Grand Master, Paul von Rusdorf. This was not the end of the territory, and the narrative will not be elaborated in this context. But it is of outstanding interest that a chapter which might have ended by exemplifying the most ordered of the principalities must even in doing so demonstrate the depth of German particularism. For within so highly articulated a territory, bonded, one would have supposed, by the comradeship of the frontier

113

and sustained by a ruthless efficiency, we have to observe how even in the face of the Slav threat the German Order was fractured within itself along divisions of dialect. Not only did the 'Low German' convents rebel against the rest, but the 'Upper German' members themselves were consciously divided into the separately organized 'tongues' of Rhineland, Meissen-Thuringia-Saxony, and Swabia-Franconia-Bavaria. It is ironical that the unifying languages of the north-east were to be a Protestant German and a Catholic Polish.

5

The Towns: Order and Conflict

(a) *The nature of German urbanization*

The enlargement of old towns and the foundation of new ones gathered speed from the later twelfth century onwards. In the thirteenth century the number of German towns increased ten-fold, and by the end of the medieval period in about 1500 there were twelve to fifteen big cities with over 10,000 inhabitants each, fifteen to twenty middling-sized cities with between 2000 and 10,000, 150 towns of between 1000 and 2000 inhabitants, and perhaps 2800 settlements which can be called towns containing a few hundred souls each. Cologne was top of the list, with some 30,000 inhabitants, and of those with more than 20,000 there were only Lübeck, Danzig and Hamburg in the north, Strassburg, Ulm and Nuremberg in the south. Just below these there was Augsburg, with 18,300 inhabitants in 1475, and properly placed in the first league by reason of its special role in the history of early capitalism.[1] In all these urban settlements together lived perhaps one and a half million people, or some 10 per cent of the German king's subjects, not counting those in the kingdoms of Bohemia and Hungary. A quick calculation will show that, even if we maximize the number who lived in the towns of more than 1000 inhabitants, that still leaves the majority of German 'town' dwellers living in places which today would only count as villages.

Of course these figures beg the long-discussed question of what a town is or was. Most of the places in this enumeration were obviously very small. Yet nowhere more than among German scholars has the matter been so painstakingly discussed, and it is proposed in the present context to accept German criteria of what medieval German towns were. These comprise both an economic function and a constitutional one based upon possession of a town law. There is also a political element which will naturally be discussed throughout this chapter. And since any criteria may fail at some test or other, it is useful to recall the remark by Professor Walter Schlesinger at the Linz conference of 1972 that a town might well be just what contemporaries believed to be one.[2]

It ought to be said at once that German towns, like all other towns, are fundamentally the creations of economic activity, and that in particular the largest medieval towns were engaged in long-distance trade. A good deal of attention is deliberately given in this chapter to other aspects of German urbanization: the need to protect frontiers, to garrison, to administer and to supply residences to kings and rulers. But to avoid misunderstanding the point should be made now that behind this medieval town expansion was the economic impetus given by population growth, intensification of trade, and especially of long-distance trade, and of manufacturing, particularly of cloth and of metal goods deriving from German, Bohemian, Hungarian and Austrian mines. Trade flourished over a network of internal routes despite the impediments of toll-stations, highway robbers and hostile lords whose frontiers had constantly to be crossed. The main arteries lay east and west along the Baltic, up and down the Rhine, over passes of the Alps into Italy and along the Danube into south-eastern Germany, Austria, Hungary and beyond. Young men from north German towns might expect to learn the business and languages through postings to the London Steelyard or some other Hanseatic trading station; many young south Germans learned business methods in the Fondaco dei Tedeschi in Venice.

The older towns, whether bishoprics or royal palaces, had castles, and a close connection between town and *Burg* endured in the thirteenth century. But new towns sometimes had no *Burg,* and in such cases the city itself acted as a fortified place. The bishop of Breslau never lived in his city, but on an island in the River Oder; the plan of Wismar shows the fortification of the whole town by 1276 and a further all-enclosing stone wall by about 1400.[3] In this age of expansion riverside towns tended to stretch out further along the bank, as at Bremen, Cologne, Magdeburg and Würzburg, to cite only a few. Settlements might coalesce to form a single town, and Brunswick is a famous example of this. Suburbs and dependent little towns were often created by charters which styled them *Weichbilder* or places of freedom *(Freiheit)* where the inhabitants might freely hold

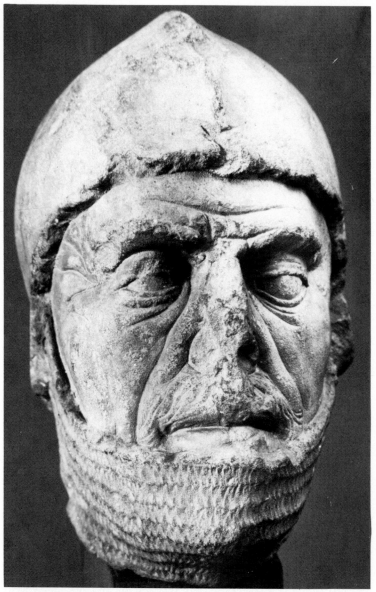

1. Head of an armed man. Sandstone. Sculptor unknown, about 1480. Found in the Swabian region (Untertückheim). Württembergisches Landesmuseum, Stuttgart.

2. The lading of a Hanseatic ship. Pen and ink drawing, about 1430, from a History of Troy.
Germanisches Nationalmuseum MS 998, fo. 197 v.

3. The Nose-Dance at Gümpelsbrunn: festivities at a peasant wedding. Engraving by Nicolaus Meldemann, *fl.* 1529–31, Nuremberg.
Agrarhistorische Bildsammlung, Universitätsarchiv Hohenheim (Stuttgart).

4. Georg, count of Löwenstein, Dean of Bamberg Cathedral.
Painting by Hans Pleydenwurff, *c.* 1456.
Germanisches Nationalmuseum, Nürnberg.

and inherit their property, possess jurisdiction and practise trade as long as they did not receive into freedom the undertenants of the founding lord against his will. A lot of these very small towns were deliberately founded, sometimes as suburbs of larger towns, sometimes on their own, in the fourteenth and even the fifteenth centuries.[4]

From all this it will be clear that Germany owed its spectacular town growth, which was so deeply to influence its political and social life, to two kinds of power, the one consciously willed, the other not. To take the last first, a town could grow or even come into existence because men collected on the site for some prior reason, perhaps as courtiers or *ministeriales* of a lord, or servants of a prelate, and these might be reinforced by men of landed wealth from the surrounding countryside who found a market ready there and were able to enlarge and extend it. Where this sort of thing happened, at Trier, say, or Mainz, the merchants came gradually to form a community which derived its first strength and protection from a Roman or ecclesiastical lordship but later struggled for mercantile independence. On the other hand, a town might be deliberately founded by a lord, and his written instrument preserved to tell the date and even the motive of the founder. There were many charters like this, from Lübeck's re-foundation by Henry the Lion in 1159 and its confirmation in 1226 by the Emperor Frederick II as *libera civitas, locus imperii,* down to tiny towns like that specified in the charter of 1311 from the bishop-elect of Münster, who created *opidulum de villa nostra Dulmene* [Dülmen, Westphalia], which was to live *absoluta libertate sub eo iure, quod vulgus 'to wicbelde' dicit.*[5]

These figures and abstract statements do not help the historian much in conveying a pictorial idea of late medieval Germany as a more urbanized land than ever it had been before. Was it a country so covered with large and busy towns that most people felt town life to be fuller, more important, more interesting than rural life, as they did in Italy? Or did Germany remain in essence deeply rural, wild and underpopulated so that towns were simply useful adjuncts to an agrarian and feudal society, ultimately ruled by landed nobilities? Or was the reality different in different places and altering at different rates? These must remain questions for the reader's reflection. They could hardly have been answered in a concise way, even by contemporaries. The famous woodcut of Nuremberg — perhaps the

117

most 'industrialized' German city of the age — which appears in Hartmann Schedel's *World Chronicle* of 1493 suggests a dense network of streets and a roofscape of crowding gables surmounted by formidable towers. Albrecht Dürer's water-colour of Nuremberg from the west, painted a couple of years later by one who was after all a sophisticated observer and a member of an industrial family, shows green and muddy lanes surrounding a toy-town. A third view is a clash of opposites, for there is in the German National Museum at Nuremberg a painting from 1516, probably by the cartographer Ehrhard Etzlaub, which portrays 'Nuremberg in the Imperial forests'. Stylized as it is in order to show the portions of the forest belonging to various Nuremberg foundations, it shows the city from a slanting, aerial angle as densely compacted, stone-built, red-roofed, securely walled, yet set like a tiny model in a green open space which itself is surrounded by vast forests.[6]

These ambiguities could be multiplied. The forces deployed by Swiss, Swabian and Rhenish town leagues could hardly have been procured from sleepy villages, and the eye-witness Italian who travelled in 1497 from Trent to England through Germany[7] wrote of Ulm as 'a big town, governed as a free republic, rich and full of merchants; the streets wide, straight and paved with cobble-stones according to the German custom', and at Cologne he was impressed by the great size of the city, its roofs of slate black along the Rhine, standing up against the intensively tilled country round about. So from these scraps of evidence the impression is gained of contrasts: of cities bigger than those in England but more widely spaced apart than in Italy, full of activity, even smoky (they were burning coal round Aachen) but belonging at the same time to a continent of fields, mountains and above all forests where the spirits might be benign but the inhabitants dangerous in the extreme. Nowhere was this contrast more strikingly made than by the fifteenth-century chronicler from humane, rich, cultivated Augsburg who wrote with horror of the ghost-filled forests just over the horizon which stretched to Hungary, and of terrible castles in the wilderness barred by thorn hedges.[8]

More scientifically, C. T. Smith, in his historical geography, described late medieval Germany as covered by a fairly large number of substantial towns of the second rank which in the south and west were within four to five hours' ride of each other, and in the north and east within seven to eight hours.[9] Putting it another way, he wrote that each town in south-west Germany served an average of forty to fifty square miles, in central and eastern-central Germany sixty to eighty-five square miles, and in the colonial east 100 to 170 square miles.

If urban Germany presents the mind and imagination with confusing pictures, it would be useful to think again about the meaning of urbanization. At the beginning of the chapter it was said that the impetus behind town building in the thirteenth century was economic, and that is obvious enough. But there are some qualifications. The creation of urban settlements was not uniform everywhere. As colonization drove eastwards, for instance, there might be chains of towns deliberately founded along routes or acquired while the hinterland was left wild. Where secondary colonization was in progress, that is, where partially settled territory was filling up with new settlers and receiving more developed economic and political form, and local princes worked to consolidate their rule, a regular honeycomb pattern of townships might be established, certainly to fulfil an economic purpose in stimulating and serving local and occasionally long-distance trade, but organized with intention and method. Again, towns might be built or acquired by lords with an even less directly economic purpose, namely, for the furthering of seignorial administration and the territory's defence. This political urbanization occurred rather often both in colonizing regions and in politically fragmented areas. There were, in fact, some features of late medieval Germany which encouraged this deliberate founding of towns by princes. Germany was becoming a land of written administration, as was shown in Chapter 1, where literate officials served their masters by bringing more immediate rule; and Germany was in a special sense a land of frontiers, not only on the further perimeter beyond which were non-Teutonic peoples, but internally too, as territories fragmented under the influence of partible inheritance, private wars or marriage settlements. To guard territories newly won you need garrisons, to administer them you need officials, to do both you need towns, even if only small ones. And as so much of Germany was in a state of fragmentation or under the direct rule of princelings, the scale tended to be small, even though the country was large: 'dwarf towns in dwarf states', as Stoob put it.[10]

Some examples will illustrate these various developments. The first comes from the Bavaria of the Wittelsbachs, who had been invested with the duchy by Frederick I Barbarossa in 1180. By strokes of fortune several families of the higher Bavarian nobility died out soon after this, leaving the Wittelsbachs as their heirs. As this happened the ducal family founded new towns in chain-like formation, mostly along river-valleys on the periphery of their existing estates, to act as points of administrative and military control along their new frontiers. Frequently the new towns were linked with seignorial castles, and the places became administrative centres developed by Wittelsbach *ministeriales.*[11]

A similar sort of development can be seen in the fragmented Franconian territory acquired dynastically by the Emperor Charles IV in order to bridge the important gap between Prague and Frankfurt-am-Main. Besides the existing towns of Auerbach, Pegnitz, Sulzbach and so on there were the simple markets of Eschenau, Gräfenberg, Lauf and Velden, to which Charles gave town law and where he constructed small towns with habitable towers where royal officials were able to lodge.[12] Here again there are very small towns (not villages) acting as defensive and administrative posts on the borders of territory which might be disputed.

A third instance is Silesia, colonized by German-inhabited towns under German law mainly in the thirteenth century, in such a way that the towns lay fifteen to twenty kilometres apart like a network over the whole part-Slavic countryside. Most of these towns were founded deliberately, under ducal privilege, by a *locator* or agent *(Erbvogt)* who possessed his own house, lands, and rights to dues and services as hereditary representative of the lord, and who administered low justice with townsmen as jurors. The towns possessed regular ground-plans on the east German colonial pattern, with square market-places near which the better-off merchants and sometimes members of the nobility lived. To each town a more or less circular district of fifteen to twenty villages was attached under that town's dominance — the so-called Silesian *Weichbild* organization — and the town controlled market, justice and administration, had the monopoly of trade and industry, and left agriculture to the countryside. Even in these towns the inhabitants were sometimes also agriculturalists, yet since they were towns they possessed the arrangements proper to towns: town councils, formed mainly by the co-optation of leading merchants and well-off occupants of houses on the market-place, and the exercise of high as well as low justice under the *Erbvogt*. It is impossible not to regard them as towns, rough and rural though they may have been.

And, incidentally, they lay closer together than C. T. Smith's general figures for town density in the east would allow.[13]

This view of German towns as political as well as directly economic creations may be extended by looking at their role as royal residences. It is well-known that the early medieval king had resided in castle or palace, moving about from one to the other. Often enough the *Burg* dominated the town or was even part of it. But in the thirteenth century the ability and need to conduct written government on a larger scale suggested that the town itself could offer more to its royal lord than money, soldiers and pledgeable goods, indeed, it might offer itself as a royal seat.[14] Germany had no London or Paris. Its older royal palaces were unimpressive. Aachen at the time of Charlemagne was little more than a ceremonial capital, a place for a lord to live, and little else. But Germany by the thirteenth century disposed of numerous fine towns over its enormous area, places where writing was done in the normal course of events, places which already performed adminstrative functions for a world which was no longer exclusively agrarian, and indeed which had begun to express in their chronicles a political self-awareness. By this time the town economies were allowing power to pass into the hands of the burghers in the form of town councils (the *Rat*). In some larger towns power flowed out beyond the walls and began to be exercised over portions of the surrounding countryside, and in defensive leagues formed from time to time with other towns in like predicaments. These developments were hastened by the collapse of the Hohenstaufen monarchy after Frederick II's death in 1250. In 1254 there was a league of Rhenish towns, and it was these which helped Rudolf of Habsburg against the weaker William of Holland. Rudolf understood the power of towns, as did certain kings after him. He gave them privileges, but in return he asked for political support. So it is not surprising that from this time began the era of town leagues, intermittently legitimate, and that big towns rather than royal palaces became the royal stopping-places on the king's endless journeyings. The leagues fluctuated, but the main groups of towns were along the Rhine, in the Wetterau (that is, round Frankfurt-am-Main), near the lake of Constance, in Swabia, and, in the north, the groups of Hanseatic towns from the lower Rhine eastward along the Baltic coastland. For good and ill, towns, especially those engaging in long-distance trade,[15] became political entities which could support or damage the king's own policies, and the king found it necessary to support or attack them, usually lived in them, and could rarely ignore them. The clever Charles IV used the towns. For instance, he won over Nuremberg from Wittelsbach allegiance, and it was Nuremberg merchants who made possible Wenzel's policies towards the Visconti. In the end this harmed Wenzel, but Nuremberg survived to make friends with Wittelsbach Rupert and also with the Luxemburg kings and to remain perhaps the most conservative and patrician of all German towns throughout the middle ages.

The thirteenth-century economic development of towns in this way attracted royal interest and the royal presence, which in turn helped town development. The king entered the market-place and made it also a palace. The most specialized examples of this change are Prague and Vienna (already touched on in Chapter 2) because they were the principal seats of the Luxemburg and Habsburg families after they had become habitually royal. As to Prague, Charles IV was the first Luxemburg to develop it, and he had royal Paris much in mind as he was doing so. There he created a city which in character could be compared with Naples and Avignon rather than with any German town. Probably this was not due to the adventitious fact that the first Master of Cathedral Works, Matthias of Arras, had come from the papal palace at Avignon, so much as to the political comparability of Charles IV with the French king (or for that matter the Avignonese pope) in requiring a fixed residence for administration and the mystique of kingly rule while he was engaged in collecting provinces under his suzerainty. Charles had, in fact, learned the need for a static centre of power, unlike the Poles and the Russians, and was deliberately building up a new royal city on the left bank of the Ultava to be a capital for Bohemia and, doubtless in his own forward vision, a capital of the empire. Prague was not, of course, the end of the story of lordly city-building. The idea that cities were royal residences was expressed again in the Golden Bull of 1356, which laid emphasis on Nuremberg, Frankfurt and Metz as proper meeting-places for the king and his princes. And what kings did was repeated by princes other than the king, so that seignorial capitals emerged, like Brunswick, Marburg or Munich. Munich, in fact, created by the Wittelsbachs, might have become a German capital if its ill-starred patronal house had triumphed in the end over Luxemburg and Habsburg. As it was, Vienna appeared as Prague's mirror-image, enlarged by Rudolf IV of Habsburg, the great outsider of fourteenth-century princely Germany. Rudolf founded his university in 1365 in rivalry to the Charles University of Prague, and took every opportunity to perform symbolic acts of state there, like laying foundation-stones of royal and ecclesiastical buildings. In such a spirit was St Stephen's church in Vienna called *Dom* before it was in fact elevated to cathedral status, and Rudolph wanted the city to be a ducal place of burial not unlike Prague for the Luxemburgs, or St Denis for the Capetians, or even Meissen for the Wettiner dukes of Saxony. The mystique of the princely necropolis is to be seen further down the social scale in the little ducal towns of Silesia.[16]

But it was for the living that fourteenth-century urbanization chiefly catered, as princely residences, like those of rich patricians, got decent glazing and could be warmed well enough to allow expensive thin clothing to be worn.[17] In 1317 the archbishop of Trier, no stranger to comfort, had already appointed a hereditary roofer for his Burg Ehrenbreitstein. By the fifteenth century fine princely building was usual, as exemplified by Albrechtsburg in Meissen, begun in 1470 by Arnold of Westphalia, mason for the whole province, who also built in Dresden and knew how to construct fan vaulting in numerous rooms on several storeys. Residences like these were linked to towns and engaged numerous craftsmen in the tasks of creation and upkeep.

In such ways German urbanization spanned an immense range of character, from the fortified outpost to the impressive capital. In this section the economic and social nature of the towns has been taken mostly for granted in order to give attention to their political significance. In particular, the relationship between the urban world and the king is important enough to merit a little more discussion, in Section (c) below. This should form a link in our understanding of towns as both political and economic environments.

(b) *Lordship over towns*

Unlike English towns, where the overlord was nearly always the king, German towns lived under a great diversity of seignorial rulers. The king himself might be far distant or immediately present. In Meissen the king was a fairly remote figure in the later middle ages and few privileges were even sought from him by towns. On the other hand, the Rhine valley and upper Alsace were Rudolf of Habsburg's dynastic homeland, a region where he stayed often and where there were few local direct lords of towns. These upper Rhenish towns pressed the electors for a decisive vote on Rudolf's behalf for the sake of their own peace (always their first priority), and after Rudolf's election they gave him taxes and received privileges from him.

This contrast between Meissen and the upper Rhine illustrates the best-known distinction between late medieval German towns, namely, those directly subject to the empire, the so-called imperial towns *(Reichsstädte)* and those subject to lords other than the king *(Landesstädte)*, which may be translated as provincial towns. In some ways the distinction is an artificial one, because it was not really one of economic character but of political accident and degree of autonomy; but it is convenient to accept and consider it, for it tells us something about urban government.

Not all towns which belonged to a king were or became imperial towns. In the twelfth and thirteenth centuries royal cities could be pledged as a whole by the king and lacked the autonomy which later made them truly imperial cities. It was, for example, Sigismund who stopped pledging Swabian royal towns and pledged, when necessary, only certain financial sources within them. As to those cities which did become imperial ones, the moment of achieving this status cannot always be easily identified. That there was such a status is undeniable. Certain large towns which became known as 'imperial' usually (but not always) retained the designation irrespective of who was emperor. But in the course of time their circumstances had changed, so that the meaning of the title was not the same in the fifteenth century as it had been in the thirteenth. At first royal towns were simply towns belonging to the king, who might do with them pretty much what he liked. At best he could describe them as imperial as an expression of royal gratitude. Frederick II, in 1226, granted that Lübeck should be 'free, that is to say, a special city and place of the empire and belonging in a special way to the imperial dominion, and at no time ever to be separated from this special dominion'.[18] At this early period, however, no assumptions can be made about such a town's autonomy. In towns not owned by the king the city documents might declare a close bond with the empire but without denying any existing rights which might be possessed there by a bishop, abbot or secular lord. In 1212 Frederick II, it seems, gave the episcopal city of Constance the right to have a council as a gesture of thanks that it had opened its gates to him and not to his rival Otto Welf; but the bishop's authority was not removed.

Before long another circumstance affected important towns as it affected every political being in Germany, and that was the Interregnum between William of Holland's death in 1256 and Rudolf of Habsburg's election in 1273. William's election in the presence of a papal legate in 1254 was not widely accepted, and the Interregnum is variously thought of as beginning in 1250, 1254 or 1256. In any case, the long vacancy at this time threatened towns, which were already stirring into self-government, with subjection to local lords or princes. Swabian cities in particular wanted no 'protection' from noblemen after their long-standing dukes, the Hohenstaufen, had been removed; so they loudly proclaimed the validity of their peaceful leagues during times of vacancy, and they played a considerable part in recognizing the new king. In 1254 the Rhenish towns noted that 'while the empire is vacant and we lack a lord and king' they should form a league and bind themselves together to conserve all the property (or good things) of the empire *(omnia bona imperii)*.[19] In this way the Interregnum pushed some towns into claiming autonomous jurisdiction in the name of an emperor who had not yet been elected.

But there was a long way to go from earlier medieval overlordship to late medieval autonomy. Even royal towns were subject to the king's detailed dominion, as has been seen. Originally a royal town was one where the king appointed the steward *(Vogt)*, whether the town was on royal territory or not. A consequence of this juridical lordship was his power to tax. In addition the king had power to conscript soldiers for campaigns: this can be traced from about 1240 right through the middle ages, though it should not be confused with the general call-up, extended even to Hanseatic towns, during the Hussite emergency. That was something quite different: an authorization by the papal legate in 1431 on the grounds that the war was a crusade.[20] Another expression of the imperial nature of towns was the oath of homage taken by all citizens and their sons over fourteen at the ceremonial entry of the emperor to the town or a ceremonial deputation of citizens to the imperial court. This oath was sometimes taken in the later medieval period. For instance, in the mid-fourteenth century the citizens of Goslar swore '...that we will be true and loving to our lord, the lord Charles, emperor of the holy empire'.[21] It was a way of recognizing the emperor's legitimate election and was sometimes tendered in return for privileges.

In the course of time most of the offices and ceremonies of subjection to the emperor lost their meaning or became pure formalities. Ultimately, to be an imperial city was to be free from all extraneous lordship. At that state, which occurred in the fourteenth century, the city council *(Rat)* under its mayor or *Bürgermeister* became the supreme body and took over the functions formerly exercised by the imperial steward *(Vogt)* and his subordinate judges *(Schultheiss* and *Richter)*.

It is not necessary to regard this development of the imperial cities' autonomy as a mere sign of German royal weakness. There were certain advantages in it for the king as well as for the cities. For example, kings who were short of money sometimes had to pledge the tolls, the Jews or some other cash-producing source in one of his towns, or even the whole town (though not in Swabia after Sigismund) to a prince who had capital to lend. In these cases the king naturally lost control of the pledged town or important parts of it, and the lord who received the pledge might move his officials in and interfere with the existing healthy economic life. But if the town was already free and self-governing it might well be able to raise the money on the king's behalf, redeem itself from pledge and return intact to its imperial lord; whereas an undeveloped royal town like Ansbach or Harburg might be lost to the king for ever if he pledged it. From the city's viewpoint it is likely that imperial status in fact conferred greater economic freedom, since it would not have to reckon with the officials of some prince interfering in the town's financial politics, which were more profitably left to the private network of the leading families.

Nuremberg provides one of the best instances of an imperial town, partly because it has been much studied by scholars and partly because it was one of the few cities of medieval Germany that approximated to a city-state, set in the midst of some twenty-five square miles of its own territory and never subject to a prince-bishop.[22] The emperor Henry III (1039–50) had lived there for a time and installed a castellan or burgrave to look after his interests and receive certain judicial profits. By the time of Barbarossa the burgrave had become a permanent resident in the *Burg* and the emperor built himself a new castle nearby *(Kaiserburg)*. Frederick II's charter of 1219 exempted the citizens from all lawsuits except before his imperial bailiff *(Schultheiss)* in the city, and allowed imperial taxes to be levied on the city corporately. During the thirteenth century the burgrave and the bailiff continued to function but the citizens were able to develop their own system of tax-collection, their police, and a complex administrative structure stemming from an oligarchic council. In 1313 a privilege of Henry VII recognized a condominium of burgrave and citizens during imperial vacancies. In 1320 the Emperor Ludwig of Bavaria gave the city council jurisdiction over capital offences and conferred numerous trading privileges, and by the end of the fourteenth century the city dominated the burgrave, who in 1427 sold it most of his remaining prerogatives. If the essence of an imperial city was to be nominally a 'place of the empire' but really self-governing, then Nuremberg is a good model. In the Golden Bull of 1356 it was designated the place where the first *Reichstag* of each reign should be held; in 1423 Sigismund nominated it as the repository of the imperial regalia; yet by the fifteenth century its council was all-powerful over every inhabitant, from its own councillors down to the charcoal-burners in the city's forests, and all residents came to be known as *Untertanen*, which means 'subjects' and denotes a modern political concept, instead of the usual variety of medieval names for status like burgess, citizen, vassal, tenant and so on.

Of the one and a half million Germans who lived in towns during this period, the great majority belonged to the small or medium-sized provincial ones and not to the large self-governing imperial cities. But the variety of lordship under which they lived was wide, and is itself a comment upon the diversity of medieval Germany. Few German towns, even imperial ones, attained in the fourteenth century the degree of self-rule achieved by Nuremberg or Lübeck. Their political importance (apart from their sheer number) lay in their relationships with the local princes. A town and its overlord were useful to each other, even in the case of small places which might be good for a few tolls, a troop or two of soldiers or an object of value which might be pledged for a term of years. More valuable still in a political sense were medium-sized towns in an up-and-coming princedom which might assist in state-building while preserving their own peace and profitability. Some further examples will illustrate these political roles.

Two alternative broad lines of development were open to provincial towns in their political life: either they acquired a certain degree of independence from their lord and lived their own economic lives with more or less help from the nobility, to the advantage of each side; or else they were firmly worked into the princely polity on the prince's terms.

As an example of the first, Meissen and Lusatia lay north of Bohemia and in the fourteenth century were still in the stage of colonization by Germanic people.[23] They correspond roughly to that part of Saxony which now lies in Eastern Germany, and were to become additionally important with the development of mining in the general area of Zwickau and Chemnitz (Karl-Marxstadt). It was a region of mixed lordships and considerable trading development. Characteristically towns and their territorial lords helped each other, the towns receiving protection even though they might be shifted about among lords through the action of pledging. The lords seem to have understood that the economic development of their towns would redound to their own advantage, not least because the towns would be able to produce the money to get themselves out of pledge and back to their original lord. Lords also understood the towns' needs of defensive walls and were prepared to reduce tolls and imposts so that such building might be carried forward. Again, lords were often able to appreciate that if they pledged their judicial rights to a town the result was likely to be healthy. The lord got the money; the town got the right to exercise judicial power over its citizens and sometimes even over people outside the town boundaries. When the king of Bohemia acquired Lusatia he used the towns against the *Raubritter* who were disturbing the peace. In this way Lusatia, rather like Silesia further east, became a region of town-lord co-operation, largely under the Luxemburgs, and to the benefit of all.

A second example of town-lord co-operation is visible in the Danube region from Passau downstream through Austria to Pressburg in Hungary.[24] Town life was already well-developed by 1246, when the ruling family of Babenberg died out. That particular princely house and many lesser lords had encouraged urbanization, and it can hardly be doubted that the Danube highway, as a bringer of wealth through common trade, dominated the political thinking of all. It certainly appears that the nearer to the Danube, the more intense the economic activity and the more precocious the development of urban institutions, with seignorial consent. Markets were encouraged, walls and bulwarks financed, communications guarded by joint endeavour. The usual landmark of urban progress is the appearance of the corporate community, represented by the town's *Rat,* which displaced the lord's judge *(Richter)*. Such a development was symbolized by the change in inscription on seals from *sigillum civium* to *sigillum civitatis*. These events started in Vienna in 1282 and in general spread to Lower and Upper Austria and thence southward to Styria in the fourteenth and fifteenth centuries. By the end of the middle ages most Danube towns still actually belonged to territorial princes but were favoured and privileged, even by the emperor (an Austrian) who, for example, awarded them the salt-monopoly. Their prosperity was in the interests of everybody: king, lords, burghers, any of whom might be wine-growers. No single interest seems to have been wholly dominant, not duke, knightly family nor any closed circle of upper burghers, which was in fact notably absent. The trade of the river was paramount, and shared in by many. It is interesting that representative members of famous families from a number of cities are found transiently scattered in the Danube towns, like Teschler from Ravensburg, Ebmer from Franconia, and Holzer probably from Pressburg. More recent research has uncovered scattered family relationships along the trade-routes, for instance Nurembergers in Linz, Vienna, Pressburg and Budapest, and Viennese families in Hungary, rather than any deep-rooted indigenous dynasties like the Stromer in Nuremberg or the Zum Jungen in Mainz. Perhaps this family mobility was natural to a strongly trading society which dwelt alongside its main route, unencumbered by the mills and workshops belonging to a Stromer concern in Nuremberg. Perhaps too the very dominance of the Danube compelled mobility and the flexibility shown by the Teschler, who took the side of Corvinus in 1485, along with others occupied in the Hungarian trade. Aeneas Sylvius, with his sharp eye and sharp tongue, noted that Vienna was a city of newcomers.

A third example, of a different kind, is provided by the towns of late medieval Württemberg, that impressive successor-territory to Hohenstaufen Swabia, because here, under the prince, the towns were woven firmly and skilfully into the fabric of a modernizing German 'state'.[25] In the thirteenth century the countship of Württemberg possessed only a handful of towns, lying on the periphery of his realm and acting mainly as protectors against the Habsburgs. Many kinds of good fortune in the fourteenth century brought an expansion of Württemberg's territory and hence the acquisition of many more towns (rather than new foundations). The count of Württemberg profited especially from the defeat of the Habsburgs by the Swiss at Sempach (1386) and the defeat of the imperial town league by its princely enemies at Döffingen (1388). Within Württemberg the nobles were not independent rivals of the count so much as his officials. As to the towns, even with their own law and administration they lived under the count's bailiffs, and some became important centres of local administration under a comital steward. In 1442 there were in fact thirty-two administrative districts *(Ämter)*, each denoted by the name of its head town. To these towns justice and administration were transferred from the castle: another good example of the point made above in Section (a) about the movement of political rule into towns. The law was administered not by the councils so characteristic of autonomous towns but by the courts under a bailiff *(Schultheiss)*, who in the fifteenth century gave way to 'discreet men' under the comital officer, now simply styled the *Amtsträger*, or office-bearer. No doubt these discreet men of Tübingen or Stuttgart were miniature oligarchies, patricians such as might be found flourishing in big cities elsewhere, yet there was here a difference, for they were the oligarchs through whom the prince ruled. They did not do their own ruling. Certainly they were privileged, freed from some dues and services, free to see their sons enter universities and even the older Benedictine houses. But they stood politically and administratively foursquare with the count (or duke, as he became in 1495). In this heartland of the Peasants' War we can see how the countryside was being engulfed by rule from the towns, and how the law *(Landrecht)* emanating from the towns obeyed more modern assumptions and evened out various differences between burgher and peasant, a process not always to the peasant's liking or advantage.

A final example, that of Switzerland, is inserted here because it supplies so sharp a contrast with the other regional town-prince politics we have been considering.[26] First and foremost it was not, like Württemberg and Silesia, a country where the towns did the prince's work for him. On the contrary, in Switzerland it was rather the towns that ate up would-be princes. Nor was it, like Bavaria or Franconia, a region of clear noble dominance. The Confederation was *sui generis,* a country which was not a country but a collection of self-governing districts, or cantons, held together by a series of sworn alliances, and unique too as a channel of trade-routes over the mountains where year by year commodities and people might pass only through the skill and permission of the inhabitants. Even this makes it sound too much a land of guides and inn-keepers. The Confederation was in fact a land of many towns in which a few great ones emerged and reached out to make lesser ones their subjects or *Untertanen,* a form of lordship of town over town rarely seen outside Italy. And yet again it was not like Italy, because the towns maintained a strongly communal sense and were always hostile to a man who thought he could rule alone. If one asks why Switzerland was so different from other regions in its numerous, proud and touchy towns, perhaps the answer lies partly in long and hopeful struggles against lords like the Abbey of St Gall and the Habsburgs, and partly in the fact that the towns called into being by the currents of a trade were none the less fed, sustained and protected by communities of peasants who had learned to fight and win with their pikes in difficult terrain. Perhaps the Swiss, great townsmen though they were, never forgot they were a peasant people too.

The tidal foundation of Swiss towns in the twelfth and thirteenth centuries ebbed a little in the later middle ages from a high point of some 200 towns and townlets in 1300 to about 150 in 1500. Many of these were very small indeed, but at the top were Basel and Freiburg in Üchtland with 5000 to 10,000, and half a dozen others including Lucerne, Schaffhausen, St Gall and Lausanne with 2000 to 5000. After 1415 Bern, Zürich and Lucerne were able to occupy Habsburg Aargau, and it was agreed that this district should in future be held in common. This was cement to the Federation, and brought numbers of small towns in pledge to the victorious Swiss. In other instances too Swiss cities gained jurisdictional rights and subject citizens from crumbling lordships which pledged their property to the towns which, as ever, were replete with cash.

In general, the fifteenth century saw for Switzerland the final release of many towns from Habsburg domination, the formation of a ring of Swiss city-states ranging from Bern's 9000 square kilometres to Zug's eighty square kilometres, and the improvement of roads, water-supply and fortifying walls. Dietrich Schwarz detects a strengthening of burgher political and social influences over the older aristocratic ones in this extraordinary confederation which could promote craftsmen to high office, tolerate no despot, and settle down behind its engineered fortifications to preside over its secure members warming themselves in their glazed houses in front of tiled stoves.

(c) *Town leagues, towns, townsmen and the king*

The king and the princes have already entered the argument of this chapter at some length in order to show the importance of urbanization to the growth of royal and seignorial administration.

But the analysis is not complete. It is time to look more closely at the king's urban contacts, especially with particular towns and individual townsmen, for these were actually more important to him and to them than the great federations of cities on which many text-books concentrate.

Of course, the existence and intermittent importance of these town leagues cannot be denied, but usually they had less to do with the king than with the protection of their own interests against hostile princes or the furtherance of their trading and fiscal advantages. Consequently, they will be treated only briefly here.

Two town associations were virtually permanent despite frequent internal shifts of policy and dominance. The Hanseatic League was almost entirely directed towards the great purpose of the Baltic trade, its furtherance and defence, while the federation of Swiss cantons was also in important respects an alliance of towns which dominated their countrysides. There is a huge literature on each,[27] but a summary explanation of the Hanseatic League may be appropriate at this point for readers of an introductory book.

Hanse originally meant a body of men. It came, of course, to denote the most prominent and enduring of the German town associations; 'Hanseatic League' as a term dates apparently from 1358.

Since the association was fundamentally commercial rather than militarily defensive like other German town leagues, this term is perhaps misleading. Ever active through the journeys of ships and cargoes, we have to think of it to some extent as a 'moving league', as Mr Scammell calls it, just as others have observed that the Italian venturing partnerships, the *societates maris,* have been called 'the commune on the move'. The vagueness of north Germany theory must not conceal the drive and persistence behind this collaboration of their towns.

The Hanseatic League developed as part of the late medieval German colonization of the east. The most celebrated and influential centre was Lübeck, founded in 1143 by the count of Holstein, acquired and re-established in 1159 by Henry the Lion, duke of Saxony. Here German merchants had settled from Saxony, Westphalia and the Rhineland and began to trade all over the Baltic Sea, founding a principal centre in Gotland and new towns in the east. The settlements were in fact often complex and partial: Königsberg, for example, was more like three towns, belonging respectively to the Hanseatic merchants, the bishop and the Teutonic Order, while in existing realms, from England and Norway to Russia, permanent enclaves were organized, usually called *Kontor(e)*, within towns.

Lübeck was important because of its geographical position on the Holstein isthmus, where the obvious route took its way between the Rhineland and the west on the one hand and the 'Wendish', Prussian and Russian settlements on the east. Medieval Hamburg was in some ways its outer harbour on the North Sea, though by the fifteenth century the sea journey round Denmark through the Skagerrak was routine.

The League was an ever-renewed series of agreements between towns, the exact number and composition of which were always changing. In its best days of the mid-fifteenth century they numbered nearly eighty, though some two hundred towns shared at one time or another in Hanseatic privileges of varying kinds. The area of this activity stretched from the Zuyder Zee to the Gulf of Finland, and between the Baltic and central Germany. Because the treaties were periodic and variable the Hanse seems to share, at least in general terms, in the characteristic expediency, hardly formal enough to be called institutional, of other German arrangements like the Public Peace movement and the knightly leagues, which served as best they could a society uncentralized, insecure but vigorous.

Piracy and the threats of princes kept the Hanse together, even if the representatives meeting in Lübeck might from time to time expel offending members. Competitive hostility from Flanders and Denmark in the fourteenth century gave a slightly firmer structure to the League, and in 1356 its first general council *(Hansetag)* was held. From the irregular meetings of this body, mostly at Lübeck, there issued a series of regulations *(Hanserezesse)*, passed by majority decision.

The victory over Denmark in 1368 and the ensuing Peace of Stralsund (1370) not only strengthened the League's privileges but gave it a potential military, or rather naval, force to supply some of the protection the king could not bestow.

Princes were not members, save for the Grand Master of the Teutonic Order, but the peasant 'state' of Dithmarschen belonged from 1468 as an ally of Lübeck. Conversely, the Hanseatic towns had no ambitions, like Italian towns, to become territorial powers, beyond looking to their bulwarks and strategic outposts required for safety, and sometimes landed properties bought by citizens as investments.

There is hence a contrast between the rather shapeless structure of the League and the frequent instability of its individual towns on the one hand, and the vast flow of its commerical enterprise on the other; this brought cloth, salt and wine from the west to the eastern depths of the Baltic region in return for westward supplies for fur, wax, herring, hard-husked grain, timber and wooden products. Of these the ship, the broad-beamed cargo-carrying cog, was the chief, the instrument of the League's being and the emblem on its seals.

The Hanseatic League was originally and principally north German, and beyond the ordinary orbit of the royal concern with which this section is intended to deal. It takes its place here, therefore, as a kind of contrast with the central and southern Germany more closely connected with the king. Yet the divide was not complete. In the late medieval period trade connections with south Germany flourished and the Baltic towns themselves began to be penetrated by south Germans, and ultimately by the Fugger. The medieval north lacked the business sophistication of the south. But its merchants called themselves 'merchants of the Roman Empire of Germany' and played a major part in the urbanization of a society which, very gradually, was moving through urbanization itself towards a political integration.

German town leagues in the more usual sense consisted in the temporary alliance of neighbouring towns, mostly in Swabia and in the upper Rhineland, with the object of protecting themselves against their natural enemies, the princes. On occasion, however, certain princes themselves joined with the towns. The Rhenish League was formed in 1254[28] to oppose princely attempts at exploiting its members, and to push forward the towns' long-term plans to become autonomous under the emperor's nominal overlordship. The Swabian League of 1376, on the other hand, was formed under the leadership of Ulm to stop the emperor pledging his towns to princes as a method of repaying his debts, to resist princely jurisdiction over them, and to combat the attacks of knightly leagues like that of St George, which often had princely allies. In 1381 the Swabian Town League was joined by the Rhenish cities, including Mainz, Frankfurt and Strassburg. In 1384 King Wenzel accorded this great urban combination a practical recognition, in response to its request, even though to do so was against the terms of the Golden Bull of 1356.[29]

But its moment of triumph ended in 1387–8 when the League fought a war, mostly with mercenary troops, on behalf of the king's ally, Archbishop Pilgrim of Salzburg. Their enemies were the Wittelsbachs and numerous lords of Swabia and Franconia. At Döffingen in Württemberg these princes were victorious, and after this 'Great Town War' the Swabian and Rhenish leagues fell apart. The failure of town leagues, however, did not imply that the German towns had lost every advantage, as will appear shortly.

The other, and last, major town combination was the new Swabian League of 1488, but this was much less exclusively an urban alliance than an attempt under princely leadership to embody cities, prelates and lesser nobility of the south-west in a permanent federation for the sake of better government and resistance to the Wittelsbachs.

Before passing from town leagues to consider towns and their inhabitants as individuals in relation with the king it would be salutary to remember that late medieval Germany was an aristocratic polity. In high politics the towns could not operate on the same scale as princes, whether singly or together. The student of the age is constantly impressed by the incoherence and inconstancy of the towns' collective will across the centuries, by their inability to form more than half-hearted alliances, by the commerical individualism which prevented more than fleeting co-operation despite the family networks which are so apparent. Like the English Commons, they could help and follow but could not rule. In a way the state of affairs is epitomized by a remark made in 1359 by the Emperor Charles IV in the hearing of the Magdeburg chronicler. When pressed by the duke of Saxony not to give a judgement against him for the city, Charles answered that whatever law (meaning the Saxon law) might have been given to Magdeburg, what really counted were the decisions taken in the royal court on the advice of the princes there.[30]

This said, it may confidently be written that the relationship between kings and financially strong towns was enormously important.[31] The beginning of such continuous relationships has certainly been traced back at the latest to the time of Lewis of Bavaria, and they were flourishing under Charles IV, Wenzel, Rupert and Sigismund. Over a quarter of all Charles IV's letters were on one matter or another to towns. The towns involved might be imperial, provincial or those of his own dynastic lands, but they were mostly within the general area of kingly lands. Royal excursions to the Baltic, for instance, were exceptional. The Swabian towns were rather closer to royal activities in the fourteenth and fifteenth centuries, but were anxious to be left alone. They gave 400,000 guilders in 1417 to Frederick of Hohenzollern for his purchase of Brandenburg. The German town heartland of royal interest in the fourteenth and fifteenth centuries was in Frankfurt-am-Main, Mainz, later in the period in Augsburg, but always and above all in Nuremberg.

The royal interest in such towns centred on money, economic expertise, the supply of goods and the reception of intelligence reports, probably in that order. It was dictated by political expedience as much as by any whimsical gratifications of the kind displayed by Charles IV's son-in-law Richard II in England.[32] Charles's political and cultural activity was closely matched by his understanding of his own economic interests. This meant, among other things, a value placed by him on trade-routes between Nuremberg, Mainz, and Poland and Hungary. The route passed through Prague, and he made efforts to settle differences between Bohemia and Hungary in order to secure easy transit for merchants. He freed from toll, completely or partially, the merchants of Regensburg, Nuremberg, Rothenburg and Sulzbach. He aimed at keeping routes safe by issuing written safe-conducts *(Geleitsbriefe)*. His charters of town-foundation refer overtly to the economic functions of the settlements he was attempting to encourage.

Just as Rudolf of Habsburg had relied upon Strassburg, so in the fourteenth century the economic centre of royal Germany was Nuremberg and neighbouring portions of Bohemia, Austria and Hungary. Their importance rested on the twin pillars of industry and long-distance commerce. It was this area which provided the kings, and kings which relied upon the area.[33]

But within this general region, different kings set great store on different individual cities. Under Lewis IV, the Munich-Nuremberg axis had naturally been important. With Charles IV Prague was pre-eminent as a capital, where in the Old Town lived the imperial princes of the court, either in their own houses or with permanent landlords, but among imperial cities it was Nuremberg which was paramount. The royal nature of Franconia made possible this Prague-Nuremberg axis. Indeed, till the mid-fifteenth century, when Austria came to the front of the historical stage, Nuremberg was the pivot of every royal political combination, save for a brief period under King Wenzel. It had a favourable position as a market and a stable patriciate. Charles IV had published most of the Golden Bull there, and had arranged for the birth of his son Wenzel to take place there. There he built the *Frauenkirche* (Church of Our Lady), stayed often within the city walls, and made it a collecting point for taxes. Even more than Prague, Nuremberg was becoming an imperial capital.

The curious thing is that after Charles IV King Wenzel neglected Nuremberg and visited it seldom. On the other hand, the counts palatine of the Rhine, and especially Rupert, Wenzel's imperial supplanter, cultivated Nuremberg for all they were worth. Their own Heidelberg was not a very great city. Rupert almost made himself a Nuremberger: he married a Nuremberg *Burggräfin*, he and his officials were often there, and Nuremberg supplied the Palatinate with iron and all manner of other goods on credit. As Wenzel, after his imperial deposition in 1400 but before his death in 1419, became an enemy of Rupert and both sides tried to recruit Nuremberg, the city stood in an embarrassing and perhaps dangerous position. This was a genuine dilemma for a great commercial community, as roads had above all to be kept safe, and princely friendships were needed for that. In the event, influential Nurembergers went over to Rupert, even those who once had blossomed in the Luxemburg sun. This was not a sudden switch of loyalty, let alone an arbitrary breach of faith. Rupert's contacts in the Upper Palatinate, where he had mining interests, went back to 1350. A letter from Ulman Stromer, the Nuremberg magnate, to a friend in 1397 expressed scepticism about Wenzel and his regime, and Stromer's *Little Book* also shows the strength of opposition to Wenzel. *Per contra*, Rupert was Stromer's guest and benefactor, and his queen held a Stromer granddaughter at her baptism.

Where great citizens led, others followed, for the Nuremberg council hesitated prudently to allow public opinion to turn from the old Luxemburg loyalties towards a franker recognition of Rupert's merits. And where Nuremberg led, so too other cities followed.

For Nuremberg was not the only town to have some importance in the eyes of kings. Already Lewis of Bavaria and Charles IV had rewarded Frankfurt highly. This was the news centre of the west, as was Nuremberg of the east, and both possessed a following of lesser imperial cities. Indeed, Frankfurt itself had a long-standing relationship with the Palatinate. For all that, Frankfurt was not joyful about Rupert's accession, and helped him remarkably little. Nor did Rupert use Frankfurt for Diets as much as Wenzel had done. It was not a question of enmities but of studied preferences. When Wenzel was king Frankfurt was more agreeable to him than Nuremberg; when Rupert deposed Wenzel, Nuremberg, further away from the Palatinate, paradoxically became home-ground to Rupert.

Other cities too had special involvements, though to enumerate them all from the writings of Dr Moraw would not add to the present argument and would perhaps be less than fair to the scholar, whose full work is available to readers specialist enough to learn German. The general truth is that Rupert, like other kings before and after him, benefited from particular cities with which he had friendly dealings, and that these friendships were partly based on suitable geographical position, but largely on the financial and economic opportunities the cities were able to cultivate with particular kings. And such opportunities imply contacts with individuals rather than with institutions.

We come, then, to the last leg of the argument. The kings got accommodation, taxes, loans, goods, news and personal service from individual townsmen and not from corporations or other abstractions. Members of leading families from Nuremberg and neighbouring towns are to be found in the chanceries of John of Bohemia, Charles IV, Wenzel, Rupert and Sigismund, and in the administration of the archbishop of Prague.[34] Nor was it strange to use as diplomats men who understood money and mining as well as writing. Likewise, the chancellors of Albrecht II and Frederick III came from city nobilities.

These bonds of personal friendship were forged with individuals from various cities within the royal ambit, not with those from Nuremberg alone. The Wölflin of Prague and the Eberhard of Brünn (Brno) were leading financial contributors and court officials to John and Charles IV. They had also in some measure served the Přemyslids, so that without exaggeration one may say that burghers had stood behind the throne of Bohemia. From Frankfurt comes an early example of courtier burgher in Siegfried Zum Paradies, councillor, supplier of horses at the king's election, and later imperial bailiff *(Schultheiss)*. In Mainz a leading counterpart was the family Zum Jungen, bankers to territorial families and to the emperor, friends of the Stromer of Nuremberg, and kinsmen to Johann Gutenberg, also a native of Mainz, one of whose presses stood at one time in their house.

In such ways a veritable financial and commercial network operated over the Franconian and Rhine-Main region. In many ways it was to the benefit of kings, yet it was controlled and owned by members of town families who knew the kings personally, as they knew one another. Duly deferential, gratified by honours, they maintained a basic independence of the crown as dynasty succeeded dynasty.

At the end it is to Nuremberg again that we must turn for the greatest number of individual townsmen who served the king. Konrad Gross was singled out for his aid and consequent reception of honours by Lewis IV, Ulman Stromer by Charles IV, Nikolaus Muffel by Wenzel, Stromers again by Rupert and Sigismund. The individualism of the relationships does not imply that they were rare. Probably most Nuremberg citizens were at one time or another in contact with kings in the fifteenth century, and not all of them were members of the top families. It was their business and opportunity to lend. Some otherwise hardly known families were granted armorial bearings as a sequel. Others, clergy too, gave time to the royal service, like Albert Fleischmann of Eggolsheim, parish priest of St Sebaldus, graduate of Prague and former notary of the bishop of Bamberg. In time he became a protonotary at the court of King Rupert, and went for him on diplomatic journeys to France and Italy.

If Nuremberg provided the most burgher friends and helpers to the German kings, the great family of Stromer was doubtless closest and longest in such service. Its role can be illustrated briefly. The setting is the reign of Sigismund, who was much concerned during his early years as emperor with the development of his Italian interests. A central problem was Venetian expansion and the emperor's protracted attempt to build up south German trade towards Constantinople and the Black Sea. This policy served his interest as king of Hungary, but also commanded wide support from south German merchants, the Stromer among them. Added to this was commercial rivalry between south Germany and Milan.

In September 1414 Sigismund was in Nuremberg on political business and took the opportunity to improve his friendship both with the Stromer and with other citizens, many of whom had been wary of the house of Luxemburg since they had stopped supporting the Wenzel regime in favour of Rupert, the Wittelsbach from the County Palatine. Anyhow, Sigismund was now making up lost ground, and he visited Germany's first paper-mill, which had been built by Ulman Stromer on the river Pegnitz where it flowed past the city's gates. Sigismund decided he wanted the secret of paper-making for himself, and persuaded the Stromer to put an executive director of their firm at his disposal. This was done, in the person of Hans Geyger, who came from another Nuremberg patrician family with interests in commerce, especially in Italy, blade-making and apothecary work. We might call them 'industrial chemists' with water-powered factories on the Nuremberg part of the River Pegnitz. Now the central point of this story is that Geyger had probably stolen the secret of paper-making from northern Italy: it was not hard to use one's eyes or bribe employees. And on his way home he had also been taken prisoner by a minor nobleman near Ingolstadt. The events are known to us through the survival in the Nuremberg archives of a letter from the city council to Geyger's captor.[35] In this web of narrative the multiple concerns which king and townsmen had in common can be seen. Sigismund's economic policy touched the interests of south German merchants at many points. The merchants themselves were also industrialists (in a fifteenth-century sense), and long-distance travellers. The Stromer were already known and privileged in Sigismund's Hungarian court. Economic service led on to other things. Young Stromer kinsmen had fought for Sigismund against the Turks at Nicopolis in 1396 with thirty-two horsemen, and had survived that disastrous day. Other members of the family became political agents at the Council of Constance for Sigismund's reforming schemes. The ramifications are wide, especially if other families, other towns and other kings are taken into account. It is again all too apparent how devastating were the effects of the Hussite wars on the fortunes of those like the Stromer, for they sealed off Bohemian mines, blocked trade-routes, subjected merchants to confiscations and losses, and at the same time expelled the king of the Romans from his Bohemian kingdom, long deprived the empire of Prague, and helped to revitalize in Luxemburg and Habsburg minds the ideal of crusade, against heretic and then against

140

Turk. The ideal was deadly to central administration, and like all war inimical in the long run to the best interests of townsmen.

(d) *Class and conflict*

A 'patrician' was one of a small group of townsmen which formed by reason of its capital wealth a city's ruling oligarchy. This wealth derived basically from long-distance trade. The word 'patrician' was in fact a fifteenth-century humanist expression: in medieval German towns they were called the *Geschlechter*, or 'the families', and the collective or plural form of this word underlines the fact that patriciates were made up of dynastic family groups, not chance collections of rich individuals. When Peter Eitel of Ravensburg was commenting in 1972 on the freedom such groups had to manage their economic affairs in their city he was not being frivolous in describing it as 'an economy of cousins' *(Vetterleswirtschaft)*.[36]

In the thirteenth century patriciates emerged in all the large towns of Europe, but those of Germany had some special characteristics which help an understanding of that country's general history. Germany had no strong, centralizing monarchy like England and France, able at an early date to bring the towns within a framework of royal law and control. Nor was Germany as urban as central and northern Italy. In some ways the German towns, in their lack of a paternalistic monarchy, were political orphans, displaying the self-centred individualism so often seen in those allowed or forced to grow into a premature adulthood, so that they might be reproved for their sectionalism and for failing in the civilizing mission of class-mingling as between country and town. It would be unhistorical to impart moral blame to communities which had no choice. They lacked any choice to contribute to social peace in later medieval Germany, not because of historical laws concerning an ineluctable class-struggle between a bourgeois and a feudal order, but because there was no overriding authority able to enforce peace and make possible a more fruitful harmony of country and town, such as existed in England.

It was in the larger towns that proper patriciates formed. Lesser ones, in Austria or Württemberg, for instance, represented more ephemeral or modest groupings, and were sometimes described as the 'worshipful' *(die Ehrbarkeit)*, that is to say, wealthy, people or as 'the hereditary citizens' *(Erbbürger)*. True patriciates were deep-rooted, ramified networks of families which by the thirteenth century were monopolizing city governments. With patrician origins we cannot be concerned here,[37] and it may simply be said that some of them had been landlords in the surrounding countryside, and some had risen to importance as servants or *ministeriales* of princes. The diversity of patrician origins may be aptly illustrated by the great Nuremberg family of Stromer, whose ancestor *(Stammvater)* was the knight Gerhard von Reichenbach, possessor of the castle of Kammerstein near Schwabach at the beginning of the thirteenth century. A son of this man, called Conrad, married a Nuremberg girl of the Waldstromer family, whose members did not yet possess citizenship but were imperial foresters in the neighbourhood of Nuremberg.[38] Their numerous descendants formed a leading patrician clan of Nuremberg throughout the middle ages and beyond.

The essential characteristic of the patrician class is that it was engaged in long-distance trade. From this commercial basis its members were able to accumulate capital, sometimes to invest in urban properties, often to become financiers as well as managing businesses of considerable diversity and long geographical connections. Naturally, the kind of commercial activity in which patricians engaged was not exactly the same everywhere and sometimes changed in the course of time. Cloth merchants were ubiquitous, but the economic character of the locality altered the balance of mercantile interests. Patricians controlled the supply of metal in mining and metal manufacturing regions. Returning once more to the Stromer of Nuremberg, they had interests in acquiring coal and iron, many mills in and around Nuremberg (driven by the water-power of the Pegnitz), metal processing, corn-grinding and eventually paper-making. But above all the Stromer were members of a mercantile house which had business over almost all Europe and in a great diversity of commodities. In this way the original specialism of a future patrician is of lesser relevance. It was his profits, his diversification, his contacts and his quasi-political nature that made him a patrician in the sense intended here. The same general rule would obtain elsewhere, though there would be more interest in salt in Lüneburg, in beer in Danzig, in the fur trade in Magdeburg, and so on.

Patricians were socially elevated. In the thirteenth century they were tending to abandon trade names and adopt family ones (patronymics and matronymics) or surnames derived from places (toponymics). The rule is far from absolute. Some important Nuremberg families were called after makers of clogs or cloth (Holzschuher, Tucher). Other leading families presumably enjoyed a secret joke in sustaining nicknames over the generations like Dämon, Mörder or Teufel. Others again, like Welser of Augsburg, soon brought such lustre to the name of 'foreigner' or 'outsider' that they were proud to keep it. These are exceptions. There is surely a strong desire in a landed society to enjoy a territorial name with the possessive particle indicating lordship. No doubt it was in this spirit that Peter Egen of Augsburg expressed gratitude that the Emperor Frederick III allowed him to change his name to von Argon.[39]

Within his city the patrician lived in noble style too. He was addressed as 'Dominus' or 'Herr', often occupied a stone house, fought on horseback and displayed a shield and coat of arms. The chivalric influence is even visible in Lübeck, that city of 'holy sobriety', where courtly literature was popular in its own Low German form. The whole of Parzival was displayed in a fourteenth-century wall-painting in Johannisstrasse, and at the same moment the surname Perceval appears, attached to a family of patrician merchants.[40] Many sons of Lübeck burghers became members of the Teutonic Order; others acquired cathedral canonries and even bishoprics which were usually out of reach of non-nobles in Old Germany.

Patrician families in German cities were usually grouped in self-privileged social clubs like the *Richerzeche* in Cologne, the *Zirkelgesellschaft* in Lübeck, or the *Rundinger* in Regensburg. In Mainz the dining-club was presided over by a mess-president called 'the abbot' by members and 'toad' by outsiders.[41] From these magic social circles were drawn in rotation the members of the city council, the town's supreme governing authority. Such council-worthy men administered all policy and all justice, and in the event went off to drink and talk and dine in their places of exclusive recreation. They were the men of substance, married to socially suitable wives. Sometimes the qualifications of a councillor included not only an approved marriage-partner but one or more children by her as well — as in Vienna in 1296 — as a sort of earnest of dynastic achievement. In the town texts they were called 'better', 'greater', 'wiser' and 'cleverer', but these epithets are no different from those accorded to the honest, discreet, legal men of the better sort one encounters in English texts too. It is easy to make fun of a plutocrat's natural assumption of superior wisdom. But any glimmer of outrage in the historian's breast may suggest that he has not understood the meaning of such correspondences in oligarchic societies. Members of such a closed circle were clearly conscious from time to time of a heavy responsibility to preserve the city, its trade and its defences. They developed a corporate sense strong enough to carry out self-assessment for taxation with a high degree of honesty. The rule was in a way proved by its exception in Nuremberg, where a chief treasurer *(Losunger)*, Muffel, was executed for embezzlement in 1469. This political class had been in existence for a long time, evolving out of the group that had founded the city, forming a family network from which the council and its officers were chosen. Obviously it had access to written records which were as the tablets of the law, and believed itself uniquely well-informed and alone capable of preserving the interests of the city as a whole against its tireless enemies outside. With respect to Professor Maschke[42] it is hard to contrast favourably the collective consciousness of city rebels whom we shall meet shortly with the selfish, inbred, family consciousness of the patriciate unless you are starting from the premiss that a patriciate was in itself bad. For Maschke a high point of the patrician ambition and its so-called individual subjectivism was the oil-painting of 'the grand old man'. This may well be. But the truth here is that the letters, diaries and autobiographies of this closed group, not to mention the official archives of the city, in fact did make them wiser and probably more discreet in arranging policy, and certainly gave them a corporate consciousness at least equal to that of resentful outsiders in the town. The fact that victorious rebels ended by themselves becoming patricians or leaving the work to them simply exemplifies once more what happens in all rebellions where former rulers and their families are not removed wholesale.

From here we may pass to the question of patrician longevity. The German experience seems to have been rather different from the English, in that rich town families in Germany were longer-lasting and stayed in the town more easily than in England, where they more often escaped to become country gentry. At this stage a comparison cannot get beyond impressions, as systematic tracing of patrician dynasties in the two countries has not yet been done. But for England both Professor Sylvia Thrupp and Professor Hoskins have argued that the lives of urban families were often short, partly because heirs failed and partly because families which were successful tended to move out into the shires and marry into country society. To these arguments have been added more lately the view that late medieval England experienced little investment either in town property or in production, that much which might have been manufactured here was bought abroad, and that perhaps the peaceful English countryside offered too great an inducement to go and live in emparked quietude and leave the balance of payments to the sheep.

Writers on German towns, on the other hand, often emphasize that many individual families continued in their own town-setting for a very long time. For example, in the lists of Lübeck mayors of the fourteenth and fifteenth centuries there are certain names which often recur: Pleskow, Castorp, Warendorp, and so on.[43] The same is true of the forty-three great Nuremberg families, such as Mendel, Holzschuher, Pfinzing, Ebner, Stromer, Muffel or Grundherr, which were holding the stage in 1521 and of which apparently even the most recent went back to the fourteenth century.[44] In the same vein, Hans Planitz wrote that in Cologne about twenty families of patricians lasted over 250 years, and the seemingly new ones which appeared in the fourteenth century were on inspection mostly co-lineals with older families. Obviously, there were disappearances due to disease or impoverishment. In Constance, of the seventy-five rich families of 1388, thirty-four had disappeared into poverty or obscurity by 1400, and some of them are traceable in the poorer quarters of the town. The monetary unions of the late fourteenth century, like those organized between the Palatinate, Nuremberg, Bamberg and Würzburg in 1396, led to the issue of better currency, which apparently caught some rich patricians with their treasuries full of the old coin which could not be exchanged at par, so that they were impoverished.[45] To what extent German townsmen acquired property outside their walls either as investment or as places to live, as happened so often in England, is the other side of this question. It is also one of those topics which is as yet insufficiently researched rather than contentious. None the less, it is worth reserving a short section for it later.[46] In the meantime we continue with the patricians within the town and the rebellions against their rule during the period under study.

The fourteenth century saw a spate of town risings which was to last until the middle of the sixteenth century at the earliest. They all shared the characteristic of being rebellions against the patrician monopoly by mixed groups of lesser townsmen, most often referred to collectively as either 'the craftsmen' *(die Handwerker)* or 'the gilds' *(die Zünfte)*. In reality the rebels were an amalgam of various social elements who either were or felt excluded from the top, hereditary management. Professor Maschke has enumerated 210 town risings, from 105 different towns, during the 250 years between 1300 and 1550, and his list is patently incomplete.[47] In north and north-western Germany alone there were over fifty urban risings between 1300 and 1500, and they were common in the west and south as well. Whether Maschke was right in saying that the northern rebellions were less bloodthirsty than those in southern towns is open to question. But the town rebels of late medieval Germany shared certain circumstances: they found themselves bearing a heavy cost of tax in keeping their town free of its enemies in a world increasingly hostile to towns and merchants, and they were people who strongly believed themselves excluded from government and even from information about government. Many town chronicles take note of these risings and, although they are mostly written from the partisan view of the patricians, the chroniclers show clearly enough that the object of the rebellions was participation not revolution, the breaking of age-old family monopolies, maintained by co-optation, not the upsetting of a constitution or the inauguration of a new gild policy. Indeed, no rebels, however angry, shouted for defence cuts, or embraced the city's enemies as friends, or halted for a moment the town's resolve to hire soldiers and maintain the walls, towers and treaties behind which alone the citizens felt safe.[48]

In 1374 Brunswick and its duke conducted an unsuccessful private war against the archbishop of Magdeburg and had to pay a ransom of 4000 marks. The town's indebtedness rose to nearly 10,000 marks and the council felt obliged to levy a special corn-tax. In April the masters of the gilds *(Gildenmeister)* were notified of this by the council. These men seemed ready to agree, and so did many of the craftsmen. But when a special meeting of tanners and shoe-menders was called an uproar broke out. There was a riot during which about eight council members were beheaded and looting took place. A new council was quickly set up and the old councillors who had fled tried to get Brunswick excluded from Hanseatic privileges. Yet by 1380 the rift in

Brunswick had been almost healed, most of the exiles had returned and hardly one rebel remained on the council. Detailed study of this rising shows the rebels themselves to have been a mixture of merchants and craftsmen, all with some possessions, a few with land, and some with business or family connections with the old council. There is evidence that there were successful craftsmen who had built up businesses. The rebels further seem to have come from a wide range of age-groups but in general to have been stronger in the surburbs, whilst the *Geschlechter* were dominant in the city centre. One of the landed rebels who later lost his property in a local feud was Eggeling van Schalling, councillor for the Brunswick suburb of Hagen, who had twelve houses there alone and more property in the city centre. Clearly this was not a straightforward conflict between the rich and the poor of Brunswick, but one ostensibly about the need for heavy taxation in which anger brought to the surface no more profound accusations than those of self-will and aggressiveness.

Cologne had a long history of city-strife which culminated in 1396–1400, when the council was overthrown and power seized by craftsmen and merchants. The strongest craft-group were the weavers, but they were divided among themselves. There were other cross-currents, such as a dispute about who might participate in the wine-trade. But perhaps the strongest demarcation was between the oldest patrician families, styled the *Schöffen*, on the one hand, supported by the archbishop, and the next most important group, who called themselves the *Greifen*. After some atrocities the patricians were forced to give way to a more widely-based council with patrician representatives and mayor but with members also drawn from the lesser merchants and gilds. The new council sent handsome presents of money to the archbishop and King Wenzel. A new council minute-book, written up by a very adroit trimmer called Gerlach van Hauwe and called The New Book (*Dat nuwe boich*, 1360–96),[49] painted a picture of scandalous patrician rule and a deeply suffering community. But the rebels were themselves made up of wine merchants and goldsmiths, conjoined with not very affluent craftsmen, and the precise complaints in the council's new book were largely about taxation, bribery and bad faith against the close family network of the patricians. Here again is the mixture of bitter personal and family politics with trade-disputes. It is doubtful if the events can be understood without reference to a rebellion of gilds in 1369–71

147

which had been suppressed by the patricians. Our knowledge of this comes from a little rhymed chronicle on 'the battle (or slaughter) of the weavers' *(Die weverslaicht)*, not by an eye-witness but written before 1400. It took a strongly partisan view on behalf of the city nobility and regarded gildsmen as terrorists. The writer may have been an educated Cologne cleric who had seen something of Flemish rebels and disliked what he saw, but he wrote calmly and pointed out faults on both sides.

Lübeck's troubles of 1403–8 sprang mostly from the high cost of maritime warfare against pirates and of constructing the Stecknitz Canal. The council decided on a once-and-for-all tax in 1403. But another feud against a local trouble-maker (Balthasar von Wenden) ate up the proceeds, so a committee of sixty was set up to investigate what were believed to be council misdemeanours of the previous twelve years. Complaints escalated into a demand that the investigators should themselves share conciliar power. Some councillors at this point left the city and a wholly new council was set up. The struggle for eight years was really between the old and the new councils. When the old council won, with the help of King Sigismund, Denmark and the Hansa towns, there were a few executions and a few former rebels were accepted on to the newly constructed council. Again, the rebels have in many cases been identified, and appear generically as second-rank merchants, craftsmen, and a handful of 'class defectors' from among the patrician families. Those who actually participated in the rebel council were mostly merchants, as were all those former rebels co-opted on to the reconstructed council. Investigation of the sources further suggests that the rebels were mainly middle-aged, had not been on the council before, and had not in most instances even held any town office. Dr Barth's analysis and use of the sources has vividly re-created the supercilious outrage of the patricians and their firm belief that outsiders would never be able to understand the true interests of Lübeck or the subtle contacts and intelligence needed to uphold them. Their power was a sacred trust and certainly not something any patrician would think of regarding as enjoyable. For their part, most of the rebel grievances were severely practical and concerned the level of prices and tolls, the slow pace of judicial procedures, the character of policies which seemed to consume taxes, but above all the conviction that Lübeck power lay in the hands of a mere half-dozen men and that election to the council depended only on favour and friendship. To this was added the radical cry that foreign policy was expensive and probably useless, and if it cost so much to defend Lübeck's remoter possessions, then the possessions should be limited to what could be defended. The greatest chasm in understanding was the rebel belief that by the charter of Henry the Lion all citizens had the right to elect the council. But the council never answered this claim.

At Mainz, to take a final example, the council in summer 1444 declared a great debt, whereupon a committee of gildsmen demanded to see the accounts. When this was granted, the gildsmen made detailed accusations of misspending, often on private consumption. A new council was forced on the city and many patricians left. This was the culmination of a century's strife between gilds and patricians; and in this case the matter was overtaken in 1462 by the archbishop's conquest of his own city, the freedom of which he removed. But it seems that again the root trouble amongst the inhabitants was a desire on the part of newly enriched yet non-patrician burghers to share in the city's government. In fact there are variations on this theme in town after town, but the main theme is the same. In Mainz the most important industry was cloth manufacture and the commerce in it was in patrician hands. The craftsmen imitated the social clubs of the rich merchants, and it was natural that inflammatory speeches should be made in them on occasion. A leading agitator was Henne Knauff, a man of independent means and a professional rebel. An interesting sidelight on this particular strife is the presence during negotiations of other German city representatives who came to support the gilds, not so much out of political sympathy but as creditors looking to the winners to get them to pay back the money they had lent in the city.

In these four instances which have been described, and in others as well, the rebels usually seem to have been lesser merchants, mercenary captains, craftsmen of different sorts, clerks, lawyers and some few political defectors from the governing side. All these were people who in one way or another had seen their interests blocked by the ruling establishment, and said so. A brief account of this mode of communication was ingeniously worked out from the sources by Dr Reinhardt Barth and described above in Chapter 1.[50] Compared with the suave and no doubt sincere objections by the patricians to violent and resentful disturbances of methods which in their own view had

149

been working well enough, there was little abstract argument on the part of the craftsmen and lesser merchants on the subject of the city's honour and prosperity. The opposition was indeed lesser bourgeois and not truly proletarian. The craftsmen who rose to the top in these movements were those who had involved themselves in trade as well as in production, and wherever new constitutional arrangements were won, trading rather than manufacture was prominently the gainer. In the Lübeck meat business, for example, there was all the difference in the world between the butchers, who were also cattle-dealers and benefited by the rising, and the *Knockenhauer* (knackers), who were simply manual labourers, and in an ill-regarded calling at that.[51]

These hierarchies of esteem in German towns were not static but, quite apart from the risings, constantly being changed upwards and downwards in ways which are sometimes hard both to chart and to account for. Every town had a particular hierarchy among its gilds, visible in the order of precedence accorded to them in civic processions and public functions, and these orders of procedure have been cleverly used by Erich Maschke to demonstrate the social order in various localities.[52] To take a few instances: in Basel, a great trading city with limited industrial development, the leading gilds in the council records were merchants, minters, shopkeepers and vintners, organized in 'gentlemen's gilds' *(Herrenzünfte)*, down to weavers and fishermen at the bottom. In Augsburg, also a trading city but prominent in fustian production, weavers had a more prominent position, amongst the merchants and the brewers, leaving carpenters and joiners at the bottom. Likewise Ulm, with its combination of trade and textiles, saw clothmakers and lesser merchants enter the patriciate in the late fourteenth century, while building workers were again left at the bottom. Strassburg gave special prominence to boatmen, shopkeepers and inn-keepers. These orders of precedence were not merely the rules of fancy-dress parties. The growth of gild influence was guaranteed, as Maschke himself said, by the costs of military-political activity, and it was the richer craftsmen and the merchants who had to bear the financial brunt in the form of imposts and loans. The basic cause of unrest was financial demand, not merely a closed and obscurantist system of oligarchy. For patriciates had already begun in various instances to co-opt new members before serious rising began, as with the furriers of Magdeburg or the goldsmiths and the money-changers in Brunswick Old Town. The whole thing was speeded up and made more acrimonious by the disorder of the late fourteenth century.

Even had there been no exceptional strife, the movement of the markets and the movements of individuals within the economic world would have created the universal problem of social mobility. Some manual workers could as individuals move from their craft into retail trade and thence into wholesale operations and finance and see, as they did so, their income rising step by step from a few hundred guilders a year to ten or fifteen thousand; in other words, a successful artisan moving into business might make himself thirty times richer than before. Then, as *nouveaux-riches (Emporkömmling)*, they developed the social antennae, biologically so closely allied with business skills, which led them to the more prestigious social parties, to make friends among such people, to frequent the appropriate *Trinkstuben* or clubs, and in general to appear about the place as acceptable husbands or fathers-in-law for patrician daughters.[53] Upward movement like this tended to deprive ordinary gilds of their quick-climbing members and hence to leave them even less desirable work-associations than before as richer craftsmen-merchants moved on and were naturally inclined to denigrate their former haunts and associates.

At this point it is reasonable to ask why there were rebellions at all of the sort that have been described if this social mobility was already at work. The answer seems to be that the risings were set off by taxation. The taxes were imposed by councils on citizen bodies which were hardly represented at all in policy making, whether they were poor people or those who had been getting as rich as the councillor-class itself. There was no modern democratic machinery for voting councillors in and out. Hence the explosions. Perhaps the eventual changes seem quite small and the issues themselves hardly dramatic. But everyone knows that strong feelings can be engendered by financial and social grievances which in another age might appear trivial. The German town risings occurred because a few important people were treated as outsiders. When they had won their point and got into the council-chambers they no longer needed the backing of the poorer classes and quickly ignored them.

So these disturbances did not involve any movement towards social equality nor any dilution of the patrician class. Quite the reverse. The consequence was to emphasize the importance of the patriciate and its mode of life in the government of the city. Whenever a rebellion led to the creation of a new constitution by giving new people a say in the election of council and officials, they said their say by choosing patricians and not small traders, let alone craftsmen, for the tasks of diplomacy and senior management. How could it be otherwise? How could a man govern, lead military contingents, sit on time-consuming committees or travel constantly on diplomatic missions unless he had not merely the income but the *kind* of income which would permit him to give his time up so lavishly? For this life he could not be detained in shop, warehouse or even office. He required 'unearned' income, that is, profits from investments, rents, or offices held as part or whole sinecures: in other words the patrician perquisites and posts *par excellence.*

So throughout the decades of uproar, despite banishments and beheadings, most councillors and mayors on reformed councils continued to be members of mercantile houses which engaged in long-distance trade, were accustomed to travel, were able to offload such administrative work as they had on to hired agents, other members of their family, perhaps their wives. Such 'natural governors' are not difficult to exemplify. Such was Hans Pirkheimer of Nuremberg, who in 1356 had sixty leased properties, nineteen freeholds, five town houses and twenty-four properties of which he was the mortgagee. Gildsmen were not of course excluded completely from city offices and embassies: after all, they had fought precisely against such exclusion from the outset. But even more certainly and successfully they had fought for the right to vote in elections, not necessarily to be elected themselves to posts they would have found insupportable. When it came to standing as a candidate or to the appointment of an emissary, it was obvious that only a man who could afford it could accept. In Augsburg, for instance, the new constitution of 1368 provided for two mayors, one of them to be a gildsman and the other a patrician. But over the next 180 years the gildsman-mayor was on ninety-four occasions in fact a long-distance merchant, and only thirty times an individual who could be called a lesser tradesman. In Lübeck the picture is exceptionally clear of how a popular gild rising resulted in nothing more than another élitist council. In 1408 the patricians had been so frightened that they dared not go out of doors, but the revolutionary council contained far more merchants than artisans, and in 1416, when the old council returned and accepted five members of the revolutionary council into its number, every one of them was a merchant.

In late medieval German towns there were many variations on this theme, but it was a simple theme: that town rulers in the upper ranks had to have leisure. Perhaps the English word leisure too easily suggests mere idleness or recreation. The requirement was rather for the classicial Greek quality of leisure $(\sigma\chi o\lambda\eta)$[54] or, in German *Abkömmlichkeit*, which was emancipation from routine engagements and appointments, so that they could be free for thought, policy-making and the necessary diplomatic travel. Such a man had, in the half-opprobrious phrase, to be one of the 'idle rich' *(Müssiggänger)*. But the truth was there with all the immobility of platitude. Only the man rich on income which at the moment others were earning could do the work elsewhere expected of kings and landed magnates. Even some public works were financially so demanding that in the age of early capitalism only the well-off could undertake them, like that of the contractor whom Magdeburg council wanted in 1422 to put up a new bridge over the Elbe: it was a task which the town book said, 'needed unspeakable work, care and loss of time.' It was undertaken by Hans Schartau, member of one of the city's oldest and richest families.[55] Likewise, in the diplomatic activity of *Landfriede* politics, in collaboration with king and princes, the leaders of big cities had to be virtual career-diplomats. Nicholas Muffel (III) of Nuremberg was constantly in diplomacy from 1447 to 1457, as 170 surviving council letters show. Similar documents from Augsburg and Frankfurt give the names, costs and duration of their envoys' journeys, and lines of travel cover the surface of Germany and beyond. These leading citizens had living standards like those of the nobility, even when they came from cities where ordinary gildsmen had a majority on the council. Sometimes they married into noble families, though it seems probable that most patrician marriage alliances were contracted, if outside the city at all, with patrician families of other cities.

Another interesting but difficult question leads out of this consideration of social conflict within the towns. If the rebellions, for all their total number and their long collective duration, never issued in revolution but permitted the richest citizens to remain at the head of political and social life, is it possible to find enough common assumptions to justify reference to a German civic mentality in the late middle ages? In other words, if the rebellions were fundamentally about heavy taxes and the social exclusiveness of those who levied the taxes, and if the rebellions simmered down and life went on under the same sort of town rulers as before, with a few personal changes here and there, can one go further and find any characteristics which were generally true about German citizens?

At the outset it must be recognized that it is probably impossible at this stage to say anything much about the poorer classes in the way so brilliantly done for a rather later period by Professor Peter Burke.[56] Dr Reinhard Barth, already quoted here, used a good technique of examining town records for oblique evidence of lower-class opinion. But the popular written expressions of such opinion are only beginning to become plentiful at the end of the medieval period and have not yet received much detailed local study.

So the urban poor must be relatively neglected here, not because they escape the writer's mind but because he knows too little about them to offer more than generalities. It is clear that their numbers and proportions fluctuated according to place and time. Affluent Nuremberg knew less of teeming slums than most large towns like Augsburg and perhaps Freiburg im Breisgau, let alone a paradise of Tuscan bankers like Florence. Another commonplace, demonstrable from late medieval tax-returns, is that the better-off lived in the city centre; the huts and shacks of the poor were more likely to occupy outskirts and suburbs. For the rest, one might respectfully differ from Professor Maschke's suggestion that only modern industrialization brought deep inner conflict between rich and poor. Medieval theologians might write calmly of the providential hierarchy of Christian society, where poverty implied no personal blame, but copious evidence, some cited in this book, leaves little doubt that to comfortable burghers the poor, being frightening and dirty, carried also the tincture of wickedness about them. To the Augsburg chronicler in 1466 there was no point in consulting even weavers about taxes, for 'the deprived man always turns to the bad'.[58]

The patrician mind can be seen in greater detail, so must be discussed. In 1958 an interesting attempt to anatomize it was made by Heinrich Schmidt [58] in his study of three chronicles, from Augsburg, Nuremberg and Lübeck respectively. All were from the fifteenth century, and each was by one or more professional scribes accustomed to handling documents on public affairs. By considering what these men wrote apart from business matters, Schmidt thought he had found a circumscribed and introspective world, and went on to claim that these chroniclers mirrored the mentality of town oligarchs who saw the whole world in terms of their own city, almost without consciousness of time, and yielding a mere mass of undifferenced events in which the (to us) trivial and important were mingled in an ever-flowing stream.

To such chroniclers, according to Dr Schmidt, Christendom and 'the holy empire' were the same, and both were bounded by the town's horizon. The Nuremberg chronicler treats Sigismund's coronation in Rome, or Maximilian's release from Bruges in 1488, as effectively Nuremberg events, known and celebrated by fireworks and the pealing of bells. The Moslem world, however menacing, was a geographical blur. Rome itself was made concrete for the reader in terms of the seven Nuremberg churches where the Roman Indulgences might be earned. Roughly the same critique was made of the Lübeck and Augsburg writers for whom politics were events of the streets, not of abstraction, and for whom the outside world offered threats looming out of a fog of incomprehension. Town rights, especially those of imperial cities, were sacred; princes were in general highly menacing. For the rest, events follow pell-mell as signs, wonders and natural phenomena, the meanings of which were mystical rather than practical, and probably known only to God in any case.

Dr Schmidt's analysis contains much that is convincing and interesting, even if much too that is only to be expected, certainly of medieval reportage and indeed of some modern. These chronicles were written for domestic consumption, and it is not astounding that a great frost which killed the birds in the surrounding forest should be noted, or that the antics of a madman in the street should be remarked alongside a comment on the emperor's movements. The same occurs in modern newspapers, even if their lay-out is more ordered. Nor would one expect the lively interest shown by patriotic citizens about their past to be matched by scientific historical knowledge. When he points out the static sense of history in the town chronicles and the geographical parochialism which allows interest in great figures only when their doings affect the home city, he seems not so much wrong as stating something obvious in the popular writings of even advanced societies.

Later medieval Germany (including Switzerland) possessed a relatively very large number of professional town scribes and chroniclers. Quite often they were appointed from another city. Many of them spent lives in travel, in all kinds of capacity from envoy or scholar to common soldier. They were sometimes eye-witnesses of important events like the Council of Constance, the Toggenburg Succession War (1436–50), imperial audiences or the defeat of the Burgundians. They might, like Wassenberch of Duisberg, have vital documents passing through their hands, like Amerigo Vespucci's letter on his voyages to his friend Lorenzo de' Medici, simply because he, Wassenberch, was a member of the Order of Knights Hospitaller with its wide-ranging geographical connections.[59] A place did not have to be very big to hear about big events far away. Again, Dürer made maps of Germany showing the way to Rome, and even if Dürer was an exceptional man, presumably he made his maps for other more ordinary people.[60] Considering all the evidence of movement, of documents, oral reports and the chroniclers themselves, it is impossible to think of the German patrician world as a closed and ignorant one simply on the basis of chronicles the purposes of which were rarely scientific understanding. Dr Schmidt did right to portray the intellectual limitations of the patricians. If perhaps he considered only part of the evidence and made them seem greater bumpkins than they were, one might show their leading fears and prejudices more constructively by referring to evidence other than the chronicles.

Some more precise notion of patrician mentality may be gained, at least for Nuremberg, through the plays acted at its annual Carnival. More specifically, it might be argued from this literary source that the sense of civic identity was strong but that it derived less from the town's positive achievements, like its fine churches or almshouses or administration, than from certain fears (and hence hatreds) projected on to groups felt to be enemies of the town's safety and order. In the case of Nuremberg in the later fifteenth century these groups would appear to be the nobles, the Jews, the peasants and the Turks.

At the end of the middle ages the metropolis of Nuremberg was ruling over twenty-five square miles of surrounding territory. The walled city was intersected by a dense network of streets, and here lived the majority of the citizens. The patricians and the richer families obviously had more space than others and probably owned several estates. Although it was a very oligarchic community, undisturbed by rebellion since 1348–9, most of the craftsmen were themselves owner-occupiers of their houses, and one-family houses at that, which might belong to the same, relatively modest, family for generations. There was plenty of money about, and food was fairly cheap.[61] In this case, therefore (though not necessarily in other cities), there is reason to think that attitudes and assumptions were widely shared between both patricians and craftsmen, and that the Carnival was a joint production in which they could demonstrate with solidarity against outsiders. And outside in particular was the margrave of Brandenburg, who not so long since had been the hated Hohenzollern burgrave of the city and was still the most dangerous of its noble enemies; outside also were peasants who would have liked to get in and share the benefits of being Nurembergers (30 per cent of Nuremberg subjects already were in fact agriculturalists); near at hand, already in their ghetto, were the Jews, and not so very far away by now were the Turks; Nurembergers had been present in 1396 on the fatal field of Nicopolis, and the rapid Turkish advance was only halted for a time by the death of Mehmet II in 1481. Hence, all four potential threats were at hand, and it was these which were symbolically attacked in the annual Carnival.

The direct origins of the Carnival lie in the fourteenth century, but its fixed form, which gives an insight into the mentality of the burghers, comes from the fifteenth and early sixteenth centuries.[62] It took place at Shrovetide and began with a running parade through the town and dances by masked and costumed characters, known as the *Schembartlauf* from the masks and beards worn by the running and capering participants. As the wild parade went round the city, money was collected, especially from Jews and keepers of brothels. At the very end a huge float symbolizing Hell was burned in the market-place, but the main part of the entertainment in between was a series of plays enacted at inns on a number of set themes. These plays well illuminate the townsmen's preoccupations. A frequently-acted one was 'The Play of the Grand Turk', which originated in the 1450s and referred to the Turkish advance and the fall of Constantinople in 1453. The sultan meets councillors from the German cities who visit him under safe-conduct. These complain that the Christian princes cannot keep order and protect merchants and peasants. The Turk appears, rather ambivalently, as the new peace-keeper. When the nobles complain that such a role should not be given to a pagan, the sultan speaks of the evil living in Christian lands, and invites Christians to submit to him. The townsmen appear respectful and accommodating towards the Turk. In view of the terror which the Turks are supposed to have inspired in late medieval Europe, and indeed of the military support against them given by Nurembergers, this attitude of respect towards a frightful and barely understood enemy throws a harsh light on social divisions within Germany between towns and princes. Most of the other plays were very anti-semitic, and likewise contemptuous of peasants. Nurembergers lived very close to a peasantry which was often portrayed by Dürer and other artists, especially in south Germany, with great skill in showing them as misshapen, almost sub-human, and engaged in crude festivities.[63] German literature too depicts them as avaricious, envious imitators of their betters, pugnacious guzzlers and naturally brutish and lecherous.[64] Another Carnival play, 'The Play of the Pope, Cardinals and Bishops', concerned the condition of the true poor in Germany as victims of internal strife, ground between knights and nobles on the one side and the peasantry on the other, in which a fool, speaking with the voice of wisdom, which was his dramatic function, accused the nobility of idleness and pleasure-seeking and warned that only when their power was limited would peace return. The peasants are shown as brutal and lustful, and yet for the Carnival occasion a light-hearted sexual freedom is expressed, as occurs in one play where some peasants seek entry into citizenship (a significant theme) and are requested to prove their qualifications, which they do by highly outspoken boasts of sexual prowess. Also in the repertoire was a more highbrow disputation between a priest and a rabbi, which called for a good knowledge of the Bible and the Talmud. Even Nurembergers who could hardly follow this one would be gratified to realize that the rabbi lost the argument. More aggressive was the play which represented a mass-baptism of Jews and thus pinpointed at least the conscious reason for local hostility. In these ways every scene and every actor in the Carnival was able to give vent to his fears, discontents and inmost wishes. The solemn burghers let themselves go — perhaps vicariously through the younger men — and under the mask of clowning poured out the city feeling that nobles did not protect the land, that Jews, though a source of money, were deicides and worshippers of a sow, and that the peasant was a gross fool.

It may seem inconsistent that this section, which has concentrated at some lengths on discords between townsmen, should end by describing feelings which citizens seemed to share. The inconsistency is more apparent than real. For one thing, Nuremberg was a city where craft rebellion had not succeeded, partly because the powerful Butchers had aligned themselves with the patricians and partly because Charles IV had helped in putting down an attempted rebellion in 1348-9. For another thing, Nuremberg does not appear to have been the scene of bitter and continuous class strife, in spite of an abortive rebellion, nor is it easy to demonstrate that the place was ruled by class terror. Gilds and combinations of craftsmen were certainly not permitted, but the lesser citizens appear to have been exceptionally well-off in respect of housing and servants. The law was harsh but not specially directed at the lesser citizens. There was a high degree of regulation of economic and personal life which was tolerated and perhaps willed by the majority of citizens. One might go further and suggest that even in other German cities where rebellions occurred from time to time, they were in effect more of a periodic manoeuvring for position among burgher social groups than signs of any universal cleft within the bourgeoisie. The attractions of town life since the mid-fourteenth century may well have increased the basic solidarity among the inhabitants and sharpened the fear felt for outsiders, whether peasants hammering at the gates, princes intent on being political masters or lesser nobility who in certain areas lived by harassment. Nuremberg's Carnival externalized certain fears; but it was not the only city to have one. With some variations, Carnivals existed in Lübeck, as an import from Nuremberg in 1415, and in Strassburg, where Sebastian Brand created his own interpretation of human folly. Such themes appear also in illustrated books — the so-called *Geschlechtsbücher* — produced for the pleasure and instruction of patrician families, incorporating the coats of arms they assumed, and testifying to their nostalgia for an order they believed, with some self-deception, to be as old as the world. So despite the rebellions it is probable that there was an identifiable German burgher outlook, and that the rebels were not attempting at any time to revolutionize the order of their society but to claim more participation in it. The German towns of the late middle ages lived in a state of immense, defensive conservatism.

(e) *Town and country*

Earlier in the previous section it was suggested that prosperous families in German towns did not take their departure when they had made money, or at least did not do so with the ready facility of English burgesses and businessmen like the Celys, the Paycockes, the Chaucers and all the others who sought dignity and tranquillity in the country life of surburb or the provinces. Whether this contrast is entirely well-founded or not cannot be safely said in the present state of knowledge. But at first glance it looks as if late medieval Germans were much more anxious to get into towns than to leave them. Private warfare made the countryside more continuously dangerous than it was in England, for villages were the first to suffer, and to suffer designedly, in the feuds. Nor was any civil disturbance in late medieval England to be compared with the systematic savagery of the Hussite wars in which unfortified villages in, for instance, Silesia had nothing to save them from flames and massacres. Village desertions in the fifteenth century had something to do with the demographic trend, but there were other motives as well behind the desire to get into, or near, a town. Towns offered the safety of their walls. They offered a better living because, as increasingly concentrated centres of manufacturing, production and sale, they gave higher prices for agricultural produce. On their side towns could be glad of extra manpower for both menial and military purposes as well as for suburban food-growing.[65] In short, town life in later medieval Germany was coming to dominate country life in the sense that there was a drift to the towns and that the towns were in many ways better places to live in than the country. The peasant whose standard of living was lagging markedly behind that of the townsman was the object of pity and scorn, and the country areas in any case offered to townsmen few of the advantages (which were to be found in the English context) of cloth-making or peaceful knightly and noble households in their deer-parks, threatened only occasionally, and affluent enough to keep the squire's dreams from being troubled by visions of the investment he might be missing.

In Germany there were, of course, exceptions to this flight from the countryside, and further research will doubtless show more. Nurembergers possessed small lordships outside their walls and were patrons of churches in the countryside surrounding their city. Meissen and Leipzig both acquired property outside their walls in the mid-fourteenth century, and some of their inhabitants were known as 'farming townsmen' (*Ackerbürger*).[66] Mühldorf and Landshut in

Bavaria lay in a fruitful and relatively peaceful countryside under the Wittelsbach dukes and the Mühldorf Annals (1313–1428) give a strong sense of the intermingling between town and countryside. Some citizens lived outside the town boundaries but owed military service to the town itself.[67] Brunswick townsmen are said to have acquired rural land, to the annoyance of the local nobility.[68] In south-eastern Westphalia the fourteenth-century depopulation brought land into the hands of townsmen,[69] some of whom became 'noble', others of whom remained landed citizens of Münster, Soest or Paderborn.

A more detailed study of town-country relationships has fortunately been made for the south-western Baltic coastlands,[70] though again it cannot be said how typical were the conditions there. The hinterland of Mecklenburg was a little agricultural state, removed from important imperial or political affairs, but rich enough to give the north-east its first university (Rostock) in 1419. The towns (Wismar, Rostock, Stralsund and Greifswald) were first colonized mainly by immigrants from towns to the west who, in moving east, formed the first élites, but by the period 1250 to 1350 it was the surrounding countrysides which supplied the new settlers in the towns. By 1400 these towns were large: Rostock and Stralsund had about 13,000 inhabitants, Wismar perhaps 8000. But at about this point the town authorities began to consider such numbers too large, to penalize citizens who introduced foreigners or peasants, and to restrict gild membership. So far this accords with experience in other German towns, that is, that the later medieval period saw a flight to the towns and a relative depopulation of the countryside. In Rostock the proportion of the poorest class rose from 24 per cent of the whole population in 1378 to 64 per cent in 1569, with of course a corresponding decline in the numbers of the 'middling' classes. Entry into the town was allowed to some well-to-do peasants, but many poor ones were rejected. The whole area was one of cereal production, and there was a high demand in the coastal towns for consumption by the inhabitants and visitors, for export and for brewing. In Wismar in 1464 there were 187 indepedent brewers who used 2900 tons of barley every year, and the figures were commensurate elsewhere. All this was turned very much to the towns' advantage. They were able to fix prices and to compel the peasantry to go to particular markets. The purchase and sale of imported goods like cloth were also monopolized by the towns with the agreement of the nobility. The routes were easy to control, and the penalty for trying to sell elsewhere was confiscation. There was a bitter little joke on the island of Rügen that geese ferried to the mainland for sale instinctively turned their heads in the direction of Stralsund on stepping ashore. The towns themselves acquired possessions in the surrounding countryside, a fact which somewhat modifies the former view that the Hanseatics were not involved in the hinterland but left it wholly to the nobility. The older towns were acquiring lands and rents in their own neighbourhoods by the later thirteenth century (a hundred years earlier in the case of Lübeck). At first, townsmen might thus find themselves tenants of country noblemen, but increasingly they acquired jurisdiction as well as lands and rents, and sometimes they bought even the *Bede,* that universal basic ground-rent payable to a German feudal lord. In this way the availability of capital in the towns enabled townsmen to fulfil a virtually noble function in the environs, though without the military and noble trappings. As time went on the number of burgher landlords increased. It was they who received rents and services from the peasants, and they who lent money to the peasants at interest of 8 per cent to 10 per cent, often to enable the peasants to buy horses and farm equipment. Towns could also receive property in pledge for loans to lords and princes. A striking example is from the year 1437, when the duke of Schleswig owed Lübeck 18,000 marks against the pledge of the island of Fehmarn just off-shore. The island was redeemed after fifty-five years. In these ways towns as corporations could become landlords. But also corporations and individuals within towns could do the same. Within Rostock and Greifswald, for example, the new universities (founded in 1419 and 1456 respectively) became the lords of land outside those towns. Turning from Mecklenburg and Pomerania to Brandenburg, Dr Fritze has shown through Charles IV's *Landbuch* that burghers possessed a considerable amount of country property. The important point, however, is that only rarely did a townsman settle in the country. Burghers wanted security, good communications under their own control, and perhaps strong-points for defence: the peasants were made to work on walls, bridges and dykes, carry stone and supply horses and fodder. The country possessions were also used for income in cash and kind and as security for borrowing. But hardly ever were they made into rural retreats or emparked gentry estates after the manner of Greenwich and northern Kent at the same period, or, for the matter of that, after the manner of Brandenburg itself as Theodore Fontane knew it and described it in a later age, with its gracious country houses.[71] With a few exceptions the country possessions formed a collection of negotiable assets which individually moved rapidly from hand to hand. They were, in fact, very like stocks and shares, used for profit-taking as well as for income. Dr Fritze considers the profitability varied between 4.4 per cent and 13.3 per cent per annum, with a tendency to decline in the later fifteenth century. The effect on the peasantry may have been bad, but in the present context it is the nature of town life that is under discussion. The city fathers rarely turned into country cousins. They stayed in the town, where they conducted their business and took their profit.

(f)   *The well-being of towns c. 1500*

A note of pessimism sounds in the pages of German town chroniclers in the fifteenth century. Behind the pride of achievement fear is to be detected, as in the book of injuries done to Brunswick or the comments of Burkhard Zink of Augsburg as he watched the self-governing city of Mainz reduced to subjection by its own archbishop, Adolf of Nassau. Zink's mind moved easily to the oppressor of his own city, the Duke Ludwig of Landshut/Bavaria, who could only too easily bar the way to Venice. Indeed, Zink generalized easily out of a kind of timidity, for he did not understand that the failure of imperial cities to stick together was nothing new and nothing in itself sinister, since towns might benefit by princely interest as well as suffer. But we for our part must not generalize too easily out of boldness when so much remains to be done before a credible and comprehensive view of German towns can be offered. Still, there are some interim views worth collecting.

First, there was no chance in 1500, even if there ever had been, that the German towns could possibly behave as a coherent estate of the realm or follow any common policy. Earlier leagues had after all been defensive and for particular occasions or situations. The Swabian and Rhenish towns' defeat in 1388 at Döffingen in Württemberg in the Great Town War against a coalition of princes was not decisive because there would have been no decision had they won. The war was really one between groups of princes. Towns could be allies of each other and of princes but were in no way an independent and universal system, least of all in so vast and rambling a country as 'Germany'. They entered leagues and *Landfrieden* with princes, and against other towns and princes, and their political fates were highly various. An attempt has already been made to illustrate this. Even the Imperial Cities had varying and fluctuating fortunes, for they could lose their very status through debt or princely hostility, as did Mainz (1462) and Erfurt (1483) and many more in the sixteenth century. If they had regular representations in the Reichstag after 1489, they had no vote till 1648, and representations and votes were no compensation anyway for loss of business or loss of population. So it is best to look at some of the variables.[72]

In the north there was some decline in overall Hanseatic influence as the fifteenth century passed into the sixteenth and less business was done in the 'factories' in Bruges, Novgorod and London; Hanseatic privileges in Bergen came under attack and their trading monopolies were contested by the Dutch. Too much should not be made of these appearances of recession. But still, the political future of north Germany was with princely power, in Brandenburg especially, which called for a relatively greater amount of Hanseatic money to be spent on defences, and in time the greater political strength of Poland-Lithuania and of Russia enabled them, the rulers of those countries, to support their own merchants, not Germans. In fifteenth-century Brandenburg the towns were in full decay: their commons were deeply subservient to the patricians, and the patricians to the Hohenzollern margraves. Professor Carsten has pointed out that since these towns were almost exclusively trading ones it was an easy matter to shut them off from the outside world.[73] There was competition between towns too: even in Lübeck and Danzig on the coast, the Nurembergers got a foot in the one, and the Fuggers soon captured some of the copper trade of the other.

The picture is so uneven that one searches for a common criterion by which to judge town vitality. One, imperfect, criterion is the demographic one. Lübeck and Rostock were maintaining a stable population, while Hamburg and Danzig were developing, the one in the Atlantic trade, the other by using the Polish hinterland as a market. The variability was present over Germany as a whole. In the extreme south-west, Freiburg-im-Breisgau, Heilbronn and Constance were losing population on account of the displacement of transalpine trade. Many Swiss cities remained stable. Bern was in a favourable position here, and displaying a special self-confidence as it expanded into a virtual state and recorded its doings with pride in the commissioned chronicles of Konrad Justinger and Diebold Schilling. In Zürich the population was increasing.

An interesting group of towns, mostly optimistic and demographically buoyant, were connected by some interest or other in mining and the metal industry and trade. These were Görlitz in Lusatia, Leipzig, Zwickau and Chemnitz (Karl-Marx-Stadt), all in high production in the late fifteenth century, and not to fall back until the influx of American silver in the later sixteenth. Mining towns, especially silver mining, show a high degree of demographic fluctuation according to the workability and profitability of the deposits, and this is particularly noticeable in the *Erzgebirge* area just referred to. But Nuremberg, a good 250 kilometres to the south-west, was in a different case. Here was a great centre of metal-work production, which did not fluctuate, which has been noted before in these pages for its solidity and conservatism and which, with its curious combination of international trade and high-value manufactures, has remained across the ages a living urban area. Its population will be discussed in a moment. Perhaps it is worth the immediate effort of returning once more to this city to ask what such a community could mean round about the year 1500. The enquiries of this chapter began with the nature of German urbanization and concentrated deliberately on the political aspect, since it was one which was usually neglected. But have we yet any clear notion of economic urbanization, beyond a consciousness that Nuremberg had a European significance in the later medieval period? Her patricians and politicians left books and archives. But the innovations and manual skill of her craftsmen, the *Kleinbürger*, are almost without record except for the magnificent if stylized series of pictures belonging to the Mendel Foundation.[74] This was an almshouse for poor and honest artisans who had worked in Nuremberg, and a careful list has been kept of admissions during the fifteenth and early sixteenth centuries, each with a contemporary coloured illustration of the skill represented. The most illuminating way of seeing this industrial centre is simply to enumerate the crafts or craftsmen mentioned, for they must be nearly comprehensive:

Textiles: wool-combing, weaving, nap-raising, shearing, dyeing, tailoring, hat-making, thread- and cord-making, rope-making.

Leather: tanning, parchment-making, furrier, shoemaking, saddle- and harness-making, strap-making, purse-making.

Metal, wool and stone:

blacksmith, tool-making, plate-armour making, armour polishing, pan-smith, blade-smith, knife-making, spur-making, file-making, ring-making, tin-smith, lantern-making, wire drawing, nail-smith, locksmith, chain-mail making, goldsmith, bronze-beater, copper-smith, mug-beater, girdler, thimble-making, pewter pouring;

carpenter, cabinet-maker, wheelwright, cooper, rosary-maker, distaffmaker, wooden shoemaker, sawyer, wood-cutter;

mortar mixer, wall-maker, colour-washer, tiler, stone mason, plasterer;

horn-worker, writing material-maker, painter.

Trade: merchant, packer, weigher, sack-carrier, carter, loader, wood and coal measurer, customs officer, messenger, assayer.

Agronomy: builder, gardener, vine-dresser, steward, servant, daily wage-labourer.

Hunting and victualling:

bird-catching, net-fishing, baking, flour-sieving, slaughtering, brewing, inn-keeping, cooking, vintner.

Other: barber-surgeon, town watchman, bell-ringer, beadle, soldier, city scribe, gentleman-official of the city.

Most of the Nuremberg houses belonged to people like this, and most of them were one-family houses. In 1438 a visiting Spaniard likened it to his native Toledo in its size, antiquity and predominance of craftsmen, and he remarked on the numbers of bronze-workers and plate-armour makers, whose products were famous throughout Europe and even in West Africa. Yet it must be admitted that, after prolonged consideration of this list, only metalworking betrays any significant sign of specialization. Every other occupation could surely be found almost anywhere else. So aside from the financial and wholesale mercantile work, it was these people who kept one of Germany's most successful and renowned cities alive and awake with their industrious clatter, content with their rising incomes, and safe with their soldiers and beadles. The population of Nuremberg was constantly reduced by plague and increased by immigration from the countryside and a relatively high birth-rate. The censuses were occasional and doubtfully complete but provide more information than is usual for towns at this period. The population seems to have grown from about 13,750 in 1363 to a maximum of perhaps 22,797 in 1431, after which it remained steady for the rest of the century. The census of 1431 was made in order to enumerate the men of Nuremberg and its countryside capable of bearing arms, that is, between the ages of eighteen and sixty. Of these there were 7146. The overall analysis was as follows:[75]

Persons over 12	15,499
Citizens' children	6,173
Jewish children	52
Children of non-citizens	692
Secular clerics	69
Members of religious orders	312
	22,797

At the same time about 3585 houses were enumerated with an average of 6.4 inhabitants per house. This was not the same as households per house, as there were 4213 households, an average of about 1.2 households per house. But the statement that most artisans lived in one-household houses is borne out. A more accurate count was made in 1449–50 on the occasion of Albrecht Achilles's attack on the city, when the census disclosed 28,378 inhabitants together with about 2000 infants but declared that 9912 were refugees from the surrounding countryside.[76]

Taken together these facts and figures suggest a marked rise of population between about 1350 and 1450 followed by a period of stability in a city which was prosperous by medieval standards and without a really severe housing problem. The wealth came from long-distance trade and from some industry, especially in metal, armour and weapons, but with no sort of development which could be called industrial even in the early modern world.

Leaving aside both demographic generalities and the single

example of Nuremberg in the search for some clues to the well-being of German towns at the end of the middle ages, it will be best to end by considering personal initiatives. The efforts of professional merchants and merchant families dominate our scene. Urban Germany still seems a society of high-value trading rather than large-scale manufacture. The greatest names are those encountered before, like the Stromer of Nuremberg, which was virtually a company, or the Ravensburg Trade Society, founded in 1380 with eighty partners coming from any south German towns, and lasting till 1530. Yet such merchants formed only a minority, if a significant one, of the total population engaged in trade. In the fifteenth century more than 355 Cologne merchants are known to have visited the Frankfurt fair, and of these 40 per cent were of the patrician class: councillors, mayors, treasurers of the city. But that still leaves 60 per cent who were lesser people, and the character of German town life would not be properly understood without realizing the part played by undistinguished individuals, such as apprentices, spinsters and servants. Many Nuremberg craftsmen patronized the fair at Nördlingen. There were small savers who became in effect non-working partners in bigger mercantile enterprises, like the working girls in late fifteenth-century Augsburg, who had investments of as little as 10 guilders in the Hochstetter business.[77] In late fourteenth-century Hamburg, Vicko von Geldersen gave his maid the opportunity to share profits by making small contributions to his enterprises. Artists were also in the business, like the ill-fated Veit Stoss of Nuremberg, creator of the Angelic Greeting which hangs to this day in the great church of St Lorenz, who lost 1265 guilders he had invested with Jakob Paner; or Albrecht Dürer himself, seller of his own creations. Mining shares were both tricky and tempting. Brokers in Leipzig and Frankfurt dealt in them, and the wisdom of spreading investment over a lot of little mines was early realized, since any one mine might become flooded or worked out or, on the contrary, yield a good deal of ore. A fine visual impression of this industry is given in the illustrated *Graduale* of Kutná Horá (Kuttenberg). The majority of investors lived in the new silver towns in Saxony. Professional merchants might couple mining investment with the metal trade, as well as maintaining an interest in other commodities, achieving thus both vertical integration and diversification. Mining shares were also bought from time to time by corporate investors like the Philosophical Faculty of Leipzig

University in 1477. The Dürer money came from shares in copper and gold. Scanning the list of share-holders in precious and semi-precious metals, one encounters representatives of all German society except peasants.

The instances of both professional and amateur investment may stand for other concerns too, from small shares in Hanseatic shipping up to loans made to cities or kings by town patricians. Augsburg is of course famous for the Fuggers, whose ancestor Hans came there in 1367 from the neighbouring village of Graben and began as a weaver, and whose descendant Jakob could be noted by the Augsburg chronicler in 1525 as 'the glory of all Germany'. Speyer was the leading capital market in southern Germany in the later middle ages and Hamburg was important in the north, but there was a network of money-lending families over the face of all Germany except the eastern territories.

Already, before Luther, criticisms were heard of mere money-making, even by reformers and humanists like Conrad Celtis, a man whose emancipated outlook did not prevent him from maintaining a medieval attitude of *dirigisme* towards economic activity. On the other hand there was Conrad Peutinger, jurist, humanist and town scribe to Augsburg, who defended the economic processes, including monopoly. So too did Willilbald Pirkheimer in Nuremberg. With this debate the present book cannot deal, other than to note that it existed as part of the urban scene. The main purpose will be served if the diverse and often intricate activity in German towns is shown in conjunction with primitive industry and dominant princes.

6

Countryside Communities

About 80 per cent of Germans lived in rural communities, but there is a major contrast between the kind of village to be found in Old Germany and that in the colonial settlements to the east. In general terms, western villages grew in irregular forms, eastern ones were planned.

From the North Sea eastwards to the rivers Elbe and Saale and in the whole vast area southward to the Danube valley the villages, whether they were large or small, were of irregular form. In most of these countrysides there was a mixture of the substantial settlement, what in England might be called the 'nucleated' village (*Dorf*), with the hamlet comprising a few buildings (*Weiler*). But in some parts of this area, for example in Westphalia, in parts of Bavaria and round Lake Constance, there were regions where the communities were smaller, formed of hamlets and single farmsteads in relative isolation. In all western and central Germany the villages and hamlets had been formed unevenly during a centuries-long tide of settlement which flooded more strongly in the twelfth and thirteenth centuries.

It was different in the east. North of Bohemia and east of the Elbe was the land of planned settlement, wherever Germans moved in. The village forms were mostly regular: circular in some frontier regions but elsewhere usually linear in shape with dwellings strung out along a green or a street. These plans were imposed by the organizing agents of settlement, the locatores, as a way of allocating regular shares to the settlers and arranging from scratch a convenient mode of cultivation. In this way a family might have its length of arable stretching away from the central line of farmsteads at right-angles, out into forest, pasture or marsh, with garden area retained close by the houses.

Both in west and east fencing and hedging were of prime importance, not just to control the cattle, as in the laws of King Ine of

Wessex, but to guard against the incursions of hostile men. Up to and beyond the fifteenth century, German villages were used to the terrors of plundering attack, whether from robber-knights, mercenaries, Hussites or other agents of destruction. In the later medieval period there was a tendency to construct rural buildings more securely and in more defensible conformation for the sake of protecting both inhabitants and livestock.[1] Anyone who looks at Dürer's sketches for 'The Prodigal Son' must be impressed by the sense of massive enclosure from the great barns standing together round the central yard.

The village communities of Old Germany can often be seen through the great series of surviving custumals described in Chapter 1. The custumal *(Weistum)* exists in many different forms and comes from many parts of western and central Germany, but as a group they read more like agreements than decrees and the question arises whether they are portraying a country where lords were fixing the conditions of rural life in writing as they wanted them, in their own interests, or whether they are a sign of peasant resistance and even liberation from the more stringent bonds of the past. It is not a question that can be answered very simply. The contents of these documents often suggest peasant liberties. On the other hand, they were lords' documents and drawn up by lords' agents, just as much as were English manorial custumals. The villagers were questioned and they answered, but sometimes insistently or abrasively. Both contents and tone of voice depend on the particular circumstances of time and place.

It need hardly be said that the village community *(Gemeinde)* was an unequal one, quite apart from any agent of a lord who might be on the spot to supervise. As in all villages everywhere there were elders who had authority, usually because they had more land or more wealth than the others, more years on their backs, and no doubt belonged to one of the leading local peasant families. Their spokesman went under different names. *Dorfgraf*, 'village count', was one such. Collective judgements and decisions were given by the 'good and legal men' who have their title in many languages: *jurati, scabini, échevins, Schöffen.*

The tests of freedom are even more complex than in England. There were still serfs here and there in Old Germany, and at the very end of the middle ages, as will be seen, there was a tendency for the conditions of bondage in some places to be aggravated. But the custumals do not say much about the serf, the *Leibeigener*, whose body

171

belongs to his lord. On the other hand, the custumals have much to say about men who are 'free'.[2] But were they really free? This is not to ask if they could go where and when they wanted, for freedom of that sort, dependent upon wealth, is a different kind of question. It is reasonable to ask, however, if men and women who appear as part of the customary community were free of dependence on the arbitrary will of a lord. The general truth seems to be that the 'free' men of the custumals were free in particular, agreed respects; if they had been totally free they would not have appeared in the custumal at all. For example, there were 'free' men on the land of St Peter's church at Soest in Westphalia, and they could inherit freely from their parents, but the four-footed animals reverted to the lord when the father died. Presumably they could be redeemed by some sort of payment and so we have a variety of heriot. Elsewhere among the custumals many individual freedoms are noted: to buy and sell produce, to marry off children as the family wished, and so on. But freedoms are taken to be both specific and to have been (graciously) granted. Sometimes it is dressed up, and a peasant community has its 'old' freedoms confirmed to it by a lord who is in fact making concessions because he wants to keep his tenantry, or has even been worsted by them in some sort of conflict, or, like the abbot of St Gall after he bought the lordship of Toggenburg in 1399, needed the favour of local men. There was often a customary freedom to move about at will, but this was a grant of free movement, not a consequence of free condition.

In short, German peasant rights, so far as they emerge from the custumals, were precise and specific rights. There is no talk of abstract right. In sixteenth-century Luxemburg there were some virtually independent men, subject to the count's court but not to any landlord, who yet had to seek out the local lord wherever they happened to be in the county and give him some small symbolic service in return for protection.

The custumals of the later middle ages were created out of two contrary pressures: 'a slow but continuing and successful struggle against specific bondages', as H. Wiessner put it; and a continuing attempt on the part of lords to keep jurisdiction over men, even when they wanted to move into a nearby town or another district. In the later fifteenth century the pressures became greater. There are more examples of peasants and lords in conflict, particularly over the crucial questions of forest use, cattle grazing and the jurisdiction of the lord's court. Peasants stand up and demand their ancient and accustomed rights to take wood and to hunt, and sometimes too the removal of a severe judge. The tone of their voices in dialogue with their lord is heard to change from poor people's request to complaint and even to refusal of submission,[3] and the change coincides with the lords' efforts to improve their own position.

Relationships between village communities and lords naturally depended to a large extent upon what kind of lords they were. English historians have often shown the greater demand of church lordships, especially Benedictine monasteries, for produce and physical services, of non-corporate lordships for cash revenue, and so on. The German scene is not a mirror-image, partly because there was less direct demesne exploitation and partly, one may guess, because jurisdiction played a more important part in a world where royal justice was not ubiquitous. A few examples will suggest the kind of impact lords in different German circumstances might have on the communities under them.

The imperial convent of nuns at Essen was aristocratic, rich, demanding and nervous. The Chapter, under its lady provost, was much concerned in 1338 that the death or departure of bailiffs should not lead to loss of farm stock, negligence of court suitors, or even dilapidation of the beds in which the serfs slept, and they required all tenants 'unfree, or those who pay wax rents, or others' to have appropriate weapons, which were never to be pawned 'on account of the danger from the local invaders of the district'. The document *(Weistum)* setting out in minute detail the equipment and livestock to be maintained on every farm was promulgated in the room over the nuns' dormitory on the morning of 7 July in the presence of the convent's bailiffs *(Schulzen)*, one of whom was also advocate of a neighbouring collegiate church *(Kirchenvogt)* and another of whom was a judge in Essen.[4]

Not all big monasteries even at that period managed their estates directly. Many German peasants were tenant-farmers under the general leasing condition (which contained variations) called *Meierrecht*. It is not an accident that Meier is so common a German name. The famous Cistercian monastery of Bebenhausen near Tübingen had some lands at Plienigen, now a pleasant suburb near Stuttgart airport, where the farmers cultivated their own grain and flax and paid a proportion of the crops to the monastery. At harvest time the monks sent a day-labourer to each farmer to collect the monastery's share. The notional agreement was that the farmers should feed the collectors and bear the cost of transporting the produce for one mile from Plienigen. That left the monks to pay for about eleven miles' transport.[5]

Even more favourable to the villagers were conditions in Pfronten and Füssen, south of Munich and on the Swiss border. These places belonged to the provost of Augsburg, who possessed high jurisdiction there but was showing himself anxious to keep his tenants at a time when there was vacant land. In 1403 he drew up with them an agreement in twenty-one paragraphs.[6] The obligations seem light. The tenants had to pay money at Whitsun, about £6 collectively, some oats at Christmas time, and to come twice a year to the steward's court, where each gave a penny. Service for their property was then completely discharged, and the tenants' land could be freely inherited or alienated. In the lord's eyes the important thing was that all transactions should be done in his court. The agreement is a good instance of a church landlord trying to hold on to his tenants in a region of big towns, other ecclesiastical landlords, and considerable mobility.

In contrast with these *grands seigneurs* of the Church is the simple lord of Kmehlen in Electoral Saxony, already encountered briefly in Chapter 3.[7] He appears to history from his tax-return, stating his possessions and income in phrases which minimize his assets and maximize his burdens, but the detail allows a vivid glimpse of the little communities whose lives revolved round their master. They seem different from those we have just been glancing at. At Essen, Plienigen and Pfronten the rural population seem somehow more distanced from their lords, who were ecclesiastical, corporate, in one case feminine, and always a good way off. But here in the person of this Saxon gentleman, Seiffard von Lüttichau, we have an almost physical impression of the local lord, master, husband, father, half farmer, half soldier who lived in danger yet in peace, could take command in a moment yet shout familiarly to his labourers about the state of the soil.

The family lived well, if roughly. Spices and southern fruits appear in the household along with veal, goose and expensive fish, though the farm buildings needed repair. Lady Seiffard was alive and mother to a son and four daughters who were tolerably well clothed. They lived in the fortified farmstead at Kmehlen (near Görlitz?) with a household staff headed by the steward and including a scribe, porter, captain of the guard and various domestics such as lady's maid and the nanny. (Across the centuries the historian hears the law of King Ine in Wessex: 'If a gesithcund man wish to depart he may taken with him his reeve, his steward and his children's nurse'.) Seiffard rode about accompanied by two esquires, and had a good expensive stove for comfort on his return. The home farm lay round about, arable and pasture with cattle and sheep, and there were about thirty peasant families there too. Seiffard had four *Hufen*, fifteen leading peasants had one each (in this area, between sixty and 100 acres), and the rest lesser amounts down to four peasants who had only gardens. The text says specifically that those who had only dwellings and gardens had to look for their livelihood as day-labourers.

As well as Kmehlen, Seiffard was lord of the villages of Blochwitz, Little Kmehlen, Great Thiemig, Frauendorf and the Frauenwald, which was presumably just forest. In all these places there were peasants holding arable and cultivating hop-gardens and vegetables, and there was also more of the lord's demesne arable and pasture on a modest scale with, that year, about a thousand sheep altogether. There were ponds, hop-gardens, and attempts at vineyards.

Even if we bear in mind the self-justificatory nature of a tax-return, Seiffard emerges as a caring lord. He remarked that many of his people were poor, and in years of bad harvest he stood surety for them when they had to borrow corn. His peasantry worked for him partly in respect of ploughing and other services they owed, and partly as paid labourers. Though some wheat was grown, of which the parish priest took fourteen bushels tithe, the document speaks more of poor, sandy soil on a hilly terrain, of oats, barley and buckwheat, of dirty ponds which were costly to repair and fill. At a guess, Seiffard was lord of about 150 peasant families amounting perhaps to 800 or 1000 souls, apportioned between five villages. His father had been there before him, and they stood in some sort of service relationship with a religious house for which he supplied a carting service, though doubtless through his own servants. It is in the main a picture of a self-subsistent lesser nobleman of Upper Saxony who kept good order, exercised minor jurisdiction and went to church in Sunday clothes. There is an eighteenth-century flavour about him.

A quarter of a century earlier this had been in the path of savage Hussite columns, and the area had been devasted in the late 1420s and 1430s. The village community described above suggests resilience and leadership. A few miles to the east was Silesia, and then the east began, with Poland beyond and further still the Teutonic Order's territory.

In that eastern German world, and pre-eminently in Prussia, the village communities were different. Here we know them not by the variegated custumals drawn up from time to time between local lords and village elders, but through a type of writing remarkable for its standard form. This was the deed of foundation, which is easier to render by its German name, the *Handfeste*. All *Handfesten* were based on the German town law of Kulm, on the river Vistula south of Danzig.[8] The Prussian area was huge and well-documented and mostly belonged to a single lord, the Teutonic Order, so it is convenient to illustrate east German communities from it, even though other eastern regions could show variations.

Here is a written deed of 12 February 1418 showing the foundation of an ordinary village. It is probable that the villagers had already collected there some time before under the leadership of Tydeman, who as land-agent or *locator* was also the *Schulz*, and no doubt their houses were already built and cultivation had started. In the middle ages written deeds usually follow the physical ones. This text is translated with some abbreviation from the German:[9]

The Marshal of the Teutonic Order says that the late Brother Werner von Tettingen had given 34 *Hufen* [perhaps 3000 acres, with boundaries named] with oral instructions that a village called Thiemsdorf should be founded, named after Tydeman, the *Schulz*, to whom he had given the land. This is now ratified by the Order, and Tydeman is to have it, according to Kulmic law, with four *Hufen* especially for himself and his legitimate heirs in inheritance. He is to have jurisdiction and a third of its profits, though jurisdiction over native Prussians is reserved to the Order. Tydeman and his heirs are to serve the Order with horse and military equipment and to render 'plough-corn', like the other bailiffs in German and Kulmic villages. As to the tenants of the other thirty *Hufen*, they are to render three farthings in ordinary Prussian coin every 2 February together with two hens, one and a half bushels of oats as 'plough-corn' on 10 November, and also to render to their parish priest one bushel of rye and one of oats as tithe on 10 November. Witnessed at Königsberg. Seal.

German peasants like these were immigrant settlers from the west, or descendants of such. They came from communities already well habituated to organizing themselves round a local court, the parish church and the communal meadows, and if they were now dwellers on the Order's land they lived under the remote sway of a known, single, corporate and unchanging lord. There was no question of a personal relationship with the lord in the annual round. In Brandenburg it was different, but for the German villager in Prussia authority was represented by the village mayor or bailiff (again it is best if possible to use the German word *Schulz*, which can have no exact equivalent in the west). He may, like Tydeman, have been the village's actual founder, under the Order's patronage and ratification, or he may have inherited or even bought the office. To him the German villagers looked for justice in all but the gravest matters. They paid him their rents and in theory received supervision of their services. But there must have been difficulties here, for above all the *Schulz* was a man with military duties.[10] It was a dangerous country, frequently at war, and war was indeed the origin and purpose of its settlement. Even the villagers could be called out from time to time for local defence, but the *Schulz* with his armour had wider obligations, and it must therefore be supposed that he could be frequently absent. That involved economic sacrifice, unless he had family and household to keep his own large holding going; and it must have meant too that the running of village affairs, agrarian and otherwise, devolved upon the village seniors. At a great battle like Tannenberg in 1410 it is likely that many hundreds of village *Schulzen* were lost. Altogether the nominal village chief must have changed quite often. It is certainly true that it could be held by a woman, though her military duties would have to be performed by proxy. The tenurial security and privileges written into the *Handfeste*, proper to the settler stage, can hardly give a clear and convincing picture of what the community was like in later generations.

We return, in fact, to the dominance of the elders, the *Schöffen*; chosen by the community, acting in court under the presidency of the *Schulz* when he was there, and able on occasion even to alter the conditions of the *Handfeste*.[11] Some of these documents use the expression 'community of the village' or 'community of the countrymen' in the context of surplus land being made over as communal meadow, wood or pasture.

There were other figures than the *Schulz* who were dominant locally. In the course of time millers became increasingly independent. The parish priest cut an important figure, endowed with twice the standard amount of land, recipient of tithe guaranteed on oath by the villagers, and served on his own land by 'church peasants'. Parish regulations too have an authoritarian ring. But then, any countryman from Scotland or England must be aware that it is rarely minister or parson who by himself imposes a quality on the community. Elders, church-wardens, parochial council are chosen for their positive or negative qualities, and there can be no enforceable laws which override the interplay of strong characters and retiring ones within small communities ruled by natural oligarchs and their wives. So in Prussia the historian can note the presence of men chosen to look after the parish church's structure and maintenance, to represent it on archidiaconal and diocesan assemblies, to exercise the moral vigilance entrusted to local officials variously called *testes*, 'jurors for the synod', and *denunciatores*. But the reality must always escape us. The historian may take account of small towns, not far away but little different from the village, of the presence of garrisons, the widely permitted private brewing, the frequency of inns, the lack of royal presence but the pervasiveness always of the military and authoritarian tone. What he will make of it must be left to individual reflection, but there is yet room for research and surmise on these eastern village communities.

Though it has not been possible to do more than sketch impressionistically how the village communities of western and eastern Germany differed from each other, the main contrasts of form and circumstance seem plain enough. But the discussion has so far been deliberately limited to a static historical comparison between the two major regions. Time, though, was not standing still. During the late medieval period considered in this book there were great economic and social changes in the German lands, as in other parts of 'Europe', and these must now be passed in review. At the same time it will be opportune to soften slightly the stark contrasts between east and west which have been sometimes accepted.

To state this case briefly at once: it has been argued, on the whole rightly, that peasant life in western Germany grew freer between the thirteenth and the fifteenth century, largely because manpower was first drawn eastwards and then reduced by plagues. Consequently, labour was at a premium and lords competed both for it and for jurisdiction. East of the Elbe, on the other hand, a reverse process occurred and a peasant society born in the relative freedom and enterprise of the frontier began a long move towards peasant serfdom under noble masters whose burdens they could not evade and towns which would not let them in. Of course this is a bare statement. Further study has suggested, and will probably go on suggesting, that even in the east there lived some peasants who prospered in relative freedom, and that even in the west the country poor suffered not only from physical and spiritual disabilities but in certain areas felt a tightening of the bonds of an actual serfdom which had never wholly disappeared. But the elementary changes must occupy us first.

After the thirteenth century, the high tide of colonization began to ebb. No one is wholly sure how this happened, but without doubt the birth-rate in Germany, as elsewhere, began to decline and the death-rate to increase. In a pre-industrial society a narrow differencing in these rates quickly changes an excess of births into an excess of deaths, and the resulting depopulation is seen in the desertion of villages, either partially so that they become smaller, or wholly so that they disappear altogether.[12]

The desertion of villages was not evenly distributed throughout Germany. Areas which had been most recently colonized were often the first to empty. There was a more or less 50 per cent loss of villages in middle Germany, that is, in parts of Hesse, Thuringia and Saxony. There was serious but less drastic loss (20 to 40 per cent) in large regions of southern Germany, that is, Swabia and Bavaria, and in the north-east colonial lands. It is interesting that there was a more negligible loss in the anciently colonized lower Rhineland and in north-western Germany.

The most severe period of this population loss and consequent retreat from cultivation was the century 1350 to 1450 or thereabouts. Professor Abel suggested that perhaps forty-seven out of 170 thousand villages were lost between the high-tide of medieval settlement and the later days of the middle ages. Although warfare and feuding must be taken into serious account in a land so afflicted with violence, it is still hard to question the accepted view that disease was the main culprit, since plague has been incriminated in the same way at the same time in almost every other region of Europe. And if Mme Carpentier was right,[13] the Bohemia which killed so many of its own people in violent strife was let off a little more lightly by the infection of disease. In short, as the proverb went, it was the plague that gave elbow-room: *Die Pest hat Raum gemacht.*

The consequences of this demographic change have often been rehearsed and are indeed simply told, but they are not without their puzzles. Labour became relatively scarce and the wages of the unskilled rose more than proportionately to those of the skilled. There was, over a longish term, a decline in both demand for and production of cereals. In this respect some work on pollen analysis has confirmed literary statements and archival reckonings. The retreat from corn cultivation did not of course mean a dramatic reinvasion by scrub and forest everywhere in Germany, but brought a tendency to relinquish inferior corn lands. Good harvests were still possible, as in the 1370s. But there was some change in land-use and in habits of diet which came to accord with the higher spending power of a diminished working population. Meat consumption rose, and cattle-raising and importing increased to supply the demand. German domestic cattle-breeding flourished in East Friesland and elsewhere. Detailed regulations survive from 1391 to show how the archbishop of Salzburg regulated his own cattle-breeding.[14] In the Cologne market of 1492 were cattle from Hungary, Poland, Denmark and Russia. Attention was paid not only to meat production but to fruit growing for the market, especially in the south-west, while wine production was attempted in Silesia and as far north as Prussia, and vegetables and hops were grown everywhere. There are therefore opposites to be reconciled: depopulated villages, together with some increase in prosperity and variety of diet. As Dr Mayhew wrote: 'Islands of prosperity and even development were found in an ocean of decay and desolation!'[15]

If this is true, then why did so many country people want to migrate to towns? Whilst there is debate about the absolute rise or fall of population in particular towns, Albrecht Timm argued that towns indeed grew as a proportion of total settlement in Germany at the expense of the countryside in the fourteenth and fifteenth centuries. In earlier days developing towns had been fed by nearby villages; their own hinterland was their reservoir. In the later medieval period urban immigrants came rather more often from further away and, if not in larger numbers, at least as a pressure of poorer folk to whose admission the towns increasingly objected. Konrad Fritze[16] has shown in some detail the attractions of Baltic towns like Rostock for country people, and the townsfolk's hardening hostility to their entry. Karl Czok too[17] has made an interesting analysis of town-suburbs in fifteenth-century Saxony and Thuringia to show how they became (as, no doubt, in other regions) places of refuge for those who had fled from the countryside. Suburbs were not so much retreats for the affluent (like Chaucer's Greenwich) as flotsam-lines between town and country. Here might be seen conflict between the two as well as some community of wretchedness between refugees from villages and the poorest of the town. In physical terms this would appear as compulsory labour on walls and fortifications, sub-standard wages, shanties within sight of garbage or gibbets. For some this was better than the conditions of the past. Erfurt at least offered the protection of its outer wall. Other towns might be glad of cheap labour or even emergency militia, and a villager whose lord had enclosed pasture or raised dues might find the trade-off acceptable.

But the attractiveness of towns must not be over-generalized. The countryside was diversified and in places productive: in vines, hemp, woad, saffron or cattle. It was usually the bigger towns which had most to offer, and longest, to the poor peasant. Middling craft towns yielded a miserable livelihood.

So the picture must be examined carefully and in detail. Towns varied and were getting harder to enter. But on the whole the German countrysides of the late middle ages were not happy places. There was increasing differentiation between richer and poorer peasants. Rural landlords, as will be seen, were turning the screw, and were the harshest enemy. The Peasants' War of 1525 is, for once, an exact description: it was a country movement.[18]

The German experience has incidentally a special lesson for those of us English historians who have been happy in the thought that the fifteenth century was a 'golden age of the wage labourer'. The limited truth embodied in Thorold Rogers's famous aphorism has stealthily been enlarged to suggest that it could be a happy fate to be born a peasant. True, the phrase was argued from a changing English scene, and the German one was plainly more unpleasant, less protected. But even at best the peasant life has earned too much vicarious enjoyment. How do even two meat meals a day compensate for a lifetime's labour on the land? And do a few more durable possessions adequately reconcile the majority of country workers and their sons to a life in which clothes are often soaking wet, toil little aided by mechanization but at the mercy of natural hazards, new faces unlikely to be friendly?

Perhaps a townsman makes himself ridiculous by writing of such matters, but it remains doubtful whether a fifteenth-century labourer would be wholly content with any explanation of the price-scissors.

There are some more precisely evidenced reasons for the towns' attractiveness to German peasants in the later medieval period. One was the relative safety of walls at times of devastating feuds and private wars, not to speak of the Hussite irruptions. However good the price of livestock or crops, it does not take long to destroy them. To take a single illustration, in a campaign between two rival brothers of the Wettin family in Saxony in 1456, sixty villages were burned in one day.[19] Some towns also offered better prices than villages for produce, and the possibility of different, better-paid or more agreeable work, hopes, even if illusory, of self-betterment, and more things to buy. The chance of escape from new or higher seignorial charges will be considered in a moment.

At one time the influx of men from the country to town was welcome there. They meant workers and defenders. But by the fifteenth century gild restrictions and other measures limited immigration, and it seems to be from this time, unless literature is putting us on a false trail, that anti-peasant satire rises to a new harshness. If a single biting phrase may do duty for the whole torrent of insult described by scholars, it could be the words of Felix Hemmerlein, canon of Zürich, during the wars of 1450 between Zürich and the Forest Cantons: 'However much you wash and comb a dog, it remains a dog, ... so peasant folk, and they are best in suffering, worst in happiness.'[20]

The restriction on country people from easy entry into towns delivered them the more readily into the hands of great landlords and princes. W. Abel has explained the seignorial problems of the fifteenth century. The price of corn and the lease-prices of land both decreased. It was difficult to get land cultivated because labourers had become relatively scarce and their wages relatively high. Seignorial income fell. Landlords could try to deal with these problems by the use of blandishments and threats, and the documents show both.

Reference has already been made to concessionary grants of freedoms of various kinds. During the later part of the fifteenth century, however, there were more occasions when the actions of lords, particularly in south-west and central Germany, distressed the rural communities. The problem has become contentious because peasant revolts in the later fifteenth and earlier sixteenth century, and the explosion of the Peasants' War in 1525, have naturally attracted scholars who wish to apply fundamental theoretical explanations.[21] To some the peasants were revolting against a demesne economy based on forced labour, though a widespread and thorough regression to serf conditions has not yet been demonstrated. To some, German peasants were egged on by the example of 'Swiss liberties', though the Swiss themselves were not free from peasant revolts. Günther Franz's general view that peasants were fighting for their rights against modernizing princes who were denying them free access to forest and river, contrary to 'the old law', has not yet been upset by fresh evidence and is suspect more because it is not new than because it is demonstrably false.

It would be foolish to suppose that there is a single and simple answer to the late medieval disturbances in peasant communities, and it is likely that threats were felt both from landlords with profits to think about and from princely rulers whose objects were political as well as economic.

The freedom of the forest for those who cleared and used it (*Rodungsfreiheit*) had a long history in Germany, where the rigour of an English forest law had not prevailed. If changes in the requirements of production called for a greater amount of timber, this kind of ancient freedom would be easily threatened. The encroachment of forest on hitherto cultivated areas was not wholly a consequence of village desertions but sometimes of a deliberate policy of afforestation on the part of lords with mining and timber interests.[22] It would be to the detriment of peasant communities when there was wholesale cutting, attempts to limit or even prevent hunting, and the exaction of high rents for the forest pasturing of animals.

A more generalized assault upon peasant communities was the quite widespread attempt to raise rents, dues, services and taxes where this seemed possible. Violent resistance to such policies does not need peasant poverty or peasant affluence to explain it, any more than rebellion in the towns against the patricians and their tax-men proves anything about the rebels except that they had the determination to resist. In England a country rebellion could expect little mercy: 'the ax was sharp'.But there were also certain safety valves, like royal protection of copyhold. German peasants were probably especially vulnerable for lack of a royal court system which might mitigate lordly excesses, and for their increasing rejection by towns which at other times might have accepted more of them within the walls. In such circumstances in the fifteenth century, lords were sometimes finding that they had the physical power to compel peasantries to pay up, and even to enserf them. The possibility is proclaimed by its very prohibition. As early as 1355 Charles IV had forbidden the oppression of the peasants in his own territory of Lusatia, especially with taxes and unaccustomed dues, whereby his land might be ruined.[23] In the fifteenth century there was no such king about, and the Habsburg stewards in south-western Germany were oppressors like other princes, such as Württemberg, Baden, and the bishoprics and great abbeys of the south. The abbots of Kempten provide a good example of lords who in the fifteenth century tried to create an unfree subject tenantry, irrespective of actual historical differences in status among their peasant population and the free customs of many. Overall prohibitions were issued against movement and against marriage outside the abbey's jurisdiction, and every tenant was reduced to the position of a rent-paying serf. This initiative was prolonged, dramatic and ultimately successful for the abbey, despite its perjury and the appeals of peasant communities to neighbouring towns, nobles and the emperor himself. There were similar cases elsewhere, aiming to unify lordship over the subject tenantry and to make the lordship personal, not just a right over certain land.[24]

Sometimes peasant communities were not so accessible, as when they lay topographically within the lands of a lord but for historical reasons not within his jurisdiction. In such cases there were often exchanges of peasant communities between lords who could then integrate their new acquisitions and enserf them with the rest. In March 1348 the count and countess of Hohenberg in Hechingen (near Tübingen) exchanged their serfs and their offspring with those of the abbey of St George in the Black Forest.[25] This kind of thing happened more frequently from the late fourteenth century onward, as towns were less willing to protect serfs who fled or grant burghal rights to villagers within the ambit of their own jurisdictions.[26]

There remain many problems to be solved, such as how some lordships could 'territorialize' their serfs and others not; for despite attacks on the freedoms won by peasant communities in the west, and despite the risings and rebellions which culminated in the Peasants'

War of 1525, it is not true that serfdom was reimposed wholesale in Old Germany. Further regional research is needed to explain the varying degrees of princely power over local peasantries. In the meantime it seems clear that in the years up to 1500 Germany displayed a painful triangular tension between peasant communities, towns, and landlord-princes. It is perhaps less than useful to look for culprits, even though it is hard not to feel a greater sympathy with the country workers than with impoverished noblemen. To understand the continued social divisions in Germany is more enlightening than simple indignation.

In the east the decline of peasant settlers into serfdom has long been studied and recognized. But just as our view of the emancipation of the western peasant must be modified as research goes on, so in the east the rise of serfdom seems not to be an unbroken tale of communities and men fallen on evil days.

To large tracts of north-eastern Europe the fifteenth century brought harsher peasant conditions. The region was affected by a declining population and falling grain prices, just as was western Europe. In the east, however, lords were evidently able to impose heavier dues and services on a peasantry which could not escape to towns or better themselves by town markets and town protection, for towns were fewer and unequal to the power of great landlords. In parts of eastern Germany the lower nobility met the problems of demographic decline and falling receipts not by abandoning direct cultivation but, on the contrary, by becoming more energetic producers for the market and increasing grain production. Peasants who could not simply run away were forced to work harder and increase their payments. As for the well-to-do burghers in places like Rostock, they found a community of interest with the landed nobility.[27] In Prussia the severe shortfall of the Order's income after the defeats at the hands of the Poles in 1410 and 1466 forced it too to increase peasant burdens, sometimes even three- or four-fold.

The fate of village communities in fifteenth-century Mecklenburg, Pomerania and Prussia is still hard to see clearly. The early published evidence has tended to include vivid literary items, and the famous instance of the Lubbe family from the Danzig region may or may not prove exceptional.[28] At all events it shows the possibility of a family chronicle of a peasant family into which one Jakob was born in about 1400. It was a household rich enough to afford pilgrimages and lavish works of charity. The central point of the tale is the desire of Jakob to sell up and go into town as a citizen. (Obviously a really prospering peasant had such an option). But filial piety, so it went, kept him on the land to marry the daughter of another peasant. Their son did indeed make it as merchant in Danzig, and the farm went to a daughter, but even she is held up as something special: the first woman in the family to be able to read and write. Forbidden to enter a convent by the family, she had her books confiscated and was married off young to another rich peasant. The tale is disagreeable and it is a pity that Herr Günther Grass has not used it with his own kind of enlightenment. But it suggests a kulak class. More scientifically, K. Fritze[29] has drawn a picture of a peasant society in fifteenth- and sixteenth-century Pomerania which though poor was not abject, contributing more to the sum of wealth than the regional towns, and though receiving less than its share not deprived of meat, good cloth and spices.

7

The Church of the German Nation

(a) *Aristocratic churches*

Nobody supposes that late medieval Germany was divided into a
multiplicity of churches separate from each other in any theological or
canonical way. The bishops were subject to Rome, just as were those
of England. On the other hand, the political decentralization of
'Germany', so much discussed already in this book, and the peculiarly
aristocratic quality of the prelates, gave the church itself a princely and
particularistic nature quite unlike that of England.[1] For one thing,
English bishops did not choose their king: it was the other way round.
German bishops, on the other hand, were most often great political
lords in their own right, not just territorial landlords, and some of
them had a vital part in electing their king. Further, when the king was
chosen, the prince-bishops still held a strong position in relation to the
pope. In 1439, at the so-called *Acceptatio* of Mainz,[2] the German
princes accepted the decrees of the Council of Basel, and only later and
with difficulty were brought to recognize the superiority of the pope.
Even then their interests were individualistic, and the Diet of 1445
made something of a special point in proposing 'a common meeting of
the German dioceses *(Kirchen)* or a national council'.[3]

The church in Germany, then, existed in varying regional guises as
well as on a number of social levels. Differences between Exeter and
Durham, say, may be felt or guessed by an experienced medievalist,
but they were hardly as great as those between Strassburg and
Lübeck. No less than in the political world, Germany was religiously a
land of multiple internal frontiers: actual jurisdictional frontiers
between bishoprics, or between principalities where the princes were
strong enough to insist on ecclesiastical jurisdiction within their
frontiers, whoever the bishop might be; and metaphorical frontiers

between Christians of different classes: cathedrals and abbeys of unrivalled noble rank; lords with their courts and chaplains in palaces or castles; burghers with the clerical and lay officials they appointed for their huge parish churches, city almshouses and hospitals; and the obscure worshippers in the countrysides.

First and foremost, ecclesiastical Germany belonged to the aristocracy. Most of the bishoprics were also principalities. This, incidentally, is why so many maps of medieval Germany are unhelpful when they announce 'ecclesiastical territories are coloured blue [or whatever]', for the fact of them being ecclesiastical does not give them important common features. If they were principalities, they are better marked as such, not standardized by a colour-wash. At the top, the political power and wealth of the Rhenish electoral archbishoprics of Mainz, Cologne and Trier make Durham and Winchester look like country estates. Other archbishoprics like Salzburg, and even ordinary bishoprics like Passau, were not far below the Rhenish standard. The roots of their political and therefore secular being penetrate deep into the Roman and Carolingian past. In the late medieval period the great bishoprics were often nourished by tolls, especially when they lay across important navigable rivers. Their inhabitants, clergy as well as lay folk, were subject to various forms of taxes and renders, and their landscapes were covered with castles, fortified posts and other signs of dominion. It must be admitted that from the thirteenth century rich townsmen not infrequently secured self-rule and drove the bishop out to live elsewhere in his territory. This helps to explain the constant friction between towns and princes, but it does not stop high ecclesiastics possessing their princely character.

By the fifteenth century there were ten provinces which may be reckoned within the German sphere, whether through massive German settlement or by reason of the emperor's personal monarchy over a substantial part: Mainz, Cologne, Trier, Salzburg, Hamburg-Bremen, Magdeburg, Prague, Vienna, Gnesen (containing Breslau and, after 1466, Ermland and Kulm as well as wholly Polish bishoprics), and Riga.[4] Within the provinces were varying numbers of bishoprics, from the thirteen of Mainz to the two and one of Prague and Vienna respectively, created late in the day as favours to the emperors Charles IV and Frederick III. Some of these bishoprics, like Strassburg, Worms or Passau, were hardly less imposing than many an archbishopric. The same may be said of the numerous great abbeys of princely character, like Einsiedeln, Reichenau or Bebenhausen.[5]

It is a commonplace that sons of noble families were sometimes provided to bishoprics in medieval England. In Germany this was the rule rather than the exception. Taking the archbishops of Mainz, Trier, Cologne and Magdeburg from AD 900 to 1500, A. Schulte found that probably 153 out of 166 were noble, four of burgher family and nine of unknown origin.[6] The list of bishops given by Hauck also contains great numbers of counts and also members of the lower nobility.[7] Cathedral chapters too were largely recruited from the lower nobility and in some, such as Strassburg and Passau, from the higher nobility. The Concordat of Worms (1122) which had confirmed the right of election to the cathedral chapters underpinned their strong, habitual aristrocratic structure. Their sense of caste is illustrated by the canons of Passau who, according to Piccolomini, refused to obey Pope Nicholas V (1449-55) on the grounds that he lacked sufficient noble ancestry to qualify him even to belong to their chapter. At Strassburg a prospective canon had to prove sixteen noble quarterings. Such rules were not universal. At Basel the chapter was noble only from 1337, and some German cathedral chapters were open to townsmen. Like the cathedrals, many Benedictine and other monastic foundations for men and women, especially those of ancient foundation, such as Reichenau, Säckingen or Einsiedeln, continued during the late medieval period to have a highly aristocratic composition, even when the numbers of religious had become quite small. When Piccolomini became Pope Pius II in 1458 he confirmed to Einsiedeln its old custom 'that no monks shall be received except from noble families, provided that there are enough monks in the monastery'.[8] In fact, the last monk, the nobleman Diebold von Geroldseck, fell on the side of his friend Zwingli at the Battle of Kappel in 1531, and only after that did the monastery become re-populated, this time by men of non-noble origin.

The reasons for the aristocratic quality of important German monasteries are complex, but in brief it may be suggested that their original recruitment from the lower nobilities of landed families was not different from what happened in England or elsewhere. In England Benedictine monasteries continued on the whole to recruit gentry (for lack of a better description), but in Germany the lower nobility who corresponded largely to 'gentry' tended to emphasize its noble status and, in the absence of primogenitary succession, to maintain it and often to rise in the social scale. Their consciousness of status became openly expressed. Monasteries in Swabia were considered *freiherrlich*; those in Westphalia were said to be the preserve of the *Dynasten*. This is just one more instance of how well-to-do German families tended to form a *de facto* caste.

The colonial German east was much freer from this family exclusiveness except, partially, in some Cistercian houses. In the medieval period it was still a frontier zone where the immense landscape was open to the enterprise of yet-unrooted men. Even Hermann von Salza, Grand Master of the Teutonic Order, was of unfree *(Dienstmann)* origin.[9]

The aristocratic nature of the German church leadership had the profoundest consequences. For one thing, it diminished the power of the lower clergy to protect their privileges and income, since their superiors were mostly not just prelates with canonical jurisdiction, and thus controlled by written church law, but independent social and political lords, and lords moreover who were not much inhibited by a king. In England the lower as well as the higher clergy could turn to the king for protection against papal demands for money, as they did in 1481.[10] In Germany the lower clergy not only lacked this buffer but were frequently subjects of a spiritual lord who could tax them himself as though they were not clerics at all.

The consequences of having a truly aristrocratic prelacy extended further. Bishops and abbots who were able to behave like secular princes (because that is in fact what they were) provided examples to secular princes who wanted to behave like prelates. After all, these men of high position were often related to each other, and consanguinity in a society ruled by rich families brought with it not just envy and rivalry but imitativeness and an understandable expectation that what one lord could do his brother or cousin might do also. Nowhere more than in Germany had the secular princes reached so eagerly for the powers to organize their churches and clergy. Bishops and counts were the same sort of men and sometimes actually the same men. Dramatic statements of this intermixture are often cited, like the exclamation of Duke Rudolf IV Habsburg of Austria (d.1365): 'I myself intend to be pope, archbishop, bishop, archdeacon and dean in my land'; or of the duke of Bavaria in 1367: 'our territories are free: pope, emperor and king have therein nothing at their disposal'.[11] In practice it is the more atrocious instances that get easily remembered. Count Otto of Brunswick was so ardent in defending his own jurisdiction against what he believed were the encroachments of the archbishop of Mainz that a Brunswick clerk who sought his father's inheritance in the Mainz court was seized by the steward of Brunswick, tried in his court, and beheaded.[12] On the other side, among prelates who exercised secular rule, may be numbered Abbot Mangold of Reichenau, who in 1366 arrested five fishermen for poaching and is said to have put out their eyes with his own fingers and sent them thus blinded to Constance, from where they had come. The abbot himself later became bishop of Constance. In the next century, Bishop Wedigo of Havelberg (d.1487), when told that his private war was destroying churches and chapels, answered, according to the *Codex diplomaticus Brandenburgensis*: 'Well, I can alway: econsecrate them if they are violated.'[13]

These may be isolated incidents, but the generality of clerical involvement in lawful violence is shown by the Mainz provincial canon of 1423 (which only repeated one published by Charles IV in 1377) that clergy without temporal domains must not engage in wars nor challenge anyone to fight *unless* it was in the interests of their church and with the permission of their superiors.[14]

The degree to which secular princes took over the functions of ecclesiastical jurisdiction cannot so readily be made the subject of generalization, because princely particularism almost by definition worked differently in different places. Such powers, too, might be taken for different reasons: the prince's belief in his duty to control abuse, the mere exercise of *force majeure*, or with the complete legality of a papal concession.

The Luxemburg lands of Charles IV yield a good example of how ecclesiastical power was a necessary adjunct of the political struggle for dominance, yet at the same time was exercised by political rulers on the spot rather than those far away. Charles created a Bohemian church, with Prague as its metropolitical centre, at some expense of Mainz, Regensburg and Salzburg. All this was done with the help of the pope at Avignon, with whom Charles needed to maintain good relations. Bohemia in fact provides an exceptionally good example of an aristocratic church, though a complex one, as it was controlled by lords of differing rank and race, from the king downwards. Church jurisdiction was largely in the king's hands and involved both Czechs and Germans. Many bishops, provided to their sees by the king's old tutor, Pope Clement VI, were foreigners and especially Germans, and mainly of high social status. The Cistercians, friends of the Luxemburgs, were largely aristocratic. As to parish priests, J.M. Klassen has shown at length the importance of the aristocracy, including the lower nobility, in the presentation of clerks to benefices. Some had Catholic leanings, some were Utraquist, but in the long run it was the nobility who emerged fortified in their power over the Bohemian church.[15]

Further north, the Brandenburg bishops (within Charles IV's area of control) none the less felt they belonged to the margrave of Brandenburg. Not far away, the bishops of Lebus were hostile to Brandenburg and felt themselves to be Silesians. Likewise, control of elections to church dignities tended to fall to local princes in Mecklenburg, Schleswig and Holstein. In the Wettin lands of Saxony the lord's consent was needed for any changes in the property of bishoprics, and the bishops anyway came mostly from a small group of noble families allied to the Wettiner.

It is interesting to show by a couple of more extended examples how far important princes in Old Germany controlled their churches. To do so will emphasize that in late medieval Germany there was a general accord between provincial *(Land)* churches and the local princes rather than the emperor. Such lordly dominance was a sequel of aristrocratic family power, rooted in the locality, helped by the huge size of the country, by royal weakness, the Schism of 1378–1417 and, latterly, by the creation of princely universities where local spiritual power might be fostered and training grounds prepared for princely servants.

The count palatine of the Rhine was massively protective towards the church in his principality, and conversely his church was throughout the fourteenth and fifteenth centuries highly dependent upon him.[16] The Palatinate was a composite territory, intricately mixed up with land belonging to the sees of Worms and Speyer, and despite some opposition the chapters of those great churches were filled with members of families loyal to the elector. Such were Sickingen, Helmstädt, and Venningen, while hostile families like the Zweibrücken were excluded. It throws a sharper light on the aristocratic church to realize that it was formed not by just any aristocrats but by those who belonged to allied or mutually sympathetic social circles. For his part the elector palatine was regarded as the protector *(Schirmvogt)* of the sees, and helped them in their struggles against the town communities. True, the electors left spiritual matters to the clergy, but acquired some control over the foundation of new benefices, indirect control of patronage, and disciplinary control over residence and clerical financial accounting. As protector of some eighty monastic foundations the count palatine supervised reforms, even in the ancient abbey of Schönau. In return ecclesiastics were expected to give payments and services and to use the electoral courts for speedy and effective justice in civil matters. The ecclesiastical influence of the count in fact reached out beyond his own principality to place close kinsmen in other western German benefices and to cultivate good relations with the Teutonic Order which had come to possess property in the region.

The most striking dependency of the count palatine was the university of Heidelberg, founded in 1385 at a moment when Christendom was in schism and Prague and Erfurt at loggerheads. It was convenient for the Wittelsbach elector to train his own lawyers and, in an age when even the intellectual life was growing more regional, to have a *studium* in his own dominions. In 1452, the year of the Arrogation by which princely primogeniture was asserted in the Palatinate, the elector reformed his university. For twenty years the professors had been arguing what kind of theology should be taught: the so-called *via antiqua* or the *via moderna*.[17] Henceforth, the elector determined, both approaches should be tolerated. Indeed, a student had to choose one course or the other, hear the lectures of one set of professors or the other, and receive one of the two qualifications in the same subject.[18] This seems an interesting experiment in complementary theologies, the sort of thing which in modern Europe might be taken for granted, as at Tübingen. In medieval Heidelberg no intellectual impetus was gained. Theological students declined in number during the fifteenth century from about 50 per cent to 10 per cent and their place was taken by lawyers, amongst whom civilians overtook canonists in about the year 1500.[19] Doctors of law took an oath to the prince. University jurisdiction was exercised in the electoral court. The rector of the university became dependent on the lay power for enforcement of decisions in both secular and ecclesiastical causes.

The story was much the same in Württemberg, that Swabian

successor state to the Hohenstaufen territories, composite yet expansive and more and more firmly directed by its rulers. The county (impartible after 1482, a duchy after 1495) contained portions of the bishoprics of Constance, Augsburg, Würzburg, Worms and Speyer, but it was the prince who dominated, even over important monasteries like Bebenhausen and Blaubeuren, and he did this while still maintaining good relations with both local churches and the papacy.[20] The secular grip of the count on the church in Württemberg was expressed in the great amount of patronage he possessed over parish churches, chaplaincies, chantries and monasteries. He had control over elections, a veto on the alienation of church property, and even the right to hospitality for men and hounds while he was hunting. Like the count palatine, the count of Württemberg was active in the foundation of a university. Tübingen (1477) was partly to serve the purpose of providing him with locally-trained clerks, but more than in the Palatinate a specifically religious motive seems to have been at work in Württemberg at large. The great Gabriel Biel, mentioned below in Section (e), was attracted to Tübingen, where he became professor of theology (1485) and then rector of the university (1489). He subsequently retired to be provost of the Brethren of the Common Life in Urach, where the count had endowed and encouraged the community. More than most secular lords, Count Eberhard was concerned with the spiritual aspect of his principality, intervening in the church courts and reforming monasteries. From 1482 prelates had to swear an oath to the count on taking office that they were loyal representatives of the count's people.

Without undue generalization, these instances are enough to show the importance of the princes' growing power over their churches in the late middle ages. Counts and dukes who exercised so paternal a hold over the churches within their principalities were paralleled in many towns by the governing civic bodies who appointed and controlled their own clergy. Nuremberg may well be atypical because its bishopric was at Bamberg, some way off, but it followed a common pattern in being controlled by secular men. By the late middle ages the city council of Nuremberg had firm patronage over the two main town parishes of St Sebald and St Lorenz, and its agents managed the financial affairs of the city's churches, convents and hospitals.[21]

We are left observing a huge and complex country, which we may call Germany, composed of principalities and noble polities large and small, oligarchic in the towns and aristocratic almost everywhere else, which comes to much the same thing. In the cartographers' search for an intelligible plan, one device has been to distinguish between ecclesiastical and secular principalities. The aim of this section has been to show that any sharp distinction is an illusion. But one may at this stage speculate whether the church in a principality like Württemberg, under a paternalist secular ruler, was not in better case than the church in a great prince-bishopric like Mainz or Constance, where the ruler's need to act the prince not only strikes a more discordant note to modern ears but seems also to have been tainted by that endemic medieval disorder called anticlericalism[22] and the violence on both sides which flowed from it as a consequence, somehow the worse for occurring in a Christian setting.

(b) *Relations with the papacy*

The political attitude of German kings towards the papacy, especially till the time of the Council of Constance, was touched on in Chapter 2, and the main attention here will be given to the epoch of the Council of Basel. By that time, in the middle of the fifteenth century, the politically fragmented nature of the German church had become more obvious.

Under Charles IV the empire, of which 'Germany' was the most important part, had already begun to have a central-east European axis rather than a German-Italian one. Papal claims to approve the emperor had been openly denied by Lewis IV in 1338, and the approval was no longer sought in advance as a matter of course. Avignon was none the less a good friend to Charles IV, and for a time it looked as though stable relations might be maintained on a sense of common interest between Avignon, France and Luxemburg.

This balance was destroyed by the almost simultaneous arrival of King Wenzel and the Great Schism. After the outbreak of the Schism in 1378 German kings, with brief exceptions, supported non-French popes. Older loyalties were broken. France, Germany and the papacy itself fell into internal conflicts, from which they began to emerge only in the time of the Emperor Sigismund (1411–37).

This king was the most effective of those who tried to reunify the Latin church, and under him something like a German church (as a concept rather than a political-ecclesiastical unity) enjoyed a brief self-awareness, drawn together by the hopes of intelligent men like Konrad of Gelnhausen (who later taught at Heidelberg), Henry of Langenstein and Dietrich of Niem. These hopes were for reform of the curia and the fiscal, unseemly regimes of rich cardinals, the renewal of Catholic life in diocese, parish and monastery, and delivery of the faith from Bohemian heretics and oriental infidels.

The dream of real unity at Constance had been brief. Religious unity was never more certainly in the hands of kings. It was fractured in Germany by rivalries of many kinds. The two main ones were, first, between 'conciliarists', who held General Councils to be superior to the popes, and their pro-papalist opponents and, second, between German princes, who effectively controlled so much of German church life, and the papal court, which thought that its rights were being thus usurped. In the end the rivalries were resolved in opposite directions. The pope was recognized as spiritual head, but princes got most of the church control they wanted.

If Constance fell short of expectations in the matter of reform, at least it produced (apart from the seven decrees of universal and very marginal reform) a German concordat which set down in writing some main points at issue between Germany and the papacy.[23] The number of cardinals was to be limited; they were to be learned, or if from noble families at least literate, and to be chosen from all parts of Christendom. The system of papal provision to benefices was to remain in being but greater attention was to be given to providing qualified graduates, according to a scheme which was spelled out in detail: a parish with more than 2000 communicants, for example, was always to have a graduate priest who might hold no other benefice. The papal taxes called 'common services' and 'annates', payable when a man received a greater or a lesser benefice respectively, should remain, as pope and cardinals were considered to need the revenue for their maintenance, but were to be restricted in various named ways. The kinds of law-suit brought before the Roman courts were to be limited. Far fewer benefices were to be given *in commendam*, that is, to some important favourite who would enjoy the revenues without residence or responsibility. Men who had committed simony by buying some spiritual office were to confess the fact. Excommunicated people were not to be treated as 'untouchables' (*vitandi*) unless it was a case where the convict was notorious for his physical attacks on clerks. There was to be a check to dispensations allowing unsuitably young or unordained men to receive benefices. An upper income-limit was set for cardinals. Indulgences were admitted to be too numerous, and were to be limited in number. This last clause was special to the German concordat, but the whole list, here rather abbreviated, gives a fair idea of the grievances against the papacy.

Obviously, these were grievances which for the most part touched bishops, monks, universities and patrons, or in other words the leaders of the German church. It is such people who naturally occupy at this time a section entitled 'Relations with the papacy'. Popular discontents were as yet more diffuse and not focused especially on the papacy. For this reason they will be indicated below in a discussion of anticlericalism.

There was never much doubt that the popes would reject the ruling of Constance, in *Haec sancta* that General Councils were ultimately the supreme authorities in the church, and Martin V in fact prohibited all appeals from pope to council. But he stood to the letter of *Frequens*, that General Councils should be called at regular intervals. He summoned the Council of Basel in 1431. It was confirmed by Eugenius IV in 1433, and lasted in various forms till 1449. The decisive conflict between pope and council was fought out at Basel, and it was one dominated by German affairs.[24] Of these matters, the chief to attract notice here is whether the German princes and king would accept the fundamental proposition of *Haec sancta*, or whether they would opt for papal monarchy as it had become known in past centuries. The Council of Basel — a smaller body than is sometimes realized[25] — supported the conciliarist position intermittently and chaotically, in the manner of a badly-chaired debating society, while the pope made efforts to dissolve it. During most of the 1430s pope and council were deadlocked. Eugenius IV scored a victory by negotiating with the Greeks for reunion at his Council of Ferrara in 1437–38. But Basel and the pope anathematized each other, and the German Reichstag which had just seen the election of Albert II Habsburg (18 March 1438) declared Germany neutral in the quarrel and called for a new, German-influenced council to settle the matter. The pope and the council were in fact each trying to gain the support of the German princes, and each had at disposal skilled representatives, like Cardinal Cesarini, friend of the pope, and Nicholas Tedeschi, archbishop of Palermo, a conciliarist. The

197

Germans themselves were advised by two clever jurists, John of Lysura, a councillor of the archbishop of Mainz, and Gregor Heimburg, a strong anti-papalist.[26] At Mainz on 26 March 1439 the Reichstag adopted the so-called Instrument of Acceptance as a provisional measure, by which it received the reforming decrees of Basel and took up an attitude favourable to the princes' own interests. The Basel decrees were in any case mostly against papal taxes and interference in ecclesiastical elections, and the princes added that German candidates ought always to be preferred in German churches. But it soon became clear that the German prince-bishops and abbots were looking for favours and advantages of all kinds whether they came from the council or from the pope, and everybody was ready to violate the Basel decrees for the sake of an ally or a privilege. The aim to preserve the empire from discord, once paramount, was forgotten in the pursuit of particular ends. In 1439 the Council of Basel deposed Eugenius IV and, while the eastern and western churches were temporarily reunited under that pope at Ferrara and Florence, the rival council at Basel elected Duke Amadeus VIII of Savoy, a married layman, as an antipope who called himself Felix V. This was in January 1440, the same year that Frederick III was elected king of the Romans. German neutrality meant divided councils and conflict, not the peace of indifference. The sees of Cologne and Münster leaned towards Basel and its antipope. Many other princes were inclined to repudiate Felix V. Frederick III himself had made some efforts towards reunification and, being told by Tedeschi that his duty was to protect the rights and liberty of the church, crisply answered that that was precisely what he was doing, though he meant the pope and his adviser meant the Council.[27] He then went off to Aachen to get crowned, leaving the experts to their debates. Nicholas of Cusa stuck out for Eugenius and argued that the partisans of Felix ought not even to be heard, and he called to witness the triumph of Florence, where Greeks, Armenians, Georgians and Jacobites had been reunited with Rome. On his return Frederick asked Eugenius to call another council, preferably in a German city, or else allow him as king of the Romans to do so. This was a move likely to irritate both sides, as each thought its own council authentic. The electors were wavering. The Basel fathers were violating their own decrees by scattering money and privileges to win partisans. Frederick III and his chancellor, Kaspar Schlick, were now intent on getting Eugenius recognized.

Chance brought Frederick III into contact with Piccolomini at Basel, where the king offered him work, and for this he left Felix. Ultimately, Piccolomini's career was greatly forwarded by the friendship he struck up with Schlick, a man who had as much influence over Frederick III concerning imperial affairs as he had had over Sigismund and Albert II. In 1443 Frederick sent Dr Ebendorffer to Basel to propose that a new council should be held at Constance or Augsburg, and it was their refusal that convinced Ebendorffer that the Holy Spirit had abandoned the fathers of Basel. From this moment the king inclined increasingly towards the pope. Certain princes still hesitated out of preference for the oligarchic principle. But in 1446 came the final agreement between Frederick III, who recognized the supremacy of Eugenius, and Eugenius, who promised Frederick the imperial crown, financial favours, and major rights over presenting to benefices in Austria and Germany. It was after Frederick's reconciliation that Piccolomini renounced his neutrality, wrote his justifications, and received major orders.

At this point Eugenius IV made the bad mistake of interfering in a Rhineland quarrel and deposing the archbishops of Cologne and Trier. This swung the princes against him. It took the hard work of skilled diplomats like Parentucelli (the future Nicholas V), Carvajal, Cusa and Piccolomini to rally a group of princes favourable to the pope. This was done in the Reichstag at Frankfurt in 1446. The leaders of Germany had appeared in number: dukes, counts, the Grand Master of the Teutonic Order, the king of Denmark, bishops and delegates of knights and towns. A general formula on the grievances of the German nation was worked out. On his very deathbed in 1447 Eugenius IV received the fealty of many German princes in return for the restoration of the deposed archbishops and a multitude of concessions already embodied in the Acceptance of Mainz. This is known as the Concordat of the Princes, to which in fact most German princes gave assent and got in exchange wide rights, actual and retrospective, over appointments to benefices in their principalities. The pope vaguely asserted the 'eminence' (not the pre-eminence) of a General Council. It was a moment of agreement and face-saving. Once Eugenius was dead, Nicholas V, who had been present at Frankfurt, confirmed the concordat. Most princes had no wish to be saddled with Felix V, but certain electors (Cologne, Trier, Saxony and the count palatine) still wanted various concessions.

Frederick III, with those princes who had already made their peace with Eugenius, assembled at Aschaffenburg, where the rest were won over. Nicholas V was recognized throughout Germany, and a more detailed and definite concordat was drawn up in 1448 at Vienna by Frederick III in the name of the whole German nation. It was much concerned with the right to provide to benefices, and while in theory it gave the pope general rights of as wide a scope as had ever been allowed, in practice the negotiations were carried on with individual princes and territories and remained contentious.

The result of these long manoeuvres was not only the defeat of the conciliar movement (ironically, very much a German achievement), but the further elevation of German princely power over the churches of their realms. The emperor had great rights in Habsburg lands. In Brandenburg and Saxony the electors nominated their own bishops. In Cologne, Salzburg and Bamberg papal rights of collation fell away. When in 1451 Cusa was sent off on his great legation through Germany by a pope who knew the country unusually well, his reforms were appreciable, and to some he appeared as an angel of light. But even he could not alter the aristocratic structure of the churches, nor indeed escape from it himself, as he found in his conflict with his chapter at Brixen and in the Tyrol. The story cannot be carried here up to Luther. But it will by now appear readily that the antipapalism which burst forth cannot be ascribed simply to the power of the pope in populating the bishoprics of Germany with his men. It was deeper than that, a fiscal protest no doubt, but a theological one which touched the hearts and minds of men and women who were not aristocrats and who had never been personally involved in political relations with the papacy.

(c) *Anticlericalism*

The remark attributed to J.A. Froude, that anticlericalism is caused by unpleasing priests, was good enough as a witticism but not historically useful. Anticlericalism is a political phenomenon. In its strict sense it has been more apparent in modern times than in medieval, as during the French Third Republic or Germany's *Kulturkampf*, where theoretical alternatives to sacerdotal Christianity existed. Conversely, clericalism is equally political, as in Eire or Poland, where the clergy at certain periods seemed defenders of the national polity by their existence more than their personal goodness. But in medieval times the historian must often accept extended meanings. In England, for instance, there was Lollardy which, being antisacerdotal, was near enough to anticlericalism in the strict sense, but it was not antichristian. There was also hostility to the papacy for its financial exactions and often its juridical claims to override local patrons. There was hostility to richly endowed clergy, whether bishops or monasteries, partly for a seemingly excessive wealth they guarded too jealously, and partly for their role as great landlords in a world grown angry with the oppressions this might involve. There was also dislike of church courts and, more widely, of priests who infringed a moral code which they imposed on the wretched laity. Indeed, the fact lay folk believed in that code intensified their dislike of its imperfect guardians. There was also the specialized hostility to highly-placed clergy in English royal service who at moments of crisis like 1341, 1376 or 1450 suffered for their political unpopularity but in an added way, because of the clerical immunities they enjoyed before the law. And there was the clerical anticlericalism of secular clergy against friars for a series of reasons, many of which might be summed up as jealousy. All this and more make up the strands of feeling and thought in England ascribed with some naiveté by so many moderns to the late medieval church's particular 'corruption'.

The German scene requires more caution still. Statements like that of Cardinal Cesarini in 1431 to Pope Eugenius IV that unless the German clergy amended their ways the people would massacre them[28] are good rhetoric rather than good evidence. Of antipapal feeling there is, of course, no doubt; the previous section has taken some account of this. But this is not exactly anticlericalism. Luther's catalogue of complaints in his *Address to the Christian nobility of the German nation*, printed in 1520, was the climax of at least a century of protest against papal and clerical practices and, more than that, a critique of the priestly church, but it was the cry of a deeply Christian people, not of sceptics and *philosophes*. The grievance literature was based on the idea that modern times were worse, not better, than the old days. The contrast was between innovations *(Neuerungen)*, which were usually bad, and the customary *(hergebrachte)* ways, which had been good.[29] Whether or not the *Reformation of the Emperor Sigismund*[30] is a typical document, it is again religious in tone, however reproachful, and prescribes how spiritual and secular authorities ought to govern.

It looks to the reform of the church and the eradication of heresy which even then (1438) was hardly a dominant feature of the German (as distinct from the Bohemian) scene. For the matter of that, even Hussites of the extremer sort can hardly be classed as anticlerical without qualification, for their priests who celebrated the Eucharist with tin cups in barns were emphasizing priesthood, not renouncing it. No more were the German humanists distinguished for antisacerdotalism. It has been well argued that fifteenth-century Germany saw numbers of educated men who were half humanist and half scholastic in outlook, drawn from all strata of society, deeply entrenched in German morality.[31]

If the identity of a German anticlericalism in the later middle ages in so elusive, why bother to give it space? The answer is because of an undercurrent in Germany of violence against the clergy, not specifically antipapal, but in practice wholly secular and expressed in a brutal disdain for clerical immunities. It was not necessarily something exclusively German: murders, lynchings, castrations, robberies and sacrileges against clerks are encountered in England too. But in Germany the impression is of harsher and more routine violence against clerks, sometimes because the government of cities was contested between townsmen and a bishop's administration, sometimes because clerks were victims, just as laymen were in bitter contest for jurisdiction between lords,[32] but perhaps fundamentally because the weakness of royal rule had permitted easy recourse to violence and a habitual blurring of the difference between laymen and clerks.In this respect the basic German anticlericalism was part of a widespread contempt for peaceful behaviour of which the Christian clergy had, theoretically and habitually, been special guardians. Much earlier the Peace of God and the Truce of God had proclaimed the importance of limiting aggressions, but success depended upon a public order provided by the king or at least some great lord of wide-ranging power. In Germany this order was especially fragile and intermittent. Furthermore, the clergy had always been deeply implicated in the German world of private war and accepted violence. It is, then, arguable that the specific German anticlericalism of the late middle ages lay in widespread practical rejection of clerical immunity.

A few instances will illustrate this contention. In 1308 the new archbishop of Magdeburg, Burchard III, imposed fresh taxes on the town to finance its fortification. The subsequent revolt became a virtual war and the citizens put their archbishop in a cage on a tower until he met their demands. Future synods of Magdeburg usually specified excommunication for violence against clergy who were regularly threatened in their persons and property by laymen.[33] The same archbishop, locked in dispute with his townsmen, had also to insist in 1320 that it was the clergy's right and not the laity's to decide the time of divine service.[34] A third synod held by Archbishop Burchard, in 1322, increased the penalties against those who took prisoner an archbishop, abbot or other prelate, and prohibited the seizure of clerical property as a means of forcing them to appear before secular courts. After this the archbishop was actually captured and killed in prison and the killing concealed for a year, until in 1325 the decomposed body was found in a dungeon.[35]

Between 1385 and 1403 a synod of Magdeburg repeated an old statute, already promulgated in a provincial council of Mainz, which tried to protect parish priests who disobeyed their bishop for fear of their temporal lords. Another made special mention of chaplains of castles where the lord rather than the bishop clearly had the effective power to lay down in detail what the chaplain should do and when.[36] In 1396 Dietrich of Nieheim (Niem), bishop-elect of Verden near Lüneburg, requested the secular authorities to cease at once from billeting soldiers in religious houses. The converse of this was the oft-repeated prohibition against clerks who wore armour and took part in wars even when the interests of their churches were not involved.[37] In 1418 the archbishop of Salzburg had it proclaimed throughout his province that no one was to be ordained or to receive a benefice if his forbears as far back as great-grandfather could be shown to have killed, injured or held prisoner a clerk in holy orders. Chaplains to noblemen were further forbidden to celebrate Mass in their lords' chapels before having taken an oath to participate in church synods and keep the rules made there, and to make such rules known to the lords and other inhabitants of the castles, 'as the parish priests rarely dare do this'. A picture emerges of these castles as islands of violence where clergy were shut up or beaten, sometimes even to compel them to lift spiritual censures.[38] Here is a perfect instance of the anticlerical mentality under discussion, which could see spiritual censures regulated with the whip. A final example illustrates violence in the heart of the clerical order itself, when a provincial council of 1428 held by Archbishop Henry of Riga, in the territories of the Teutonic

Knights, complained that six messengers sent by the council to the Apostolic See to denounce the many oppressions practised by the knights on the church (men under religious vows) had been arrested on the frontier of Livonia, their letters confiscated, and themselves thrown into the water and drowned. The aggression against the synod of Riga was compounded by the complaint of the Knights to the archbishop that the messengers had been executed as traitors and public enemies.[39]

(d) *Priestly initiatives*

The earlier sections of this chapter have presented a black picture of vast provinces and dioceses dominated by landed nobilities, with bishops and clerks feuding and subject to assaults as though they were laymen, and hardly members of a Christian society at that. There seemed few voices even raised in petition for reforms, and few reforms which came.

Yet there are more positive themes to follow in the work of Germans for the Christian life, whether through institutions, scholarship or personal piety. Something has already been said about the holding of provincial and diocesan councils. The more dramatic abuses they denounced should not mask the efforts they made to produce or maintain a canonical routine of discipline and attitude. Despite the monumental labours of Hefele and Leclercq, it is probable that even more councils were held than those of which record has survived. The records which exist show a leading part taken by the great province of Mainz. Its statutes were frequently repeated and copied in other provinces, and they were naturally echoed in the diocesan synods of Mainz's own bishoprics. The content of these conciliar canons is largely of an ordinary nature and corresponds in range to virtually the whole subject-matter of the canon law, but their repetition at fairly frequent intervals over the area of the German-speaking provinces indicates that the bishops were at least awake to pastoral matters, as in England, save in the worst periods of the Schism. It is the non-existence of church synods which seems to signalize and encourage church disorder, as happened in early thirteenth-century Languedoc.

The application of German prelates to this basic task may be given a few illustrations. In 1349 it was noted at Mainz that an ancient custom allowed archdeacons, if qualified in law, or if they had competent assessors, to judge causes of matrimony and usury which were normally prohibited to them. All other ecclesiastical causes in Mainz were reserved to the archbishop or his official.[40] In 1381 Archbishop John Jenstein of Prague published a decree in the synod of Prague obliging the clergy of Bamberg, Regensburg and Meissen, over which he had jurisdiction as papal legate,[41] to observe the statutes of his predecessor, Ernest (1349), to which he added various decrees about pursuing heretics like the Vaudois and 'sarabaites', by which he seems to have meant Flagellants or Fraticelli. Measures were also to be taken against the antipope Clement; benefices were not to be endowed with money obtained usuriously; monks were to stay in their monasteries; clergy were not to live with concubines and were to teach their people the Our Father and the Creed.[42]

These are routine matters which may be paralleled elsewhere. Sometimes provincial councils were held even though a number of diocesan bishops were absent at the wars or engaged in political disputes, like the provincial council of Trier held in 1423 by Archbishop Otto von Ziegenhain, from which all his suffragans (Metz, Toul and Verdun) were absent.[43] In spite of this, many lower clerics, regular and secular, were present and helped to ratify canons against Wycliffites and Hussites, against carelessness in saying Mass, and against the maintenance of clerical concubines and their children by clerical revenues. Such children were to be kept discreetly in their own houses. Clergy were not to practise the trade of inn-keeper nor give light penances in return for presents. If the picture is one of loose discipline, it is of a more peaceful character than the savageries already encountered in Magdeburg and Prussia.

Study of the *Histoire des Conciles* leaves the impression (and no more than that) of a change in ecclesiastical Germany during the later fifteenth century. This may be summarized by saying that fewer councils were held, that bishoprics had been impoverished by war, especially the Hussite wars, and that the concurrent papal drive for revenue (partly on account of the Turkish threat) aroused greater ill-feeling against the papacy than had been felt before. In view of the future pattern of Christian allegiance, it is interesting that antipapal feeling was now stronger in Bavaria and the Rhineland than in the far north, where the pope was regarded, certainly in Lübeck, as a guardian of Christianity, along with the king of Poland, against the outrages of the Teutonic knights.[44]

The activity of councils, legatine, provincial and diocesan, was a routine medieval instrument of church discipline. Every now and then a burst of activity by some outstanding man lifts the church above a humdrum level. One such man was Nicholas of Cusa,[45] who according to the Abbot Trithemius appeared in Germany as an angel of light and peace amidst shadows and disorders. Much of the work relevant to the present theme concerned his legatine visitation of Germany, undertaken in a land fragmented by circumstances and uncertain of its direction after the Hussite wars and the Council of Basel.

As soon as Pope Nicholas V was established he named legates to go into the countries of Latin Christendom to publish the indulgence of jubilee (to persuade the faithful to come to Rome in 1450), to preach the crusade against the Turks, give help to the Greeks, and to work for reform, especially of the clergy. For Germany the legate was Nicholas of Cusa, who had played so considerable a part in restoring recognition in Germany for papal supremacy. Cusa had been a cardinal since 1448 and bishop of Brixen in southern Germany (directly subject to the emperor) since 1450. He was a German bishop, but not an aristocrat. His father had been a man of moderate property on the lower Mosel. The village of Cues is now joined with the better-known Bernkastel, but even then the family owned vineyards. The story is that the father was harsh and the boy ran away and found a friend and patron in Count von Manderscheid. Anyhow, Nicholas matriculated at Heidelberg as a clerk of Trier diocese, migrated to Padua, where he graduated doctor of canon law at the age of twenty-three, and went on to Rome before returning to Germany. He owed his promotion and public career (given his lucky patronage) to a native brilliance of that rare kind combining speculative and practical ability. This context is concerned with the practical, and in particular with his legatine visitation of Germany during 1450–52, undertaken when he was just approaching fifty. He was chosen partly for his attitude and services to the papacy, but also because he was a native German speaker, and as *Cardinal Teutonicus* something of a wonder in a land accustomed to prince-bishops who were Germans but not cardinals, and to cardinals who were Italian and not very welcome. The mission comprised a modest retinue and followed the itinerary: Rome — Salzburg — Vienna — Regensburg — Nuremberg — Bamberg — Würzburg — Erfurt — Halle — Magdeburg — Halberstadt — Wolfenbüttel — Brunswick — Hildesheim — Hanover — Corvie —

Minden — Holland (he could not reach Münster or Osnabrück, embroiled in a private war) — Cleves — Cologne — Trier, and thence to his own Cues, where he founded the hospital for poor men which bears his name.

In the course of his tour he was made aware of the great hostility felt in Austrian and South German monasteries towards Rome, and the equally harsh feeling between the secular and the mendicant clergy in most of the German-speaking lands. Amongst his injunctions, Cusa included the obligation to add prayers to Sunday Masses for the pope, the diocesan bishop and the Church as a whole. He encouraged the holding of councils and visitations, and insisted on the rule made in 1215 that all adult Catholic Christians should go to confession to their parish priest and receive communion at least once a year (IV Lateran: *Omnis utriusque sexus*). Details of his life and thought may be read elsewhere, but in respect of Germany's religious life as a whole the principal evils were gross superstitions, like bleeding hosts, and a variety of simony which consisted in the habit of monasteries charging money for appointment of priests to benefices in their gift. The monastic reform which Cusa worked so hard to extend had wider implications and is known from its result as the reformed Congregation of Bursfeld. Very briefly, the objects were to promote study, to improve service in choir, and to form a disciplined congregation under an abbot elected by a chapter-general of the congregation. In 1430 Duke Otto of Brunswick had given the monk John Dederoth of Northeim the mission to reform the abbey of Klus, near Gandersheim and subject to the formidable nuns of that place. Dederoth had been to Rome on the business of Northeim, and had got to know various monastic reformers. In 1433 he was proposed as abbot for Bursfeld, and before long Bursfeld, Trier (St Matthias), Reinhausen and Klus formed the first nucleus of the new congregation. It opened for its subjects a seminary in Cologne and received juridical approval in a legatine bull at the council of Basel in 1446. Other houses joined, to the number of at least eighty-eight abbeys as well as convents for women, and they were spread over Saxony, Thuringia and the Rhine and Mosel valleys. It was in general a north and north-west German phenomenon (like the Brethren of the Common Life), and its fruits were an ordered monastic life and numerous liturgical and ceremonial books.

It is of some interest that the two outstanding priestly figures of late medieval Germany, Nicholas of Cusa and Gabriel Biel, should both have had connections with the Brethren of the Common Life, should both have possessed keen theological intellects (not a necessary consequence), and should both have concerned themselves with the administration of reform. Cusa was possibly schooled at Deventer, and the reforms of both him and Biel were influenced by the ideas of Gerard de Groote, especially in his high view of the role of preaching and gentle practical example.

Gabriel Biel, a few years younger than Cusa, was born at Speyer and ordained in or before 1432. He too matriculated at Heidelberg and he graduated MA in 1438. He paid brief visits to the university of Erfurt and in 1453 went to study theology at Cologne. At about this time he received the licenciate in theology, which permitted him to teach the subject.

Although it is beyond the present scope to enter into intellectual history, it should be noted that the universities attended by Biel taught different and, in fact, rival courses of theology: Erfurt followed the *via moderna*, which looked more to Ockham and his school, Cologne the *via antiqua*, which held rather to the mental philosophy of Aquinas and his followers. Whether or not the first was ruled by a greater metaphysical scepticism, it is important to grasp, even if only superficially, that there was no question of a tired old scholasticism in fifteenth-century Germany, kept alive by boring and trivial men for the sake of their vested interest. There were enemies of scholasticism, some for good reason like a passion for pure, original texts, others out of positive uninterest. But fifteenth-century Germany was intellectually self-renewing, and it could have been said of many that they were not wholly either scholastics or humanists but something of both. The greatest figures, like the two now under discussion, had something original of their own to give as well, both intellectually and personally.

Biel followed the *via antiqua* at Cologne yet saw it as a good sign that the canonized Aquinas could be openly contradicted in the schools. Likewise, he elsewhere and later acknowledged Ockham and Gerson as authorities: '... now I follow the opinion of the master which also that most profound investigator of truth did follow, that is, William Ockham, whose teaching I represent as most renowned.'[46]

Biel's debt was to the whole medieval tradition. But his performance was more than this again, for he was both academic and a popular preacher; his *Sentences* and *Exposition* were works of specialist scholarship, his Mainz sermons were directed to a devout congregation, his *Defence of apostolic obedience,* touching on polemic, was of even a third kind. In another age, using his ability to make known publicly what he thought out in his secret mind, he might have been a Dominican by token of their motto *contemplata aliis tradere,* though there would have been trouble about his respect for the *via moderna.* But in the 1460s he joined the Brethren of the Common Life. Perhaps this is a shock for those who imagine these north European communities merely as simple-minded book-binders or at most practical educators with a programme of unintellectual holiness. But there it is. They attracted few people with the gifts and interests of Biel. Yet in the end we have to wonder at the variety of Biel's nature rather than the many-sidedness of the Brethren. Biel studied latterly at Tübingen, notable for a certain compatibility between the *via nova* and humanism; he served as the university's rector in 1485 and 1489, and at the last, still interested in both logic and Pico della Mirandola, he retired to the new Brethren's house nearby, in Schönbuch, where he died in 1495. Even Schönbuch lived a kind of social catholicity (small c) hardly typical of Germany, in that the brethren lived together whether they came from the estate of nobility, burgess or cleric.

Even a short account of Biel should not end without reference to the high view he took of preaching for, as he explained, faith at the beginning comes from hearing. He considered the word of God in preaching created the setting for acceptance. His talk of 'semi-arguments' may move a philosopher to laughter, but the psychology is understandable. Nor was he an anti-sacramentalist. In Holy Communion, he argued, the Christian simply receives an increase in the grace he has already been granted by coming from faith to contrition.

This glance at the specifically clerical work for religion in pre-Reformation Germany reveals a confused picture with many blank areas. It is not hard to track down Christian scholars, their movements and meetings with Italians and others, for this is the kind of thing that has attracted modern scholars themselves. The difficulty is to say anything brief and convincing about the parochial clergy of the great and varied German-speaking provinces. An impression exists of a lively parish life in many cities where the abler clergy clustered. Here, furthermore, clerical life appears to quite a large extent to be controlled by the citizens of the ruling families. If this is true, this lay character of burgher churches corresponds within city walls to the laicized tone of the aristocratic church of the cathedrals and great religious houses. This is anyhow true of Nuremberg, which was divided by the River Pegnitz into the two main parishes of St Sebald (on the north side) and St Lorenz (on the south). St Sebald received its parochial status in 1255 and St Lorenz from about 1277. The clerical superior of each was given the rank of provost by Pope Sixtus IV in 1477, but the patronage was managed by the city council, which also saw to all revenues and expenses of the city's churches, hospitals and convents.[47] The bishop was sixty-three kilometres away at Bamberg, and the rich patricians had no difficulty in controlling all land-use in the city and consequently putting great power into the hands of the lay superintendents *(Kirchenpfleger)* of church institutions. Such a structure of authority led easily to a situation in which religious allegiance as well as discipline was determined by laymen rather than clergy.

The state of country clergy must await further researches, though we have glimpses of village churches run by the leaders of the local rural community.

(e)   *The world of lay piety*

As a bridge between the life of clerical mission and the piety of lay people stands the practice — we may even call it the organization — of the *Devotio Moderna*[48]. The name itself was given in the fifteenth century to this rule of life which was neither a technically 'religious' one, inaugurated by permanent canonical vows, nor wholly a routine committed to the currents and eddies of daily life in the world. The Modern Devotion was lived by groups of dedicated men and sometimes of dedicated women. The men were known as Brethren of the Common Life, and owed the origin of their houses to Gerard de Groote, who was born in 1340 in Deventer, now in Holland. Groote's education was mainly in Germany, and the appeal of his way was chiefly confined to western Germany, the Low Countries and northern France. The early preaching of New Testament Christianity in everyday language, dwelling on straightforward morality and simple meditations on the life and teaching of Christ, moved before long also towards a directed spirituality for lay people, and from the 1390s can be discerned this twin strand of devotional life, the layman's and the brethren's. Its best-known product is the *Imitation of Christ* by Thomas à Kempis, so popular to this day that it hardly needs description.

The organized life itself spread into Germany from Westphalia, where it had early been most popular. Contemporary records speak of Westphalians as 'rough and raw', but the north German houses seem to have been anything but that, and to have created establishments of modestly prosperous appearance which on occasion stirred up some hostility from the existing clergy. The method was for small numbers of priests to come together in communal houses which they acquired or built, and to maintain themselves by the copying and binding of books, sometimes by keeping schools, occasionally by working their own vineyards, never by begging. There were similar houses of women, sometimes former groups of Beguines who had transformed themselves into sisterhoods of the Common Life and attended the regular meetings.

The moving force in the German expansion was Heinrich von Ahaus, the illegitimate son of a Westphalian count, who achieved his principal aim at the general meeting or *colloquium* at Münster in 1431. This created a 'neighbourly fraternity' bound together by mutual visitations to ensure peace and solvency. The Brethren did not allow married couples to separate in order to enter their houses (as could be done by religious orders), and they discouraged over-zealous clerics or elderly people, who might be anxious to give up benefices or property for the sake of joining a community where they would find company in their loneliness. If this sounds harsh, the wisdom is surely undeniable. 'We are not monks but we aim to live piously in the world', said Peter Dieburg, leader at Hildesheim. Their vocation was not a light one simply because it was modern and untrammelled by particular customary conditions. Certainly it rejected the usual canonical compulsion of vows. It even took a rather reserved attitude towards the sacrament of penance. The keynote of their spirituality was personal contrition, as a habitual but not excited frame of mind. Work for a living was an everyday necessity. Extraordinary mortifications were not desired, nor the extreme experiences of mystical prayer, but their meditations fastened without intellectual agonizings or abstruse speculations upon the plain imaginings of the Gospel scenes. The Gospel precepts were practised, and the Brethren encouraged to apply themselves lovingly to the people and society about them.

211

It is interesting that they were supported by both local noblemen and well-to-do citizens, and that they prayed both for the dead and for living benefactors. For all their anti-intellectualism they belonged to the old world, and did not long survive the Reformation.

How much influence they had is hard to decide. The arrival of printing removed one of their means of livelihood and perhaps of impact. Some historians have made them sound second-rate,[49] and perhaps they were. but it is not wholly irrelevant that they could attract men of profound intellect — Groote himself had had a wide education — and they are at least something to set in the scales against the violence and crudities with which this chapter has been concerned.

Despite the excesses and the defects which have been reviewed, the Germany of the later fifteenth century was a religious country. Something is heard of witchcraft and of unrewarding fables put about by the sillier friars in misguided but not novel efforts to demonstrate the superiority of their order. But as the century moved towards its end not much is heard of real heresy. Friedrich Reiser, a German Hussite, said in 1456: 'Our cause is like a fire going out'.[50] Even the main part of the *Bundschuh* risings, let alone the more obvious heretical social movements, lay the other side of the fifteenth century's ending. It is hard to deny that German piety was mostly orthodox, even if it is not immediately appealing to us, or that it was largely lay in inspiration. The endowment for private Masses increased markedly in Upper Austria from 1450, and fell drastically only from 1518. There were ninety-nine confraternities in Hamburg in about 1500, most of which had been set up since 1450. There was a tendency to ascribe particular powers to particular saints, as elsewhere in the Christendom of that time, yet at the same time a habit of naming altars, windows and furnishings in churches after the benefactor who had donated them. Indulgences were very numerous, but as much because there was a 'consumer-demand' for them as because they were hawked by a mercenary clergy.

Religious art considered religiously is too delicate a matter for the historian's pontifications, but to the present writer it seems that the sacred art of late medieval Germany, so largely commissioned by laymen, was not so much generically 'bad' or 'good' as astonishing in its variety. Against the expressionistic agonies of the 'Grünewald' crucifix on the Isenheim altarpiece in Colmar, or the physical threats offered the faithful in an uncontestably orthodox way by the paintings

212

of Hieronymous Bosch, may be placed the radiant and tranquil forms of Cologne iconography from the fifteenth century, such as that by Stephan Lochner and others, to be seen in Cologne's Wallraf-Richartz and Schnütgen Museums, or the grave beauty of the *Pietà* by 'Master P' (1471) in the Württembergischen Landesmuseum at Stuttgart.

Assessment of lay piety is, in fact, very much a matter of travelling round Germany, either physically, to museums and churches, or mentally, through books and pictures. The voyager will become aware not only of a longing for salvation evinced by the country and the age, and sometimes of fear or bitterness at the experience of death, but also of an earnest respect for the work of the world, for those who do it, and for those who are seen to have earned their retirement from it.

The Ploughman from Bohemia (Der Ackermann aus Böhmen) was written in about 1400 by a married clerk from Prague called Johann von Tepl, and its popularity is attested by sixteen surviving manuscripts and numerous early printings.[51] In some respects this German dialogue between death and the ploughman is reminiscent of the English contemporary Langland's *Piers Plowman* — 'from the pen I take my plough' — but Tepl has a more personal bitterness, even if it is true that the piece was written as an exercise in humanistic composition. The ploughman's loved wife, Margarethe, has just died and he argues the cruelty of being made to give love when the beloved will be seized by death. It is a motif of all ages, from Francis Bacon's essay on marriage to Keith Douglas's *Time Eating:*

But Time, who ate my love, you cannot make
Such another, you who can remake
The Lizard's tail and the bright snakeskin
Cannot, cannot...

So Death to the ploughman: '...the more you have of love, the more sorrow will befall you...' True, the lesson deteriorates into medieval bathos as Death quotes Hermes the philosopher that a man should guard against fair women, for they are hard to keep; and within a few stanzas we receive again the old medieval tirade against the foul corruption of the flesh and the abominable bossiness of wives. The ploughman's arguments for the excellence of a good wife are all too feeble, and the familiar medieval theme grinds on in sombre Germanic form.

Popular though he was, we may think him a strange enough ploughman to get mixed up in humanistic exercises, not to say the *querelle des dames*. No doubt there were other and simpler ploughmen as exemplars of humble lay piety in Germany, but we have the familiar irritation of seeing them only through the dark glasses of the literate. Thus the sentiment, not rare among the devout, that 'the peasant is closest to God'.[52] There is not a lot to prove or disprove such worrying propositions, but their expression seems rather more usual in the south of Germany, as in Bavaria, where Hans Leinberger embodied peasant culture and where simple Marian motifs are to be found as on a pillar in Landshut church:

Mary, pray to God for us,
Thou who art duchess in Bavaria.[53]

More securely documented ways to judge lay piety in medieval time are the consideration of almshouses for the old and a tour round a great town church.

The 'brotherhood hospital' appeared in the canon law of the twelfth century, organized under a master and according to some variant of the Augustinian rule. The objects were to care for the poor, the sick, pilgrims and others in need.[54] Houses of Third Orders of the friars sprang up in the thirteenth century as poverty increased. This was not, of course, an exclusively Germanic development, but they were very common in German-speaking lands. Even the Teutonic Order had its hospitals, but from the thirteenth century onward hospitals in general came to be administered by laymen. At first canon law emphasized the necessary jurisdiction of the bishop even when laymen were in actual charge, and quite often the hospital itself and the church buildings were physically separate. But by the fourteenth century the canon law changed in accordance with the frequent wish of townsmen that the lay founders and organizers should be in legal as well as factual control. At this point not clerics but suitable laymen (*viri providi*) were granted the ecclesiastical rights of the Ordinary, as in the Mendel Foundation to be encountered below. Such houses enlarged the property and influence of the town and show one more side of lay dominance in German medieval Christianity.

Bavaria as much as anywhere in Germany was well served with 'brotherhood houses' or 'hospitals of the Holy Ghost', to which noblemen and burghers were generous.[55] Some began as so-called *Seelhäuser* for Beghards and Beguines where men and women could live unworldy lives without taking canonical vows. Some turned into Third Order houses of Franciscans and Dominicans, to avoid suspicion of heresy. In Nuremberg by 1500 there were twenty-two such *Seelhäuser*, but since 1478 the city council had been forbidding them to house Beguines and ordering that they look after the sick. The particular interest of the Mendel Twelve-Brother Foundation[56] is that it was a new type of hospital, appropriate above all to a place like Nuremberg, where the aged and especially aged craftsmen might spend a dignified retirement. But it was not unique. Similar foundations were made in nearly two dozen other Bavarian towns. They were religious communities, yet lay, whose members wore similar dress, though this changed gradually with fashion. The brother in tricorn hat would have been as familiar a sight in eighteenth-century Bavarian towns as the gowned brother of St Cross in Winchester today.

The Mendel Brotherhouse was founded in 1388 by Konrad Mendel the elder, a leading patrician of the city, as an almshouse for artisans who could not otherwise afford a suitable retirement. At first he contributed sixty-two guilders a year for its upkeep, but in 1397 the Nuremberg city council took it over and applied certain rents to its endowment. Pope Boniface IX confirmed the endowment, and the curator *(Pfleger)* was to be a Mendel as long as the senior line of that family lasted. Thereafter the curator was to be chosen by the city council.

The foundation flourished and acquired rents in forty-four places outside Nuremberg. The purpose was to house and care for twelve old and infirm but not bedridden men, subject to Nuremberg law, who were unable to earn their own living. The rules excluded idlers, vagrants, foreigners, drunkards and executioners, and prescribed that the men accepted should be of good reputation, honest, hard-working and able to say the Our Father, the Hail Mary and the Apostles' Creed.

The life was not, of course, lived under vow, but a candidate was expected to tell the curator what property he had, and to inform the master of his craft that he had been granted a place for the sake of God and the craft. As each applicant became a brother a picture was painted of him, not as a true likeness but as a more or less standardized figure wearing the habit and cowl and engaged in his former craft. It is a little difficult to tell if some sort of likeness were intended, for the faces in fact differ somewhat from each other, though they were crudely done and wear almost without exception an expression of concentrated gloom which doubtless was meant to demonstrate the required virtues. The series of pictures forms, however, a priceless record of numerous manual operations, possibly unique at this date for their geographical and industrial coherence.

Needless to say, obedience and regularity were demanded under sanction of short rations and ultimately of expulsion. The latter penalty was rare. As to arrival, every brother brought with him a long fur coat and felt shoes, but received other clothing and bedcoverings from the foundation. If the men had families, they were left behind at home, and might not come drinking with the brother in the almshouse. Here the brethren dined and drank together, as a community. The diet was of two meals a day and included beef, veal, pork and rye bread. All this tells us something familiar even today about regional cuisine but, more interestingly, suggests again the usually high standard of living enjoyed in a great city of upper Germany, the more remarkable when we are assured that the number of really poor and homeless was few in Nuremberg. During the fifteenth century numerous contributions from the citizens allowed the living-standards of the brethren to be improved still further.

The ages of the brethren are first given in 1501, when the youngest is found to be only thirty-two, the oldest over 100, but most between sixty and eighty. They were expected to live celibate lives even if married, but resignations from the almshouse were rare. Occasionally a brother could not accustom himself to the life or wanted, if a widower, to remarry.

The position of the curator is interesting. He received certain perquisites and had an office in the buildings, but he mostly administered the foundation from his own home. At the same time he possessed the equivalent of episcopal jurisdiction, granted by papal letter, over the almshouse, and this presumably meant in practice the authority to administer the rules and the finances. For worship the brethren attended daily Mass and certain canonical hours at the Carthusian church, where the Germanisches Nationalmuseum now stands. On some feast days they would repair to the church of St Lorenz in the parish of which the almshouse lay.

The offices of steward and cellarer were supplied from among the brethren, in return for remuneration, and their duties were not only to look after clothing and shoes but to help the feebler old men to church. There was also a sort of prefect appointed by the curator from among the brethren, whose tasks were to say grace, keep order, ring the bell for church and marshal his fellows two-by-two for church. The only female on the scene was the cook, who was adjured to treat each brother fairly and not to be irritable. Most cooks left quickly to get married.

One further point may engage our attention. The overwhelming number of brethren were former artisans, and however much contemporaries, including themselves, may have considered their social status to have differed amongst themselves according to their former occupation,[57] they lived as equals. The warden and his wife, however, were clearly thought of as socially superior, for their pictures too were painted along with the others, but always as kneeling together before an altar and always with shields bearing the family arms of both husband and wife propped up against the figure of the owner. The one exception to the simple status of the brethren occurs in 1481, when the picture and the inscription record the death of Paulus Voytt, gentleman (Edelmann), at one time in the service of Sigmund vom Eglofstein, imperial bailiff *(Reichsschultheiss)* of Nuremberg. The exception proves the rule. These men lived together irrespective of social origins just as did the Brethren of the Common Life according to the prescriptions of their founder. To us this is nothing. In a society so sundered by status as medieval Germany it is of much interest.

This consideration of lay piety may end, with a sense of fitness rather than of paradox, in an ecclesiastical building in the heart of Germany: the parish church of St Lorenz in Nuremberg. Its position as one of the two great parochial churches of the city has already been noted above.[58] But we must return to it as a home of lay piety, not only because the clergy were appointees of the city council, nor yet for the fact that its financial administration was largely in lay hands, but because it was physically the creation of rich, lay Nurembergers whose names rather than their sacred subjects identify altars, windows and furnishings. These were almost all masterpieces. As the eye travels round the enormous interior the mind is filled with a strong sense of both wealth and of political co-operation between emperor and rich burghers of upper Germany, in the church setting no less than the secular one.

There is the Krell altar, given by Jodocus Krell (d.1483), a patrician like all the others, and painted most probably by a Nuremberg master who had learned some of his art in the Netherlands. It shows the oldest known view of Nuremberg, in front of which are depicted the Virgin with Saints Barbara, Bartholomew, James and Helen. By the northern choir loft the Imhoff altar of about 1420 shows the coronation of the virgin, the apostles Philip and James and, of a decently smaller size, the donor Konrad Imhoff and his three successive wives, born Rotflasch, Hörndl and Schatz, each with a shield of her family arms. In a choir window is a scene of the people of Israel coming out of Egypt, given by the brothers Sebald and Peter Rieter, after a pilgrimage to the Holy Land. Another window, directly behind the high altar and showing King Heraklius before Jerusalem, was given by the Emperor Frederick III, no less, whose own pilgrimage to Jerusalem had been worked into a sketch for the window by Michael Wolgemut, Dürer's master. Most famous of all, the ornate sandstone tabernacle, given by Hans Imhoff, stands to the north of the high altar, borne up by the self-carved figure of master Adam Krafft and two of his apprentice masons. High above hangs Veit Stoss's Angelic Salutation, a romantic figure of astonishing sweetness, encompassed by an oval crown bearing carvings of the seven joys of Mary, and blessed overall by the figure of God the Father. All this was carved out of a linden tree taken from the neighbouring imperial forest of Nuremberg. It was the gift of Anton Tucher (1457–1524), patrician and tax-collector.

At the end of this final chapter there remains the problem of how to sum up the being and activity of the German church in particular, and the society to which it was supposed to minister in general. Even the first portion of this task is daunting enough.

As far back as we can see, up until the end of the middle ages, Germany was an aristocratic society. The great bishoprics and to some extent the great monasteries had begun and continued, whatever else they were, as complex noble dominions. Cities had repeated the leadership motif in a different key: obligarchic churches in which rule was of civic rather than purely sacerdotal temper, whatever the theological destiny of the region. The papacy which in a political way had been largely the creation of Franks and Saxons came to attract hatred in many parts of Germany, yet did not cease to retain the allegiance of numerous Germans. The dominant impression at the end of medieval times is of a deeply religious society which was becoming simultaneously more consciously German.

To condense the messages of this little book as a whole appears not so much difficult as both impossible and superfluous. When its composition was begun Yeats's *The Second Coming* ran in the mind:

Things fall apart; the centre cannot hold;

Mere anarchy is loosed upon the world...

How glib this soon seemed! Germany before Luther was as unlike Yeats's Ireland as could be. A huge, ramified and urbanizing society rolled along on institutions of makeshift or even relatively primitive manufacture. It was more under-governed than over-governed. Violence was endemic but discontinuous and fired by no unified ideology. Political regionalism and social disharmonies were characteristic. The Rhine, the Danube and the Vistula swept through different worlds. Noblemen, burghers and peasants, though not without many contacts, lived further removed from each other than in the west.

Perhaps the shifting frontiers of lordships did not matter very much, but beneath these were the more consequential frontiers created by the movements and settlements of people who spoke non-German languages: French, Baltic, Polish, Czech, Hungarian.

The positive impression of this negative picture is that Germany had become a society created through its language. This was said at length in the first chapter. Added to this must come the realization, also invited in the pages above, that Germany was filled and traversed by people of all sorts — merchants, princes' diplomats and scholars above all — who spoke a language that had become common, who transacted business with each other across political frontiers, and who were often related to each other by kinship or interests. This is how late medieval Germany must be seen even as we are explaining the well-known problems of political fragmentation.

Appendix

Dynastic diagrams of the principal royal families of 'Germany'
between the twelfth and fifteenth centuries. ✳

1 WELF (Guelf) and (HOHEN) STAUFEN

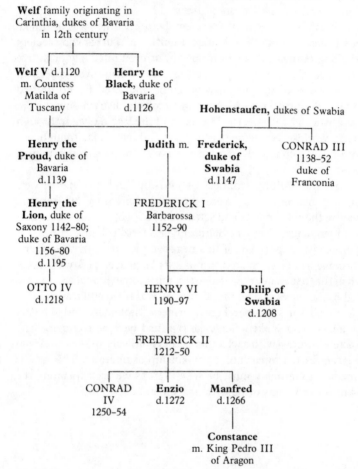

Welf family originating in
Carinthia, dukes of Bavaria
in 12th century

Welf V d.1120
m. Countess
Matilda of
Tuscany

Henry the
Black, duke of
Bavaria
d.1126

Hohenstaufen, dukes of Swabia

Henry the
Proud, duke of
Bavaria
d.1139

Judith m. **Frederick,**
duke of
Swabia
d.1147

CONRAD III
1138–52
duke of
Franconia

Henry the
Lion, duke of
Saxony 1142–80;
duke of Bavaria
1156–80
d.1195

FREDERICK I
Barbarossa
1152–90

OTTO IV
d.1218

HENRY VI
1190–97

Philip of
Swabia
d.1208

FREDERICK II
1212–50

CONRAD
IV
1250–54

Enzio
d.1272

Manfred
d.1266

Constance
m. King Pedro III
of Aragon

✳ 1. The diagrams have been deliberately simplified.
   2. Elected kings are shown in capital letters.

220

2 HABSBURG✳

Lord on the upper Rhine, friends of the Hohenstaufen in 13th century; had been designated Counts of Habsburg from 1090.

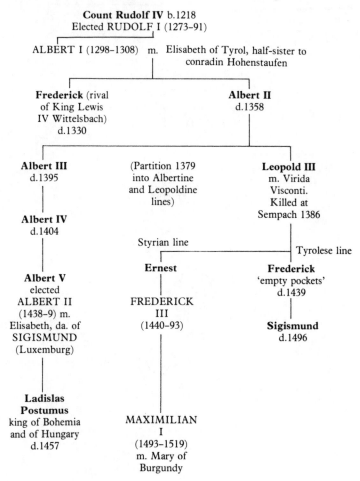

Count Rudolf IV b.1218
Elected RUDOLF I (1273–91)

ALBERT I (1298–1308) m. Elisabeth of Tyrol, half-sister to conradin Hohenstaufen

Frederick (rival of King Lewis IV Wittelsbach) d.1330

Albert II d.1358

Albert III d.1395

(Partition 1379 into Albertine and Leopoldine lines)

Leopold III m. Virida Visconti. Killed at Sempach 1386

Albert IV d.1404

Styrian line

Tyrolese line

Ernest

Frederick 'empty pockets' d.1439

Albert V elected ALBERT II (1438–9) m. Elisabeth, da. of SIGISMUND (Luxemburg)

FREDERICK III (1440–93)

Sigismund d.1496

Ladislas Postumus king of Bohemia and of Hungary d.1457

MAXIMILIAN I (1493–1519) m. Mary of Burgundy

✳The Laufenburg and Kiburg branches are not followed.

221

3 LUXEMBURG

Counts of Luxemburg since c. 1160.

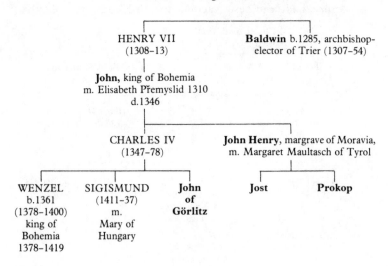

HENRY VII
(1308–13)

Baldwin b.1285, archbishop-
elector of Trier (1307–54)

John, king of Bohemia
m. Elisabeth Přemyslid 1310
d.1346

CHARLES IV
(1347–78)

John Henry, margrave of Moravia,
m. Margaret Maultasch of Tyrol

WENZEL
b.1361
(1378–1400)
king of
Bohemia
1378–1419

SIGISMUND
(1411–37)
m.
Mary of
Hungary

**John
of
Görlitz**

Jost

Prokop

4 WITTELSBACH

Counts of Scheyern, Bavaria, by eleventh century.
Family seat moved to Wittelsbach, nr. Augsburg, 1124.✳

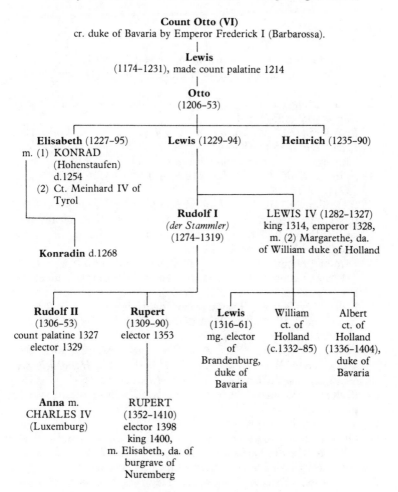

Count Otto (VI)
cr. duke of Bavaria by Emperor Frederick I (Barbarossa).

Lewis
(1174–1231), made count palatine 1214

Otto
(1206–53)

Elisabeth (1227–95)
m. (1) KONRAD
(Hohenstaufen)
d.1254
(2) Ct. Meinhard IV of
Tyrol

Konradin d.1268

Lewis (1229–94)

Heinrich (1235–90)

Rudolf I
(*der Stammler*)
(1274–1319)

LEWIS IV (1282–1327)
king 1314, emperor 1328,
m. (2) Margarethe, da.
of William duke of Holland

Rudolf II
(1306–53)
count palatine 1327
elector 1329

Rupert
(1309–90)
elector 1353

Lewis
(1316–61)
mg. elector
of
Brandenburg,
duke of
Bavaria

William
ct. of
Holland
(c.1332–85)

Albert
ct. of
Holland
(1336–1404),
duke of
Bavaria

Anna m.
CHARLES IV
(Luxemburg)

RUPERT
(1352–1410)
elector 1398
king 1400,
m. Elisabeth, da. of
burgrave of
Nuremberg

✳ 1. Most reference works, including the *Encyclopaedia Brittanica*, are vague and
ambiguous even on the main lines of this dynasty.

2. Main details here have been taken from *Stammtafeln zur Geschichte der
europäischen Staaten*, (2nd edn. Marburg, 1953), by Wilhelm Carl, Prinz von
Isenburg, esp. Plates 26a, 26d, 27 and 31.

No details have been given of the partitions.

Notes

Chapter 1

1 Jacob Grimm, *Kleinere Schriften* (1864–90), vol.1, p.227, cited by Peter Ganz, *Jacob Grimm's conception of German Studies* (1973), p.22.

2 Carlo Malagola (ed.), *Acta Nationis Germanica universitatis Bononiensis* (1887), p.4.

3 Paul Stapf (ed.), *Walther von der Vogelweide: Sprüche, Lieder, Der Leich* (Die Tempel-Klassiker, 1967), p.120 (top enumeration). The attempts at translation are mine.

4 Philippe Wolff, *Western Languages, AD 100 to 1500* (Engl. transl. 1971), pp.167–8.

5 P.G. Thielen, *Die Verwaltung des Ordensstaates Preussen* (1965), p.56. The regionalism of German speech is comically yet brilliantly treated by Günter Grass in *The Meeting at Telgte* (Engl.transl.1981), pp.21–22.

6 Otto of Freising, *The Deeds of Frederick Barbarossa* (transl. C.C. Mierow: Records of Civilization No. 38, Columbia University Press, 1953), Book 3, p.204, para.28.

7 F.R.H. Du Boulay, 'The German Town Chroniclers', in R.H.C. Davis and J.M. Wallace-Hadrill (eds.), *The Writing of History in the Middle Ages* (1981), p.463.

8 Ferdinand Seibt, 'Die Zeit der Luxemburger und der hussitischen Revolution', in Karl Bosl (ed.), *Handbuch der Geschichte der böhmischen Länder* (1967), p.461, n.5.

9 Walter Schlesinger in *Der Deutsche Territorialstaat*, vol.2, pp.101–26.

10 Wolff, op.cit., p.218.

11 Ottokar Lorenz, *Deutschlands Geschichtsquellen im Mittelalter seit der Mitte des 13. Jahrhunderts* (3rd edn., 1886–7), 2 vols., gives a general review of later medieval German chronicles.

12 For some of what follows see Heinrich Schmidt, cited in Bibliography; also Hans Patze in *Der Deutsche Territorialstaat*, vol.1, pp.9, 64.

13 Gerhart Burger, *Die südwestdeutschen Stadtschreiber im Mittelalter* (1960).

14 Fritz Ernst, 'Die Schweizer Chronisten' (cited in Bibliography).

15 For the memoirs of Götz von Berlichingen, see also p.70.
16 See Chapter 5 Note 48 for references.
17 The fundamental modern collection of these *Weistümer* is by Jacob Grimm (7 volumes, 1840–78, reprinted 1957). A comprehensive modern interpretation of these from a legal-social viewpoint is by Hermann Wiessner, *Sachinhalt und wirtschaftliche Bedeutung der Weistümer* (1934), but since updated by Dieter Werkmüller, *Über Aufkommen und Verbreitung der Weistümer* (1973) and Peter Blickle (ed.), *Deutsche ländliche Rechtsquellen* (1977).
18 Wiessner, op.cit., p.7.
19 ibid.,p.10, citing Grimm, op.cit., vol.3, p.823.
20 Patze, note 12 above.
21 *Der Deutsche Territorialstaat*, vol.1, p.36; vol.2, p.34.
22 In conversation with the author in October 1980.
23 Victor Scholderer, *Johann Gutenberg* (The Trustees of the British Museum, 1963) provides an excellent short account and further bibliography.
24 W.L. Schreiber, *The Illustrated Book in the fifteenth century* (1929), pp.10 ff. Albert Schramm, *Der Bilderschmuck der Frühdrucke* (Deutsches Museum für Buch und Schrift, 23 vols., Leipzig, 1920–), vol.1, Introduction. This great work supersedes that of Schreiber, though the latter remains useful.
25 Albert Boeckler, *Deutsche Buchmalerei der Gotik* (1959).
26 *Das mittelalterliche Hausbuch* was first fully published by the Germanisches National-Museum, Nuremberg, in 1866. A scholarly edition was made by Helmuth T. Bossert and Willy Storck for the Deutscher Verein für Kunstwissenschaft (1912), of which there is a copy in the Palaeography Room, University of London Library. A handy edition of the illustrations with commentary and bibliography to date was issued as vol.8 of the *Bibliothek des Germanischen National-Museums Nürnberg zur deutschen Kunst- und Kulturgeschichte*, ed. Ludwig Grote (1957).

Chapter 2

Where full citation of a work is not found here, it will be placed in the Bibliography.
1 E. Schubert, *König und Reich*, pp.239–40 and esp. n. 81.

2 For positive attitudes towards studying medieval Germany and its kingship, see, for example, Tim Reuter, 'A new history of medieval Germany' in *History*, vol.66 (1981), pp.440-4, as well as Schubert, cited above.

3 For a masterly account of this subject by the leading English expert, see Karl Leyser, 'Ottonian Saxony', *English Historical Review*, vol.96 (October 1981), pp.721-53.

4 Schubert, p.230.

5 R. Folz, p.49.

6 Schubert, pp.29-32, 230-4, and 230 n. 24.

7 For much of what follows, Schubert, pp.147-89.

8 Ibid., citing the Colmar Chronicle, MGH SS 17, p.246.

9 Schubert, p.156.

10 Ibid., p.182. Admittedly, he was great-grandson, through his mother, of Lewis IV.

11 Schubert, pp.178, 250 ff.

12 Ibid., pp.187, 188.

13 S. Rowan, 'Imperial taxes and German politics...'

14 P. Moraw, 'Kanzlei und Kanzleipersonal...'

15 H. Patze, *Der Deutsche Territorialstaat*, vol.1, ch.1.

16 Lechner; Trusen; Moraw, 'Zum königlichen Hofgericht' and 'Noch einmal...'

17 Lechner, p.70.

18 Ibid., p.100. See also Georg Gruber, *Die Verfassung des Rottweiler Hofgerichts* (1969).

19 Schubert, p.268.

20 Lhotsky, *Das Haus Habsburg;* Wiesflecker, vol.1, ch.2.

21 Elizabeth Wiskemann, *Czechs and Germans* (2nd ed.1967), ch.1 and map.

22 J.M. Klassen.

23 H.S. Offler, 'Empire and Papacy...'

24 For the Autobiography, Eugen Hillenbrand, *Die Autobiographie Karls IV: Einführung, Ubersetzung und Kommentar* Stuttgart, 1979. For other work on Charles IV see F. Seibt, *Kasser Karl IV: Staatsmann und Mäzen* (2nd ed. Munich, 1978).

25 S.H. Thompson.

26 P.W. Knoll, esp. p.215.

27 For the text of the Golden Bull, Zeumer, *Quellensammlung* (2nd ed.1913), no.148; see also Zeumer, *Die Goldene Bulle*, and Leyser, 'A recent view...'

28 This thesis is argued persuasively by Schubert, esp.pp.162-7, who regards it as characteristic of Charles IV to have acquired the Holy Lance for Prague but never to have bought any addition to the imperial regalia.

29 Bosl, p.486 n.2; Klassen, ch.4.

30 There are some curious parallels between Richard II and Wenzel IV, their characters and failures, but they are too speculative to discuss here.

31 Schubert, pp.254-76; Angermeier, p.317.

32 Moraw, 'Beamtentum...', and 'Kanzlei...'

33 I owe this reference to the kindness of Dr Martyn Rady, who has written an interesting dissertation on medieval Buda.

34 Schubert in 'Die Stellung...' argues that electors had begun to propose that they and not the emperor, with the Estates, were the embodiment of the Empire.

35 *Avisamentum pro reformatione sacri imperii* in *Acta Concilii Constantientis*, ed. K. Finke et al., 4 vols. (Munster, 1896-1928).

36 For an English translation and discussion see Strauss, *Manifestations;* see also Dohna and Koller in Bibliography; also Tilman Struve, 'Reform oder Revolution...?', *ZGO* 126 (1978), pp.73-129.

37 For Frederick III see esp. Lhotsky, *Das Haus Habsburg*, vol.2, pp.119-63, and Wiesflecker, vol.1.

38 On the portraits see *Frederick III: Katalog* and Pearce.

39 «Wer spricht von Siegen?/Uberstehn ist alles» (R.M. Rilke: *Requiem für Wolf Graf v. Kalckreuth* (1908)).

40 Wiesflecker, p.61.

41 For this wise motto see F. de Reiffenberg, *Histoire de l'orde de la Toison d'or...* (Brussels, 1830), p.94, cited by Wiesflecker, vol.1, p.503 n.36.

42 Mühlich, the Augsburg chronicler, regarded Corvinus and Podiebrady with contempt as usurpers. Here is another sidelight on the developing feeling of German-ness among Augsburg and Strassburg chroniclers in the fifteenth century *(Die Chroniken der deutschen Städte*, vol.22, p.xxvii). For the episode see Karl Nehring, *Matthias Corvinus, Kaiser Friedrich III, und das Reich* (1975).

43 Wiesflecker, vol.1, pp.58-9.

44 Ibid., p.96.

45 Ziehen, and H. Baron.

46 Wiesflecker, p.353.

Chapter 3

1 For example, Fritz Ernst, *Eberhard im Bart* (Stuttgart, 1933, repr. 1970), Foreword.

2 H.H. Hofmann, 'Territorienbildung in Franken im 14. Jahrhundert', in *Der Deutsche Territorialstaat im 14. Jahrhundert*, vol.2 (1970), ch.19.

3 A good summary explanation of the 'princely estate' *(Reichsfürstenstand)* is given by Th. Mayer, *Fürsten und Staat* (1950), pp.307 ff. He describes princes as *primi inter pares* with the king and, up to the twelfth century, confined to a more or less closed circle of families. Dukes were the essential type of the princedom *(der Grundtypus des Fürstentums)*. Counts were originally only delegates and officials of the king, but after the twelfth century some of these became elevated to princely status as full members of imperial Diets and possessors of the highest jurisdiction. Like Otto of Freising, Mayer speaks rather condescendingly of such new princes.

   See also Georg Sante, *Geschichte der deutschen Länder* «Territorien-Ploetz», vol.1: *Die Territorien bis zum Ende des alten Reiches* (1964), esp.pp.23 ff.; and J.W. Stieber, *Pope Eugenius IV, the Council of Basel and the secular and ecclesiastical authorities in the empire* (Leiden, 1978), esp. pp.122-4, 123 n.16, and Appendix H.

4 *Gesta Friderici I imperatoris*, Book I, paras. 7, 9, 20. Paperback edn., pp.41, 50, 53.

5 On knighthood, see Eberhard Otto, 'Von der Abschliessung des Ritterstandes', *HZ*, vol.162 (1940), pp.19–39 and, a more popular treatment, Alexander Freiherr von Reitzenstein, *Rittertum und Ritterschaft*, ed. Ludwig Grote (Nuremberg, 1972). See also Ph. Dollinger, 'Aspects de la noblesse allemande, XIe eau XIIIe siècles', in *La Nobless au moyen âge... essais à la mémoiré de Robert Boutruche*, ed. Ph. Contamine (1976), pp.133-49.

6 H.S.M. Stuart (ed.), *The Autobiography of Götz von Berlichingen* (1956) is an edition of the original text in its Franconian dialect of Early New High German with survivals of MHG. See also Helgard Ulmschneider, *Götz von Berlichingen, ein adeliges Leben der deutschen Renaissance* (1974).

7 Otto Brunner, *Land und Herrschaft* (see Bibliography).

8 Op.cit., p.20: '...wann wir aus rechter sippzal und von plut an

einander gefrundet und gewont, darumb dann sunderlich unser jeder furste dem andern frundschaft, liebe und alles guten wol pflichtig sein'.

9 Op.cit., p.77.

10 Albert K. Hömberg, *Westfälische Landesgeschichte* (1967), p.193: 'Der Adel der verschiedenen Fürsten und Landesherren war...eng miteinander verwandt, versippt und sonstwie verbunden...'

11 It is interesting here to recall the Count von Mölln who in Thomas Mann's *Buddenbrooks* is portrayed as a working farmer on a contemptibly small property, though of course that was in nineteenth-century Mecklenburg.

12 *Quellen*, no.228.

13 Herbert Obenaus (see Bibliography).

14 Op.cit., pp.183-4.

15 Op.cit., pp.194-5, 202.

16 Op.cit., pp.222-3.

17 See especially Angermeier.

18 Op.cit., p.102: 'die strazze befriden und aller mengelich auf wazzer und auf lande beschirmen, als verre sie mügen...jeder...in sinem gebite und gerihte'.

19 *CDS* vol.7, pp.XV,228: '...des sprak de Keiser, he kerde sik an nein recht, wenn wat sine vorsten in seinem hove vunden, dat scholde bliven...'

20 Angermeier, p.201.

21 Ibid., pp.403,443.

22 F.R.H. Du Boulay, 'Law Enforcement...' (see Bibliography) and references there given. The *Grosser Historischer Atlas* (also see Bibliography), Plate 71b, provides a good map of the Westphalian courts' extent of activity and of some of the organized opposition to them.

23 *Quellen*, no.228.

24 Ibid., no.172.

25 Ibid., no.182.

26 Ibid., no.170

27 Ibid., no.203. See also Hans Patze, 'Die bäuerliche Gemeinde im Ordensstaat Preussen', in *Die Anfänge der Landgemeinde...*, vol.2, esp. p.165. It is here explained brilliantly how a new community could not exist without a fixed law *(ohne schriftlich fixiertes Recht*

keine Gemeinde). I owe this and other Prussian references to the kindness of my pupil, Dr M.C.B. Burleigh.

28 On *Stadtrecht*, see Planitz, op.cit., esp. pp.331 ff. Nuremberg is discussed by Gerald Strauss, *Nuremberg in the Sixteenth Century.*

29 For some of this, see Georg Dahm, 'On the reception of Roman and Italian law in Germany', in G. Strauss (ed.), *Pre-Reformation Germany*, pp.282–315.

30 G. Aubin, 'Die Einfluss der Rezeption des römischen Rechtes auf den deutschen Bauernstand', *JNS* vol.99 (1912), pp.721–42.

Chapter 4

1 Georg W. Sante and A.G. Ploetz, *Geschichte der deutschen Länder* «Territorien-Ploetz», vol.1, 'Die Territorien bis zum Ende des alten Reiches' (Würzburg, 1964), Introduction, p.xi.

2 *Grosser Historischer Weltatlas*, Part 2: Middle Ages, ed. Josef Engel, Bayerischer Schulbuch-Verlag (2nd edn., 1979), pp.22–3 for the property of the Salians. A convenient English atlas, though less detailed and learned, is *The Hamlyn Historical Atlas* (ed. R.I. Moore) (1981), esp. Plates 23 and 34.

3 For the number of princes, see J.W. Stieber (listed in Bibliography), Appendix H. A rough and ready list of countships may be compiled from the index of names in Angermeier.

4 Alan Mayhew, Fig.18. See also K.S. Bader (Bibliography) and Bruno Gebhardt, *Handbuch...*, vol.2, which provides a politico-geographical round-up of the German territories, invaluable for reference.

5 E. Christiansen, *The Northern Crusade* (1980), p.149.

6 Volker Press, 'Die Ritterschaft...'

7 Günther Franz, *Geschichte des Bauernstandes*, pp.80–99; also Franz, *Quellen*, no.213.

8 Below, chapter 5.

9 *Der Deutsche Territorialstaat*, vol.1, no.9.

10 Diestelkamp, 'Lehnrecht...', pp.65–96.

11 For Trier, see esp. Laufner; also W. Hess and, on the great fifteenth-century archbishop, Stieber.

12 Laufner, op.cit., p.142.

13 For Württemberg, see esp. Fritz Ernst, *Eberhard im Bart* (1933); K.S. Bader, op.cit. above, n.4; and *Ausgang*.

14 Ernst, op.cit., esp. chapters 2 and 3, and most particularly p.110: '...*Diese Räte oder ein Teil von ihnen bilden eine diplomatische Zunft. Sie kennen sich im ganzen Reich...*'

15 Ibid., p.48: '*Immer ist es aber der Graf, der zuletzt regiert.*'

16 *Stadt und Stadtherr*, pp.283–300.

17 For Saxony, see principally Hans Patze, 'Die welfischen Territorien im 14. Jahrhundert' in *Der Deutsche Territorialstaat*, vol.2.

18 For Brandenburg, see Gebhardt, op.cit., vol.2; also Georg Droege, 'Die Ausbildung der mittelalterlichen territorialen Finanzverwaltung' in *Der Deutsche Territorialstaat*, vol.1, and esp. Walter Schlesinger, 'Zur Geschichte der Landesherrschaft in den Marken Brandenburg und Meissen während des 14. Jahrhunderts', in ibid., vol.2.

19 Schlesinger, op.cit., p.111: '*res enim tantum valet, quantum vendi potest*'.

20 F.L. Carsten, 'Medieval democracy in the Brandenburg towns and its defeat in the fifteenth century', *TRHS* 4th series, No.5 (1943), pp.73–91.

21 Ernst, op.cit., p.221: '*Recht, Münze und Landfrieden*'; also H.W. Koch, *A History of Prussia* (1978), p.31.

22 There is a large amount of printed work, sources and historical writing, on the Teutonic Order. The texts are mostly first-rate, though the history has for obvious reasons been singularly at the mercy of political aspirations. Of major use here must be cited Prof. Peter Thielen, *Die Verwaltung des Ordensstaates Preussen im 15. Jahrhundert* (1965), and Prof. Reinhard Wenskus, *Das Ordensland Preussen als Territorialstaat des 14. Jahrhunderts*, in *Der Deutsche Territorialstaat*, vol.1. Also Eric Christiansen, *The Northern Crusades* (1980). I owe a special debt to Mr Michael Burleigh, who has written a doctoral dissertation on the Order from its archives, now in Berlin, and who has shown me his characteristic generosity and learning.

23 Wenskus, op.cit., esp. pp.351 ff. and 352 n.24.
A portion of the text here cited runs:
He wart ein vragin drate
Nach Alexandri state
Nach sines heres geleginheit...
[i.e. Porus wanted to find out quickly about Alexander's state of

military preparedness.]

Chapter 5

1 Erich Keyser, *Bevölkerungsgeschichte Deutschlands* (2nd edn., Leipzig 1941), pp.264–6. For the problems of urban demography in Germany, see Roger Mols, *Introduction à la démographie historique des villes d'Europe du XIV e au XVIII e siècle* (Louvain, 1954), esp. I, 30–43.

2 *Stadtherr*, 349–50: "...Finally, it has been said, although only in private conversations, that in the fourteenth century a town was simply what was called a town...what was founded by a lord with the intention of founding a town, a settlement of which the inhabitants *(Bürger)* felt themselves self-consciously to be burghers of a town..."

3 Hans Planitz, *Die deutsche Stadt im Mittelalter* (Graz-Koln, 1954), Part II, para.1.

4 Heinz Stoob, 'Minderstädte: Formen der Stadtentstehung im Spätmittelalter', *VSWG* 46 (1959), pp.1–28.

5 *Op.cit.*, 4. *to wicbelde = das Weichbild* = a small town or suburb of a larger one, enjoying burghal freedoms.

6 Convenient reproductions of early views of Nuremberg are to be found in Gerhard Pfeiffer and Wilhelm Schwemmer (eds.), *Geschichte Nürnbergs in Bilddokumenten* (2nd ed., Verlag C.H. Beck, Munich, 1971).

7 C.V. Malfatti, *Two Italian accounts of Tudor England* (Barcelona, 1953), from a Latin MS in the Escorial Library.

8 Heinrich Schmidt, *Die deutschen Städtechroniken als Spiegel des bürgerlichen Selbstverständnisses im Spätmittelalter* (Schriftenreihe der Historischen Kommission bei der bayerischen Akademie der Wissenschaften, Schrift 3, Göttingen, 1958), p.38.

9 C.T. Smith, *An historical geography of western Europe before 1800* (1967), pp.305–6.

10 Stoob, op.cit., p.22: '...in dwarf states powers and apparatus were in any case appropriate to dwarf towns. Here town life was lived in miniature...'

11 Wilhelm Störmer, 'Stadt und Stadtherr im wittelsbachischen

Altbayern des 14. Jahrhunderts', in *Stadtherr*, pp.257–82. (The page enumerations given here include the often valuable printed discussions which took place after the reading of the conference papers.)

12 Johannes Bischoff, 'Die Stadtherrschaft des 14. Jahrhunderts im ostfränkischen Städtedreieck Nürnberg-Bamberg-Coburg-Bayreuth, in ibid., esp. pp.108–9.

13 Josef Joachim Menzel, 'Die schlesischen Städte am Ausgang des Mittelalters', *Ausgang*, pp.251 ff.

14 For what follows, see H. Patze, 'Die Bildung der landherrlichen Residenzen in Reich während des 14. Jahrhunderts', in *Stadtherr*, pp.1–54.

15 See pp.132–40.

16 Menzel, op.cit., p.255: '…Verschiedentlich wurde…auch die örtliche Pfarrkirche zur Kollegiatkirche oder Hofkirche erhoben, in der der Fürst und seine Familie ihre Grablege wählten.'

17 Patze, op.cit., pp.20–5.

18 *Stadtherr*, p.301.

19 Ibid., pp.318–9.

20 See Gerhard Pfeiffer, 'Stadtherr und Gemeinde in den spätmittelalterlichen Reichsstädten', in *Ausgang*, 201–26.

21 Ibid., p.203: '…dat we unserm herrn, herrn Karl, keyser des hilgen rikes, willen tru und hold wesen.'

22 Two convenient modern works are: Gerhard Pfeiffer (ed.), *Nürnberg — Geschichte einer europäischen Stadt* (Munich, 1971), and Gerald Strauss, *Nuremberg in the Sixteenth Century* (New York, 1966).

23 Karlheinz Blaschke, 'Städte und Stadtherren im meissnischlausitzischen Raum während des 14. Jahrhunderts', in *Stadtherr*, pp.53–78. For Silesia, see p.120.

24 Peter Csendes, 'Die Donaustädte von Passau bis Pressburg im 15. Jahrhundert', in *Ausgang*, pp.95–108; also Karl Gutkas, 'Das Städtewesen der österreichischen Donauländer und der Steiermark im 14. Jahrhundert', in *Stadtherr*, pp.229–50.

25 For what follows, see largely Rudolf Seigel's stimulating paper, 'Die württembergische Stadt am Ausgang des Mittelalters — Probleme der Verfassungs- und Sozialstruktur', in *Ausgang*, pp.177–200.

26 Dietrich W. H. Schwarz, 'Die Städte der Schweiz im 15.

Jahrhundert', in *Ausgang,* pp.45–62.

27 For introduction to the literature, see Select Bibliography under Dollinger; also *Hanse in Europa;* Scammell and Schildhauer. For Switzerland see pp.130-1 and D.W.H. Schwarz in *Ausgang;* also E. Bonjour et al., *A short history of Switzerland* (1952).

28 See pp.134-5.

29 See p.45.

30 For this story, *CDS* VII (Magdeburg *Schöppenchronik*), XV, 228.

31 Peter Moraw, esp. in 'Deutsches Königtum und bürgerliche Geldwirtschaft um 1400', *VSWG* 55 (1968), pp.289–328.

32 For Charles IV, see U. Dirlmeier, 'Mittelalterliche Hoheitsträger im wirtschaftlichen Wettbewerb', *VSWG* Beiheft nr. 51 (1966), pp.164–79; and P. Moraw, 'Monarchie und Bürgertum' in *Kaiser Karl IV: Staatsmann und Mäzen* (ed. F. Seibt, 1978), 43–63. For Richard II, see esp. Caroline Barron, 'Richard Whittington: the man behind the myth', in W. Kellaway and A. Hollaender (eds.), *Studies in London History* (1969), pp.197–248.

33 Peter Moraw, 'Königtum und Hochfinanz in Deutschland, 1350-1450' in *ZGO* 122 (New Series 83) (1974), pp.23–34.

34 Moraw, *ZGO* art cit. above.

35 For much of this see Wolfgang von Stromer, 'Ein Wirtschaftsprojekt des deutschen Königs Siegmund' in *VSWG* 51 (1964), pp.374–82; also Lore Sporhan-Krempel and W. v. Stromer, 'Das Handelshaus der Stromer von Nürnberg und die Geschichte der ersten deutschen Papiermühle' in *VSWG* 47 (1960), pp.81–104.

36 *Ausgang,* pp.226.

37 This debate is outlined by A.B. Hibbert in *Past and Present* vol.1 No.3 (1953), who argues as against Pirenne that patriciates were not exclusively composed of newcomers, hostile to existing aristocracies, but were formed partly by the entry of older families into commerce.

38 The ancestry is shown in the Stromer book of family memoirs *(Püchel von meim geslechet und von abentewr)* begun in 1360 by Ulman Stromer, CDS, vol.1.

39 *CDS* vol.4, p.338.

40 A. von Brandt, *Geist und Politik in der lübeckischen Geschichte* (Lübeck, 1954), chs. 1, 3, 6. The phrase 'holy sobriety' — *heilige Nüchternheit* — is von Brandt's but a foreigner who admires the

works of Thomas Mann may be forgiven for stealing it.

41 *CDS* XVII, esp. pp.315–20.

42 'Während sich in den Unterschichten ein Kollektivbewusstsein ausbildete, das bis zu radikalen Handlungen führte, entstand in der Oberschicht ein Individualbewusstsein, dessen Zeugnisse in einem bisher unbekannten Ausmass Briefe, Tagebücher und Autobiographien bzw. Familiengeschichten sind... Für alle diese Zeugnisse ist der überaus subjektive Gehalt kennzeichnend...' (From *Ausgang,* pp.23–4).

43 A. von Brandt, op.cit., Part III.

44 Gerald Strauss, *Nuremberg in the Sixteenth Century* (New York, 1966), ch. 2.

45 Bernhard Kirchgässner, 'Die Auswirkung des rheinischen Münzvereins im Gegenspiel von Reich und Territorien Südwestdeutschlands und der angrenzenden Eidgenossenschaft', in *Der Deutsche Territorialstaat* 1 (Sigmaringen, 1970), pp.225–56, esp. p.241. The author notes of the Esslinger family disasters: 'sie waren also nicht ausgestorben, sondern nur völlig verarmt.'

46 See p.160-3.

47 *Ausgang,* p.40 n.206; see ibid., pp.19–24.

48 See Baxandall, ch.4; Maschke, 'Verfassung...'; and Barth, *Argumentation.*

49 *CDS* XII.

50 See pp.9-10.

51 For the 'infamy' of certain trades, see W. Danckwerts, *Unehrliche Leute* (Munich, 1963). A knacker was more or less in the same class with an executioner. On the other hand a man like Merkel Metzeler (butcher) of Speyer made money by delivering pigs to the royal court and found himself on the Council from 1393 to 1408 (Maschke, op.cit.).

52 Erich Maschke, 'Verfassung und soziale Kräfte in der deutschen Stadt des späten Mittelalters, vornehmlich in Oberdeutschland', *VSWG* 46 (1959), pp.289–349; 433–76.

53 These remarks cannot be applied with equal force to all cities. Constance and Esslingen were less rigid about prohibiting their patricians from trade. Ravensburg and Strassburg, on the other hand, were more rigid and snobbish (Maschke, op.cit., pp.454 ff.).

54 Cf. Aristotle, *The Politics*, Book II, ch 11, paras. 10–12.
55 Maschke, op.cit., p.333.
56 Peter Burke, *Popular Culture in early modern Europe* (1978). But for the material conditions of the poorer groups, see E. Maschke, 'Die Unterschichten der mittelalterlichen Städte Deutschlands' in *Veröffentlichungen der Kommission für geschichtliche Landeskunde in Baden-Württemberg* (Reiche B, Forschungen, Bd. 41).
57 Maschke, 'Unterschichten', pp.7 and 72–4. He cites *CDS* vol. 22, p.209: '...*der verdorbene Mann kehrt sich zu dem Bösen*'.
58 Schmidt, see Bibliography.
59 *CDS* XXIV, pp.185–189.
60 E.g. British Library, The Map Room, MAPS C.2.a7(2); another copy is in the National Gallery of Art, Washington, DC, USA.
61 Wilhelm Treue and others (eds.), *Das Hausbuch der Mendelschen Zwölfbrüderstiftung zu Nürnberg* (Munich, 1965), vol. I, pp.74 ff.
62 Joël Lefebvre, *Les Fols et la Folie: études sur les genres du comique et la création littéraire en Allemagne pendant la Renaissance* (Paris, 1968); also Werner Lenk, *Das Nürnberger Fastnachtspiel des 15. Jahrhunderts* (Berlin, 1968). For a wide-ranging essay on carnival origins, M.J. Rudwin, 'The origin of German Carnival comedy', in *Journal of English and German Philology*, vol. 18 (1919), pp.402–54.
63 E.g. Campbell Dodgson, *Albrecht Dürer. Masters of Engraving and Etching. A chronological catalogue* (London and Boston, 1926), No.79. Also '*The Village Feast*' (*Kirmes*) by Daniel Hopfner (1470–1536) of Augsburg (Berlin Kupferstichkabinett).
64 For a summary of this view, see Günther Franz, *Geschichte des deutschen Bauernstandes* (1970), ch.8.
65 For some discussion of these themes in relation to central Germany, see Albrecht Timm, *Studien zur Siedlungs-und Agrargeschichte Mitteldeutschlands* (Cologne, 1956), pp.117–72.
66 Karlheinz Blaschke, 'Städte und Stadtherren im meissnisch-lausitzischen Raum während des 14. Jahrhunderts', in *Stadtherr*, pp.63 ff.
67 *CDS* XV.
68 Rhiman A. Rotz, 'Investigating urban uprisings with examples from Hanseatic towns, 1374–1416', in *Order and Innovation in the Middle Ages: essays in honour of Joseph R. Strayer*, ed. W.C.

Jordan et al. (Princeton, 1976), pp.215–33.

69 Albert Hömberg, *Westfälische Landesgeschichte* (Münster, 1967), ch.9.

70 Konrad Fritze, *Bürger und Bauer zur Hansezeit* (Studien zu den Stadt-Land Beziehungen an der südwestlichen Ostseeküste vom 13. bis zum 16. Jahrhundert. Weimar, 1976). Other treatments of townsmen acquiring property in the surrounding countryside are E.J. Schneider on Metz, D. Herlihy on Pistoia, D.M. Nicholas on Flanders; but these seem not to show townsmen settling down as country gentry in the English (or Westphalian) manner.

71 Theodore Fontane, *Wanderungen in die Mark Brandenburg,* written during the years 1862 to 1889.

72 For some of what follows, see Erich Maschke, 'Deutsche Städte am Ausgang des Mittelalters', in *Ausgang,* pp.1–44.

73 F.L. Carsten, 'Medieval democracy in the Brandenburg towns and its defeat in the fifteenth century', *T.R.H.S.* Fourth series, No.25 (1943), pp.73–91.

74 See note on p.61 above. More about these people has been brought to light by Michael Toch, *Die nürnberger Mittelschichten* (1978) since this chapter was written.

75 For these figures see the article by Wilhelm Treue and Rudolf Kellerman on 'The social and economic significance of the Nuremberg crafts in the fifteenth and sixteenth centuries', in *Das Hausbuch der Mendelschen Zwölfbrüderstiftung zu Nürnberg,* ed. W. Treue u.a. (Munich, 1965), pp.71–91.

76 Gerald Strauss, *Nuremberg in the Sixteenth Century* (New York, 1966), ch.1.

77 Quoted by E. Maschke in *Ausgang,* p.6 from the Augsburg chronicle of Clemens Sender in *CDS,* XXIII, p.219

Chapter 6

1 Albrecht Timm, *Studien zur Siedlungs- und Agrargeschichte Mitteldeutschlands* (1956), pp.136–50.

2 Hermann Wiessner, *Sachinhalt und wirtschaftliche Bedeutung der Weistümer* (1934), pp.75–96.

3 Ibid., ch.7: '*so bitten die armen Leute;... beschweren;... ablehnen.*

4 *Quellen,* nos. 169, 170.

5 Ibid., no.183.

6 Ibid., no.196.

7 Ibid., no.228 and pp.73-74.

8 The *Kulmer Handfeste* was drawn up in 1233, not as a noble landlaw but a communal townlaw, originally from Kulm. For all this, see H. Patze, 'Die deutsche bäuerliche Gemeinde im Ordensstaat Preussen', in *Die Anfänge der Landgemeinde*, vol.2, pp.149-200.

9 *Quellen*, no.203.

10 The *Handfest* of Schlochau in 1382, for example, in appointing Klaus Virchow as *Schulz* of Crampczk, said 'that Klaus and his heirs and successors shall serve us against heathendom and other enemies, as do other *Schulzen* who are settled in the district of Schlochau' (Patze, op.cit., p.161, n.40).

11 As at Wapczh in 1288 *de consilio et consensu rusticorum* (Patze, op.cit., p.171).

12 The major scholar in this work has, of course, been Wilhelm Abel, to whose writings (see Bibliography) this chapter is heavily indebted. An interesting English interpretation is by Alan Mayhew, *Rural settlement and farming in Germany* (1973).

13 Elisabeth Carpentier, 'Autour de la peste noire', *Annales, Economics, Sociétés*, vol. 17 (1962), pp.1062-92.

14 *Quellen*, no.191a.

15 Mayhew, *op.cit.*, ch.3.

16 Konrad Fritze, *Bürger und Bauer zur Hansezeit* (1976). See also pp.161-2.

17 Karl Czok, 'The socio-economic structure and political role of the suburbs in Saxony and Thuringia', in Scribner (see Bibliography).

18 Tom Scott, 'The Peasants' War...'

19 Timm, op.cit., pp.132-3.

20 *Quellen*, no.214. For an interesting if somewhat confused discussion, see Kurt Uhrig (Bibliography).

21 For a summary to the date of publication, Peter Blickle, 'Peasant revolts in the German empire in the late middle ages', *Social History* vol.4, no.2 (May 1979), pp.223-39.

22 Timm, op.cit., pp.136-68.

23 *Quellen*, no.181.

24 As well as instances in Franz, *Bauernkrieg*, there is a good example in the suit of Hans Hay, citizen of Waldsee, against the

abbot of Schussenried who was trying to claim him as a serf (Obenaus, ch.3).

25 *Quellen,* no.175.
26 See the review by Tom Scott in *English Historical Review,* vol.96 (1981), pp.135-8 of Claudia Ulbrich, *Leibherrschaft am Oberrhein im Spätmittelalter* (1979), which I have not yet seen.
27 Konrad Fritze, op.cit., ch.5 modifies the very general statements of Jerome Blum, 'The Rise of Serfdom in Eastern Europe', *American Historical Review,* vol. 62 (July 1957), pp.807-36.
28 Franz, *Geschichte,* ch.7, and *Quellen* no.237.
29 Op.cit., pp.45-8.

Chapter 7

1 The 'royalist' quality of the English church even before the Reformation is well brought out by Denys Hay in 'The Church of England in the later Middle Ages', *History,* vol. 53 (1968), pp.35 ff; also A. Hamilton Thompson, *The English Clergy in the later Middle Ages* (1947), ch.1.
2 Hefele-Leclercq, vol.VII, Part 2, p.1062.
3 '...*gemeyn versamenung der germanischen Kirchen adder eyn concilium nacionale.*' (Werminghoff, p.163.)
4 Gnesen might be omitted from a list of German provinces as it was largely Polish, but has been included here for the sake of the partly German dioceses noted above. Gran has been omitted despite the Habsburg rule of Hungary.
5 A full description will be furnished by the great work now in progress: *Germania Sacra: Historisch-statistische Beschreibung der Kirche des Alten Reichs* (Max-Planck-Institut für Geschichte, 1929–).
6 Aloys Schulte, *Der Adel und die deutsche Kirche im Mittelalter: Studien zur Sozial-, Rechts- und Kirchengeschichte* (Darmstadt, 3rd edn., 1958) pp.61-73.
7 Albert Hauck, *Kirchengeschichte Deutschlands* (Leipzig, 1887-1920), vol.5, part 2, pp.1137-94.
8 Schulte, op.cit., pp.7-8.
9 Ibid., pp.299-300.
10 F.R.H. Du Boulay (ed.), *Registrum Thome Bourgchier archiepiscopi Cantuariensis* (Canterbury and York Society, vol. liv,

1954–5), xxx, pp.136–7, 146–50.

11 Cited by Werminghoff, op.cit., pp.166–7.
12 Naendrup-Reiman in *Der Deutsche Territorialstaat,* vol.1, p.163.
13 Werminghoff, pp.168, 169 n.4.
14 Hefele-Leclercq, vol. VII Part 1, p.605.
15 No account of the Hussite revolution is attempted in this book, which is intended to be about Germany, but reference may be made to the work shown in the Select Bibliography by Kaminsky, Klassen and Heymann.
16 Ibid., p.145; also H.J. Cohn, *The Government of the Rhine Palatinate in the fifteenth century* (1965), ch.vi.
17 For a few words on this distinction, see p.208.
18 Ex inf. Prof. Dr Peter Classen of Heidelberg, April 1980.
19 Cohn, op.cit.
20 Naendrup-Reiman, op.cit; Fritz Ernst, *Eberhard im Bart,* ch. 7.
21 Gerald Strauss, *Nuremberg in the Sixteenth Century* (New York, 1966), I.
22 See Section (c).
23 The same was true of the roughly similar concordats for Italy, France, Spain and England. See Hefele-Leclercq, *Histoire des Conciles* VII, 1, pp.536–49. An agreed version of the German concordat was written in the register of the papal chancery under the date 15 April 1418, intended to be valid for five years, though it fell into oblivion.
24 This is more fully dealt with in the newly published work by J.W. Stieber, *Pope Eugenius IV, the Council of Basel and the secular and ecclesiastical authorities in the Empire: the conflict over supreme authority and power in the Church* (Leiden, 1978).
25 At its peak in 1436 it comprised some 500 to 600 members, but that included barely twenty bishops and thirteen abbots (Hefele-Leclercq, op.cit., VII, 2, p.926).
26 Hefele-Leclercq, op.cit., pp.1061 ff.
27 Hefele-Leclercq, op.cit., VII, 2, p.1089.
28 Hefele-Leclercq, op.cit., VII, 2, p.702.
29 Gerald Strauss, *Manifestations of Discontent in Germany on the eve of the Reformation* (Indiana, 1971).
30 See pp.201-2.
31 Lewis W. Spitz, 'The Course of German Humanism' in *Itinerarium Italicum* (Leiden, 1975), pp.371–436.

32　See p.191.

33　Hefele-Leclercq, op.cit, VI, 2, pp.728-9.

34　Ibid., p.788.

35　Ibid., p.793.

36　Ibid., pp.1430-1; cf. VII, 1, pp.594-6.

37　Ibid., VI, p.605.

38　Ibid., VII, p.597.

39　Ibid., VI, pp.649-50.

40　Hefele-Leclercq, op.cit., VI, 2, p.903.

41　These churches belonged, of course, to neighbouring but different provinces.

42　Hefele-Leclercq, op.cit. VI, 2, p.1401.

43　Ibid., VII, 1, pp.603-10.

44　E.g. Hefele-Leclercq, op.cit., VII, 2, 1274 ff; also the Lübeck chroniclers, especially Johann Hertze, printed in *CDS*, vol.30.

45　There is, of course, an enormous literature on Cusa. For non-specialists the English *Life* by Henry Bett (1932) is still serviceable; in French the study by E. Vansteenberghe (Paris, 1920) is much more comprehensive. More up to date is Paul E. Sigmund, *Nicholas of Cusa and medieval political thought* (1963).

46　Cited in Heiko Oberman, *The Harvest of Medieval Theology* (Harvard, 1963), p.54 n.77: '...sequor nunc opinionem magistri, quam etiam sequitur profundissimus veritatis indagator Guilhelmus Occam cuius doctrinam tanquam clariorem frequentius imitor.'

47　Gerard Pfeiffer (ed.), *Geschichte Nürnbergs in Bilddokumenten* (2nd edn., 1971), p.32; Gerald Strauss, *Nuremberg in the Sixteenth Century* (New York, 1966), esp. ch. 4.

48　William M. Landeen, 'The beginnings of the *Devotio Moderna* in Germany', *State College of Washington Research Studies*, vol.19 (1951) pp.162-202, 221-53; vol.21 (1953) pp.275-309; vol.22 (1954) pp.57-75. See also A.G. Dickens, *The German Nation and Martin Luther* (1974), esp. pp.19-20.

49　R.W. Southern, *Western Society and the Church in the Middle Ages* (Pelican History of the Church, 2, 1970), esp. p.356.

50　B. Moeller, 'Religious life in Germany on the eve of the Reformation', in Gerald Strauss (ed.), *Pre-Reformation Germany* (1972), p.15.

51　A useful modern translation is that by K.W. Maurer (London,

1947).

52 *'De bur ist om dichsten bi uns Hergoot'*, cited in Fliche et Martin, op.cit., vol.14(1), p.404.

53 *'Maria, bitt Gott für uns/Du hertzogin in Bayen bist'* (Benno Hubensteiner, *Bayerische Geschichte: Staat und Volk, Kunst und Kultur* (2nd edn., Munich, 1952), ch.15.

54 Jürgen Sydow, 'Spital und Stadt in Kanonistik und Verfassungsgeschichte des 14. Jahrhunderts', *Der Deutsche Territorialstaat* 1, pp.175-95.

55 Hubensteiner, op.cit., ch.15. For their importance in Württemberg, see *Ausgang*, 199.

56 Wilhelm Treue et al., *Das Hausbuch der Mendelschen Zwölfbrüderstiftung zu Nürnberg* (2 vols., Munich, 1965).

57 Cf. E. Maschke, 'Verfassung und soziale Kräfte in der deutschen Stadt des späten Mittelalters, vornehmlich in Oberdeutschland', *VSWG* 46 (1959), pp.289-349.

58 See p.210.

Select Bibliography

Abel, Wilhelm. 'Wüstungen und Preisfall im spätmittelalterlichen Europe', *JNS*, vol.165 (1953), pp.380–427.

Abel, Wilhelm. *Die Wüstungen des ausgehenden Mittelalters* (2nd edn. 1955). *Agrarkrisen und Agrarkonjunktur in Mitteleuropa vom 13. bis zum 19. Jahrhundert* (2nd edn 1966). Also transl. into English by O. Ordish.

Abel, Wilhelm. *Geschichte der deutschen Landwirtschaft vom frühen Mittelalter bis zum 19. Jahrhundert* (2nd edn. 1967).

Angermeier. See Abbreviations.

Atlas. See under *Grosser.*

Aubin, Gustav. 'Der Enfluss der Rezeption des römischen Rechtes auf der Deutschen Bauernstand', *JNS*, vol.99 (1912), pp.721–42.

Ausgang. See Abbreviations.

Bader, K.S. *Der deutsche Südwesten in seiner territorialstaatlichen Entwicklung* (1950).

Baron, Hans. 'Imperial Reform and the Habsburgs, 1486–1504', *American Historical Review*, vol.44 (1939), pp.293–303.

Barth, Reinhard. *Argumentation und Selbstverständnis der Bürgeropposition in städtischen Auseinandersetzungen des Spätmittelalters* (1974).

Baxandall, Michael D.K. *The Limewood Sculptors of Renaissance Germany* (1980).

Berlichingen, Götz von. *Autobiography,* ed. H.S.M. Stuart (1956). See also under Ulmschneider.

Bett, Henry. *Nicholas of Cusa* (1932).

Bischoff, Johannes. 'Die Stadtherrschaft des 14. Jahrhunderts im ostfränkischen Städtedreieck Nürnberg-Bamberg-Coburg-Bayreuth', in *Stadtherr.*

Blaschke, Karlheinz. 'Städte und Stadtherren im meissnisch-lausitzischen Raum während des 14. Jahrhunderts', in *Stadtherr.*

Blickle, Peter. 'Peasant revolts in the German empire in the late middle ages', *Social History*, vol.4, no.2 (May 1979), pp.223–39.

Blum, Jerome. 'The Rise of Serfdom in Eastern Europe', *American Historical Review*, vol.62 (1957), pp.807–36.

Boeckler, Albert. *Deutsche Buchmalerei der Gotik* (1959).

Boockmann, H. 'Zur Mentalität spätmittelalterliche gelehrter Räte, *HZ* vol.233 (1981), pp.295–316.

Bosl, Karl (ed.). *Handbuch der Geschichte der böhmischen Länder* (1967).

Brandt, Meyer. *Handbuch der deutschen Geschichte,* begun by Otto Brandt, continued by A.O. Meyer, new edn. by Leo Just, vol.1 by Karl J. Narr and others (Constance, 1957).

Brandt, A. von. *Geist und Politik in der lübeckischen Geschichte* (1954).

Brodek, Th. 'Lay community and church institutions of the Lahngau in the Late Middle Ages', *Central European History* (Emory University, Atlanta, Georgia), vol.2 (1969), pp.22–47.

Brunner, Otto. *Land und Herrschaft: Grundfragen der territorialen Verfassungsgeschichte Österreichs im Mittelalter* (5th edn. 1965).

Burckhard, A. 'Veit Stoss, German sculptor', *Speculum* 1935.

Burger, Gerhart. *Die südwestdeutschen Stadtschreiber im Mittelalter* (1960).

Burleigh, M.C.B. *The German Order and Prussian Society: a noble corporation in crisis, 1410-1466* (Unpublished Ph.D. thesis, University of London, 1982).

Carpentier, Elisabeth. 'Autour de la peste noire: famine et épidémies dans l'histoire du XIVe siècle', *Annales, Économies Sociétés,* vol.17 (1962), pp.1062–92.

Carsten, F.L. 'Medieval democracy in the Brandenburg towns and its defeat in the fifteenth century', *TRHS* 4th series no.25 (1943), pp.73–91.

Carsten, F.L. 'The origins of the Junkers', *English Historical Review,* vol.62 (1947), pp.145–78.

Carsten, F.L. *The Origins of Prussia* (1954).

Carsten, F.L. *Princes and Parliaments in Germany from the fifteenth to the eighteenth century* (1959).

Christiansen, Eric. *The Northern Crusades* (1980).

CDS. See Abbreviations.

Cohn, Henry J. *The Government of the Rhine Palatinate in the fifteenth century* (1965).

Conrad, H. *Deutsche Rechtsgeschichte,* vol. 1 (1966).

Csendes, Peter. 'Die Donaustädte von Passau bis Pressburg im 15. Jahrhundert', in *Ausgang.*

Czok, Karl. 'The socio-economic structure and political role of the suburbs in Saxony and Thuringia', in Scribner and Benecke (see below).

Dahm, Georg. 'On the reception of Roman and Italian law in Germany', in Strauss, G. (ed.), *Pre-Reformation Germany* (see below).

Danckwerts, W. *Unehrliche Leute* (1963).

Der Deutsche Territorialstaat. See Abbreviations.

Dickens, A.G. *The German Nation and Martin Luther* (1974).

Die Anfänge der Landgemeinde und ihr Wesen. 2 vols (Vorträge und Forschungen 7, 8, hg. vom Konstanzer Arbeitskreis für mittelalterliche Geschichte, 1964).

Diestelkamp, Bernhard. 'Lehnrecht und spätmittelalterliche Territorien', in *Der Deutsche Territorialstaat*, vol.1.

Dirlmeier, U. *Mittelalterliche Hoheitsträger im wirtschaftlichen Wettbewerb, VSWG*, Beiheft no. 51 (1966).

Dodgson, Campbell. *Albrecht Dürer: Masters of Engraving and Etching: a chronological catalogue* (1926).

Dohna, L. *Reformatio Sigismundi: Beiträge zum Verständnis einer Reformationsschrift des 15. Jahrhunderts* (1960).

Dollinger, Philippe. *The German Hansa* (Engl. transl. by D.S. Ault and S.H. Steinberg, 1970).

Droege, Georg. 'Die Ausbildung der mittelalterlichen territorialen Finanzverwaltung' in *Der Deutsche Territorialstaat*, vol.1.

Du Boulay, F.R.H. 'Henry of Derby's Crusades in Prussia', in *Richard II: Essays in honour of May McKisack* (ed. F.R.H. Du Boulay and Caroline Barron, 1971).

Du Boulay, F.R.H. 'Law enforcement in medieval Germany', *History* vol.63 (1978), pp.345–55.

Du Boulay, F.R.H. 'The German Town Chroniclers', in *The Writing of History in the Middle Ages: essays presented to Richard William Southern* (ed. R.H.C. Davis and J.M. Wallace-Hadrill, 1981), pp.445–69.

Ehbrecht, Wilfried. 'Bürgertum und Obrigkeit in den hansischen Städten des Spätmittelalters', in *Ausgang*.

Ehrenberg, Richard. *Capital and Finance in the Age of the Renaissance* (Engl. version, 1928).

Elsas, J. *Umriss einer Geschichte der Preise und Löhne in Deutschland vom ausgehenden Mittelalter bis zum Beginn des 19. Jahrhunderts*, 2 vols. (1936).

Ernst, Fritz. 'Die Schweizer Chronisten: ein biographischer Versuch', *Neue Zürcher Zeitung* no 12(1), Sunday, 3 Jan. 1954, p.6.

Ernst, Fritz. *Eberhard im Bart: die Politik eines deutschen Landesherrn am Ende des Mittelalters* (1933, reprinted 1970).

Finke, K. and others. 'Avisamentum pro reformatione sacri imperii', *Acta Concilii Constantientis*, 4 vols. (1896–1928).

Folz, R. *The Concept of Empire in western Europe from the fifth to the* fourteenth century (1969).

Franz, Günther. *Der Deutsche Bauernkrieg* (10th edn. 1975).

Franz, Günther. *Quellen zur Geschichte des deutschen Bauernstandes.* See Abbreviations.

Franz, Günther. *Geschichte des deutschen Bauernstandes* (1970).

Franz, Günther and Roessler, H. (eds.). *Sachwörterbuch zur deutschen Geschichte* (1958).

Freytag, Gustav. *Bilder aus der deutschen Vergangenheit: II, vom Mittelalter zur Neuzeit* (grangerized edn. by G.A.E. Bogeng, 1925).

Friedrich III: Kaiserresidenz Wiener Neustadt. (Ausstellung Katalog National-Österreichisches Landesmuseum, New Series 29, 1966).

Fritze, Konrad. *Bürger und Bauer zur Hansezeit: Studien zu den Stadt-Land Beziehungen an der südwesten Ostseeküste vom 13. bis zum 16. Jahrhundert* (1976).

Fryde, Matthew M. 'Studies in the history of public credit of German principalities and towns in the middle ages', in *Studies in Medieval and Renaissance History,* vol.1 (University of Nebraska Press, 1964), pp.221–92.

Gebhardt, Bruno. *Handbuch der deutschen Geschichte,* 2 vols. (9th edn., 1970–72).

Germania Sacra: Historisch-statistische Beschreibung der Kirche des Alten Reichs. (Max-Planck-Institut für Geschichte, 1929–).

Grimm, Jacob (ed.) *Weistümer,* 7 vols. (1840–78, reprinted 1957).

Grosser Historischer Weltatlas, Part 2: Middle Ages (ed. Josef Engel: Bayerischer Schulbuch-Verlag, 2nd edn. 1979).

Gutkas, Karl. 'Friedrich III. und die Stände des Landes Österreich', in *Friedrich III* (q.v.).

Gutkas, Karl. 'Das Städtewesen der österreichischen Donauländer und der Steiermark im 14. Jahrhundert', in *Stadtherr.*

Hanse in Europa: Brücke zwischen den Märkten 12. bis 17. Jahrhundert. (Ausstellung des Kölnischen Stadtmuseums, 1973).

Hartung, Fritz. *Deutsche Verfassungsgeschichte vom 15. Jahrhundert bis zur Gegenwart* (9th edn. 1969).

Hauck, Albert. *Kirchengeschichte Deutschlands* 5 vols. (1887–1920).

Hefele, C.J. *Histoire des Conciles,* transl. by H. Leclercq, 11 vols in 22 (1907–52).

Hess, Wolfgang. 'Das rheinische Münzwesen im 14. Jahrhundert und die Entstehung des Kurrheinischen Münzvereins', in *Der Deutsche Territorialstaat,* vol.1.

Heymann, Frederick G. 'The Crusades against the Hussites' in *A History of the Crusades,* ed. Kenneth M. Setton, vol.3 (Wisconsin, 1975).

Hofmann, Albert von. *Politische Geschichte der Deutschen,* vol.3 (1923).

Hofmann, H.H. 'Territorienbildung in Franken im 14. Jahrhundert' in *Der Deutsche Territorialstaat,* vol.2.

Hömberg, Albert. *Die Entstehung der westfälischen Freigrafschaften als Problem der mittelalterlichen deutschen Verfassungsgeschichte* (Habilitationsschrift, Münster, 1953).

Hömberg, Albert. *Westfälische Landesgeschichte* (1967).

Hubensteiner, Benno. *Bayerische Geschichte: Staat und Volk, Kunst und Kultur* (2nd edn. 1952).

Jenks, Stuart. 'Judenverschuldung und Verfolgung von Juden im 14. Jahrhundert: Franken bis 1349', *VSWG* vol.65 (1978), pp.309–56.

Kaminsky, Howard. *A History of the Hussite Revolution* (California University Press, 1967).

Keyser, Erich. *Deutsches Städtebuch: Handbuch städtische Geschichte,* 4 vols. (1939–62).

Keyser, Erich. *Bevölkerungsgeschichte Deutschlands* (2nd edn. 1941).

Kirchgässner, Bernhard. 'Die Auswirkung des rheinischen Münzvereins im Gegenspiel von Reich und Territorien Südwestdeutschlands und der angrenzenden Eidgenossenschaft', in *Der Deutsche Territorialstaat,* vol.1.

Klassen, J.M. *The nobility and the making of the Hussite revolution* (1978).

Knoll, Paul W. *The Rise of the Polish Monarchy: Piast Poland in East Central Europe,* 1320–1370 (Chicago, 1972).

Koch, H.W. *A History of Prussia* (1978).

Koeppler, H. 'Frederick Barbarossa and the Schools of Bologna', *English Historical Review,* vol. 54 (1939), pp.577–607.

Koller, Heinrich. 'Kaiserliche Politik und die Reformpläne des 15 Jahrhunderts', in *Festschrift für Hermann Heimpel zum 70. Geburtstag am 19. September 1971* (Veröffentlichungen des Max-Planck-Instituts zu Göttingen für Geschichte 36/II 1972), pp.61–79.

Koller, Heinrich. 'Die Aufgaben der Städte in der Reformatio Friderici, 1442', *Historisches Jahrbuch,* vol. 100 (1980), pp.198–216.

Konstanzer, Arbeitskreis. See *Die Anfänge* and *Der Deutsche Territorialstaat.*

Kristeller, Paul. *Kupferstich und Holzschnitt in vier Jahrhunderten* (4th edn. 1922).

Lambert, Malcolm. *Medieval Heresy: popular movements from Bogomil to Hus* (1977), Chapters 16–18.

Landeen, William M. 'The beginnings of the *Devotio Moderna* in Germany', *State College of Washington Research Studies*, vol.19 (1951), pp.162–202; 221–53; vol.21 (1953), pp.275–309; vol.22 (1954), pp.57–75.

Laufner, Richard. 'Die Ausbildung des Territorialstaates von Trier', in *Der Deutsche Territorialstaat*, vol.2.

Lautemann, W. (ed.). *Geschichte in Quellen*, vol.2 (1970).

Lechner, Johann. 'Reichshofgericht und königliches Kammergericht im 15. Jahrhundert', *MIÖG* vol.7 Ergänzungsband, pp.44–185.

Lefebvre, Joël. *Les Fols et la Folie: études sur les genres du comique et la création littéraire en Allemagne pendant la renaissance* (1968).

Lenk, Werner. *Das Nürnberger Fastnachtspiel des 15. Jahrhunderts* (1968).

Leyser, Karl. 'A recent view of the German College of Electors', *Medium Aevum*, vol.23 (1954), pp.76–87. 'Ottonian Government', *English Historical Review*, vol.96 (Oct. 1981), pp.721–53.

Lhotsky, Alphons. *Das Haus Habsburg*, 2 vols. (1971).

Lhotsky, Alphons. *Aufsätze und Vorträge*, 3 vols. (1972).

Lindner, Th. *Die Veme* (Paderborn, 1888).

Lindner, Th. *Deutsche Geschichte unter den Habsburgern, 1273–1437*, 2 vols. (1890–1903).

Lorenz, Ottokar. *Deutschlands Geschichstquellen im Mittelalter seit der Mitte des 13. Jahrhunderts*, 2 vols. (3rd end. 1886–7).

Malfatti, C.V. *Two Italian accounts of Tudor England* (Barcelona, 1953).

Maschke, Erich. 'Verfassung und soziale Kräfte in der deutschen Stadt des späteren Mittelalters vornehmlich in Oberdeutschland', *VSWG* vol.46 (1959), pp.289–349; 433–76.

Maschke, Erich. 'Die Unterschichten der mittelalterlichen Städte Deutschlands' in *Gesellschaftliche Unterschichten in den südwestdeutschen Städten* (ed. E. Maschke und Jürgen Sydow, 1967), pp.1–74.

Maschke, Erich. 'Deutsche Städte am Ausgang des Mittelalters', in *Ausgang*.

Mayer, Th. *Fürsten und Staat* (1950).

Mayhew, Alan. *Rural settlement and farming in Germany* (1973).

Meiss, M. See under Pearce, S.M.

Menzel, Josef Joachim. 'Die schlesischen Städte am Ausgange des Mittelalters', in *Ausgang*.

Metcalf, D.M. *The coinage of South Germany in the thirteenth century* (1961).

Das mittelalterliche Hausbuch ed. H.T. Bossert and W. Storck (1912).

Moeller, Bernard. 'Religious life in Germany on the eve of the Reformation', in Strauss, G. (ed.), *Pre-Reformation Germany* (1972).

Mols, Roger. *Introduction à la démographie historique des villes d'Europe du XIVe au XVIIIe siècle* (1954).

Moraw, Peter. 'Beamtentum und Rat König Ruprechts', *ZGO* vol.116 (1968), pp.59 ff.

Moraw, Peter. 'Deutsches Königtum und bürgerliche Geldwirtschaft um 1400', *VSWG* vol.55 (1968), pp.289–328.

Moraw, Peter. 'Kanzlei und Kanzleipersonal König Ruprechts', *Archiv für Diplomatik* vol.15 (1969), pp.428–531.

Moraw, Peter. 'Gedanken zur politischen Kontinuität im deutschen Spätmittelalter' in *Festschrift für Hermann Heimpel* (1972).

Moraw, Peter. 'Zum königlichen Hofgericht im deutschen Spätmittelalter', *ZGO* vol.121 (New Series 82) (1973), pp.307–17.

Moraw, Peter. 'Königtum und Hochfinanz in Deutschland, 1350–1450', *ZGO* vol.122 (New Series 83) (1974), pp.23–34.

Moraw, Peter. 'Noch einmal zum königlichen Hofgericht im deutschen Spätmittelalter', *ZGO* vol.123 (New Series 84) (1975), pp.103–14.

Moraw, Peter. 'Personenforschung und deutsches Königtum', *Zeitschrift für Historische Forschung*, vol.2 (1975), pp.7 ff.

Näf, Werner. 'Frühformen des «modernen Staates» im Spätmittelalter', *HZ* vol. 171 (1951), pp.225–43.

Naendrup-Reiman, Johanna. 'Territorien und Kirche im 14. Jahrhundert', in *Der Deutsche Territorialstaat*, vol. 1.

Nehring, Karl. *Matthias Corvinus, Kaiser Friedrich III und das Reich* (Munich, 1975).

Obenaus, Herbert. *Recht und Verfassung der Gesellschaften mit St Jörgenschild in Schwaben: Untersuchung über Adel, Einung, Schiedsgericht und Fehde im 15. Jahrhundert* (Veröffentlichungen des Max-Planck-Instituts für Geschichte, no.7, 1961).

Oberman, Heiko. *The Harvest of Medieval Theology* (1963).

Oberman, Heiko. 'The Gospel of Social Unrest' in Scribner and Benecke (q.v.).

Offler, H.S. 'Aspects of Government in the late medieval empire' in *Europe in the later Middle Ages* (ed. J.R. Hale and others, 1965).

Offler, H.S. 'Empire and Papacy: the last struggle', *TRHS* 5th series vol.6 (1956), pp.21 ff.

Nellmann, E. *Die Reichsidee in deutschen Dichtungen* (Berlin, 1963).

Orth, Elsbet. *Die Fehden der Reichsstadt Frankfurt- am- Main im Spätmittelalter* (1973).

Otto, Eberhard. 'Von der Anschliessung des Ritterstandes', *HZ*, vol.162 (1940), pp.19–39.

Otto of Freising. *Die Taten Friedrichs oder richtiger Cronica*, transl. Adolf Schmidt, ed. Franz-Josef Schmale (1965); also *The Deeds of Frederick Barbarossa* (Columbia Records of Civilization, 1953).

Patze, Hans. 'Die deutsche bäuerliche Gemeinde im Ordensstaat Preussen', in *Die Anfänge der Landgemeinde* (q.v.), vol.2.

Patze, Hans. 'Neue Typen des Geschäftsschriftgutes im 14. Jahrhundert' in *Der Deutsche Territorialstaat*, (q.v.), vol.1.

Patze, Hans. 'Die welfischen Territorien im 14. Jahrhundert' in ibid., vol.2.

Patze, Hans. 'Die Bildung der Landherrlichen Residenzen im Reich während des 14. Jahrhunderts', in *Stadtherr*.

Pearce, S.M. and Meiss, M. 'Letters about portraits of Frederick III', *The Burlington Magazine*, vol.103 (1961), pp.189 ff.

Pfeiffer, Gerhard, and Schwemmer, Wilhelm (eds.). *Geschichte Nürnbergs in Bilddokumenten* (2nd edn. 1971).

Pfeiffer, Gerhard (ed.). Nürnberg — Geschichte einer europäischen Stadt (1971).

Pfeiffer, Gerhard (ed.). 'Stadtherr und Gemeinde in den spätmittelalterlichen Reichsstädten', in *Ausgang*.

Planitz, Hans. *Die Deutsche Stadt im Mittelalter* (1954).

Press, Volker. 'Die Ritterschaft im Kraichgau zwischen Reich und Territorium, 1500–1623', *ZGO* vol.122 (New Series 83) (1974).

Prutz, H. *Die geistlichen Ritterorden: ihre Stellung zur kirchlichen, politischen, gesellschaftlichen und wirtschaftlichen Entwicklung* (Berlin, 1908).

Rabe, Horst. 'Stadt und Stadtherrschaft im 14. Jahrhundert — die schwäbischen Reichsstädte', in *Stadtherr*.

Rausch, Wilhelm. See *Ausgang* and *Stadtherr* under Abbreviations.

Reitzenstein, Alexander, Freiherr von. *Rittertum und Ritterschaft* (1972).

Rörig, Fritz. *The Medieval Town* (translated by Don Bryant from *Propyläen-Weltgeschichte*, ed. W. Goetz, vol.IV, 1932, which subsequently appeared as *Die europäischen Stadt im Mittelalter* (4th edn. 1964).

Rosen, Josef. 'Prices and Public Finance in Basle, 1360–1535', *Economic History Review*, 2nd series, vol.25 (1972).

Rotz, Rhiman A. 'Investigating urban uprisings with examples from Hanseatic towns, 1374–1416', in *Order and Innovation in the Middle Ages* (ed. W.C. Jordan and others, 1976), pp.215–33.

Rowan, Steven. 'Die Jahresrechnung eines Freiburger Kaufmannes, 1487/8', in E. Maschke and J. Sydow (eds.), *Stadt und Umland* (Veröffentlichungen der Kommission für geschichtliche

Landeskund in Baden-Württemberg, Series B, vol.82, 1974), pp.227–70.

Rowan, Steven. 'The Common Penny (1495–99) as a source of German social and demographic history', in *Central European History*, vol.10, no.2 (June 1977), pp.148–64.

Rowan, Steven. 'A Reichstag in the Reform Era: Freiburg im Breisgau, 1497–98', in James Vann and Steven Rowan (eds.), *The Old Reich: studies presented to the International Commission for the history of representative and parliamentary institutions*, vol.48 (1974), pp.33–57.

Rowan, Steven. 'Imperial Taxes and German Politics in the fifteenth century: an outline', *Central European History*, vol.13, no.3 (Sept. 1980), pp.203–17.

Rudwin, M.J. 'The Origin of German Carnival Comedy', *Journal of English and German Philology*, vol.18 (1919), pp.402–54.

Sante, Georg Wilhelm. Geschichte der deutschen Länder «Territorien-Ploetz», vol.1: *Die Territorien bis zum Ende des alten Reiches* (Würzburg, 1964).

Scammell, G.V. *The World Encompassed* (1981).

Scherer, C.W. *Die westfälischen Femgerichte und die Eidgenossenschaft* (1941).

Schildhauer, J., Fritze, K. and Stark, W. *Die Hanse* (Berlin, 1974).

Schlesinger, Walter. 'Zur Geschichte der Landesherrschaft in den Marken Brandenburg und Meissen während des 14. Jahrhunderts', in *Der Deutsche Territorialstaat*, vol.2.

Schmidt, Heinrich. *Die deutschen Städtechroniken als Spiegel des Selbstverständnis im Spätmittelalter* (1958).

Scholderer, Victor. *Johann Gutenberg* (1963).

Schramm, Albert. *Der Bildschmuck der Frühdrucke*, 23 vols. (1923–).

Schreiber, W.L. *The Illustrated book in the fifteenth century* (1929).

Schröder, Richard, and Künssberg, E.V. *Lehrbuch der Deutschen Rechtsgechichte*, Part 1 (6th edn., 1919–22).

Schubert, Ernst. 'Die Stellung der Kurfürsten in der spätmittelalterlichen Reichsverfassung', *Jahrbuch fur westdeutsche Landesgeschichte*, vol.1 (1975), pp.97–128.

Schubert, Ernst. 'Königswahl und Konigtum im spätmittelalterlichen Reicht', *Zeitschrift für Historische Forschung*, vol.4 (1977), pp.257–338.

Schubert, Ernst. *König und Reich: Studien zur spätmittelalterlichen deutschen Verfassungsgeschichte* (1979).

Schulte, Aloys. *Der Adel und die deutsche Kirche im Mittelalter: Studien zur Sozial-, Rechts- und Kirchengeschichte* (3rd edn. 1958).

Schultz, Alwin. *Deutsches Leben im XIV und XV Jahrhundert* (Grosse

Ausgabe [Library Edition] Prague, Vienna, Leipzig, 1892).

Schwarz, Dietrich W.H. 'Die Städte der Schweiz im 15. Jahrhundert', in *Ausgang*.

Scott, Tom. 'The Peasants' War: a historiographical review', *Historical Journal*, vol.22 (1979), Part 1, pp.693–720; Part 2, pp.953–74.

Scribner, R.W. and Benecke, Gerhard (eds.). *The German Peasant War, 1525: New Viewpoints* (1979).

Seibt, Ferdinand. 'Die Zeit der Luxemburger und der hussitischen Revolution', in Bosl (q.v.).

Seigel, Rudolf. 'Die württembergische Stadt am Ausgang des Mittelalters — Probleme der Verfassungs- und Sozialstruktur', in *Ausgang*.

Sigmund, Paul E. *Nicholas of Cusa and medieval political thought* (Harvard, 1963).

Smith, C.T. *An Historical Geography of western Europe before 1800* (1967).

Spitz, Lewis W. 'The course of German Humanism' in *Itinerarium Italicum* (1975), pp.371–436.

Stadtherr. See Abbreviations.

Stieber, J.W. *Pope Eugenius IV, the Council of Basel and the secular and ecclesiastical authorities in the empire: the conflict over supreme authority in the Church* (1978).

Stoob, Heinz. 'Minderstädte: Formen der Stadtentstehung im Spätmittelalter', *VSWG* vol.46 (1959), pp.1–28.

Stoob, Heinz. 'The role of the civic community in central European urban development during the twelfth to the fifteenth centuries' (transl. by Susan Gold), *Transactions of the Ancient Monuments Society* vol.23 (1978–9), pp.67–91.

Störmer, Wilhelm. 'Stadt und Stadtherr im wittelsbachischen Altbayern des 14. Jahrhunderts', in *Stadtherr*.

Strauss, Gerald. *Nuremberg in the sixteenth century* (1966).

Strauss, Gerald, *Manifestations of Discontent in Germany on the eve of the Reformation* (1971).

Strauss, Gerald (ed.). *Pre-Reformation Germany* (1972).

Stromer, Wolfgang von. 'Ein Wirtschaftsprojekt des deutschen Königs Siegmund', *VSWG* vol.51 (1964), pp.374–82.

Stromer, Wolfgang von. *Oberdeutsche Hochfinanz, 1350–1450 VSWG* Beiheft 55 (1968), Part 3; Beiheft 57 (1970), Part 1.

Stromer, Wolfgang von and Sporhan-Krempel, Lore. 'Das Handelhaus der Stromer von Nürnberg und die Geschichte der ersten deutschen Papiermühle', *VSWG* vol.47 (1960), pp.81–104.

Stuart, H.S.M. (ed.). *The Autobiography of Götz von Berlichingen*

(1956).

Suhle, A. *Deutsche Münz- und Geldgeschichte von den Anfängen bis zum ausgehenden 15. Jahrhundert* (1979).

Sumberg, S.L. *The Nuremberg Schembart Carnival* (1941).

Sydow, Jürgen. 'Spital und Stadt in Kanonistik und Verfassungsgeschichte des 14. Jahrhunderts', in *Der Deutsche Territorialstaat.*

Thielen, Peter G. *Die Verwaltung des Ordensstaates Preussen vornehmlich im 15. Jahrhundert* (Ostmitteleuropa in Vergangenheit und Gegenwart, hg.von Johann Gottfried Herder — Forschungrat Schriftleitung: Ernst Birke, 11) (1965).

Thielen, Peter G. 'Die Rolle der Uhr im geistlichen und administrativen Altagsleben der Deutschordenskonventen in Preussen', in *Studien zur Geschichte des Preussenlandes: Festschrift Erich Keyser* (1963).

Thomson, S.H. 'Learning at the court of Charles IV', *Speculum* vol.25 (1950), pp.1–20.

Timm, Albrecht. *Studien zur Siedlungs- und Agrargeschichte Mitteldeutschlands* (1956).

Toch, Michael. *Die nürnberger Mittelschichten* (1978).

Treue, Wilhelm and others. *Das Hausbuch der Mendelschen Zwölfbrüderstiftung zu Nürnberg,* 2 vols. (1965).

Trusen, Winfried. *Anfänge des gelehrten Rechts in Deutschland* (Wiesbaden, 1962).

Tumler, Marian. *Der Deutsche Orden im Werden, Wachsen und Wirken bis 1400* (1955).

Uhrig, Kurt. 'Der Bauer in der Publizistik der Reformations bis zum Ausgang des Bauernkrieges', *Archiv für Reformationgeschichte* vol.32 3/4, pp.71–225, esp. Part 1.

Ulmschneider, Helgard. *Götz von Berlichingen, ein adeliges Leben der deutschen Renaissance* (1974).

Vansteenberghe, E. *Nicolas de Cues* (1920).

Veit, L. *Nürnberg und die Feme: der Kampf einer Reichsstadt gegen den Jurisdiktionsasnspruch der westfälischen Gerichte* (1955).

Vorträge und Forschungen. See *Die Anfänge der Landgemeinde* and *Der Deutsche Territorialstaat.*

Waugh, W.T. *A History of Europe, 1378–1494* (3rd edn. 1949), esp. chs. 4, 6, 13, 14.

Weltsch, R.E. *Archbishop John of Jenstein, 1348–1400* (1968).

Wenskus, Reinhard. 'Das Ordensland Preussen als Territorialstaat des 14. Jahrhunderts' in *Der Deutsche Territorialstaat,* vol.1.

Werminghoff, A. 'Neuere Arbeiten über das Verhältnis von Staat und Kirche in Deutschland während des späteren Mittelalters',

Historisches Vierteljahrschrift, New Series 11 (1908), pp.153–93.

Wieser, P.K. (ed.). *Acht Jahrhunderte Deutscher Orden in Einzeldarstellungen* (Quellen und Studien zur Geschichte des Deutscher Orden I, Godesberg, 1967).

Wiesflecker, Hermann. *Kaiser Maximilian I*, vol.1 (1971), vol.2 (1975).

Wiessner, Hermann. *Sachinhalt und wirtschaftliche Bedeutung der Weistümer* (1934).

Wolff, Philippe. *Western Languages, AD 100 to 1500* (Engl. transl. 1971).

Zeumer, K. *Die Goldene Bulle Kaiser Karls IV* (1908).

Zeumer, K. *Quellensammlung zur Geschichte der deutschen Reichsverfassung im Mittelalter und Neuzeit* (2nd edn. 1913).

Ziehen, Eduard. *Mittelrhein und Reich im Zeitalter der Reichsreform, 1356-1504*, 2 vols. (1934-7).

Zöllner, Erich. *Geschichte Österreichs* (1961).

Further Reading in English

If this could have been a richly filled section, the present book would probably not have been written. But despite the relative scarcity of books and articles on medieval Germany in the English language, it is obvious that there are some to which attention ought to be called by reason of their fame, merit or both. It is not a question of merely referring to works listed in the bibliography above, but of the more daring task of offering a few comments. Publications alluded to here which are also in the book's Select Bibliography above will be given a short form of reference on the present page.

To a reader who wants a straight, factual treatment, the oldish textbook by W.T. Waugh is still useful, though coloured by a traditionally-expressed pessimism. The book still most often recommended by tutors is Professor Geoffrey Barraclough's *The Origins of Modern Germany*, first published in 1946, and often reprinted. It is a book to be read in the light of subsequent research. Germans themselves apparently use the text-book by Joachim Leuschner (1978), now translated into English by Sabine MacCormack as *Germany in the late middle ages* (North Holland Publishing Co., 1980). This is a useful little book, short and simple. But half of it is taken up with the thirteenth century, and the treatment appears very general. The fourteenth and fifteenth centuries are dealt with very lightly, though the (mainly German) bibliography is impressive.

For learning and insight into later medieval Germany and the Empire, the articles by H.S. Offler are unequalled. For early medieval Germany the same may be said about Karl Leyser's work. His pupil, John Gillingham, has published a skilful and well-informed pamphlet, *The Kingdom of Germany in the High Middle Ages* (Historical Association pamphlet G.77, 1971).

English-language works on particular principalities are few. There is a first-rate treatment of the Rhine Palatinate in the fifteenth century by Henry Cohn; the older work by F.L. Carsten is to be recommended strongly: the introductory sections to each chapter of *Princes and Parliaments* give useful introductions to the medieval background. There is a good book on the see of Speyer by L. Duggan. Those interested in Prussia and the Baltic lands should read the works listed above by Christiansen and Burleigh. Switzerland, essentially part of our story till the end of the fifteenth century, is best approached through E. Bonjour and others, *A short history of Switzerland* (Oxford, 1952), especially the first six chapters.

On towns the reader may find Fritz Rörig in the listed translation stimulating but scrappy, and Dollinger on the Hansa reasonably thorough. The present writer's paper on 'German Town chroniclers' enlarges on one of the present book's basic themes.

Cultural and artistic history, without which 'general history' appears unintelligible, are finely treated by Baxandall and Spitz.

Economic and social history of recent vintage is mainly confined to the very end of the medieval period and seems often pledged to attempt interpretation in ideological terms. But there are excellent things in Scott, and in Scribner and Benecke. Gerald Strauss, *Manifestations,* is a valuable source-book, and his book on Nuremberg is as illuminating about the fifteenth century as the sixteenth.

No English writer has yet done for German popular religion what R.W. Scribner has done for the Lutheran period in *For the sake of simple folk* (1981). But Norman Cohn, *The Pursuit of the Millennium,* a classic first published in 1957, paints the fringes in bright colours. On church politics and consequently on German politics in general there is the big, diffuse book by Stieber, full of learning not easily found elsewhere.

Index